Develo͟   ͟ ͟ ͟ ͟iry f͟ ͟ ͟ hn ͟ ͟ ͟ n Se͟ ͟

Developing Inquiry for Learning shows how university tutors can help students to improve their abilities to learn and to become professional inquirers.

The number of students participating in higher education increases every year, along with the assumption that learning is a relatively passive process. University tutors need to have the tools to be able to respond to a modern teaching environment that demands a diverse spectrum of skills. They must be able to help students become collaborative learners and independently motivated rather than subsisting on a spoon-fed approach.

In the innovative and practically proven approach developed by the authors of this book, students are guided to implement action research into their learning practices and reflections. Using a rolling programme of cyclical inquiries and whole group 'conferences' on improving learning, students write 'patches' on learning development which are then shared across the year group online. Each student's cumulative set of patches, together with their regular reflective writing, provide the basis for assembling a composite final assignment, a 'Patchwork Text', for assessment. This style of curriculum and assessment organisation encourages regular peer feedback and formative assessment, as part of the whole module process. This is a dynamic approach which builds personal confidence within students, both as learners and as professionals.

Providing teaching materials and examples of students' responses, including the use of blogs, wikis and discussion boards, *Developing Inquiry for Learning* analyses and theorises on the deeper characteristics of the difficulties being addressed. With the provision of relevant frameworks of theory and values, readers are amply equipped to adopt, adapt and experiment within their own developments of teaching and curricula.

Peter Ovens was Principal Lecturer in Professional and Curriculum Development at Nottingham Trent University and is now Senior Research Fellow at the University of Cumbria.

Frances Wells is Principal Lecturer in Education at Nottingham Trent University.

Patricia Wallis is a Senior Lecturer in Professional Studies at Nottingham Trent University.

Cyndy Hawkins is a Senior Lecturer in the School of Education, Nottingham Trent University.

Developing Inquiry for Learning

Reflecting collaborative ways to learn how to learn in higher education

Peter Ovens
with Frances Wells,
Patricia Wallis and
Cyndy Hawkins

Routledge
Taylor & Francis Group

LONDON AND NEW YORK

First published 2011
by Routledge
2 Park Square, Milton Park, Abingdon, Oxon OX14 4RN

Simultaneously published in the USA and Canada
by Routledge
711 Third Avenue, New York, NY 10017

Routledge is an imprint of the Taylor & Francis Group, an informa business

British Library Cataloguing in Publication Data
A catalogue record for this book is available from the British Library

Library of Congress Cataloging in Publication Data
Developing inquiry for learning: reflective and collaborative ways to learn how
to learn in higher education / Peter Ovens ... [et al.].—1st ed.
    p. cm.
1. Study skills—Great Britain. 2. Inquiry-based learning—Great Britain.
3. Action research in education—Great Britain. 4. Tutors and tutoring—Great
Britain. I. Ovens, Peter, 1944– II. Title.
LB2395.D46 2011
378.1'794—dc22   2010054209

ISBN: 978–0–415–59876–7 (hbk)
ISBN: 978–0–415–59877–4 (pbk)
ISBN: 978–0–203–81806–0 (ebk)

Typeset in Galliard
by Book Now Ltd, London

Contents

Illustrations

Figures

Tables

Acknowledgements

We are grateful to the many students with whom we have worked in Inquiry Into Learning for the cheer with which they have often greeted our better teaching and the tolerance they have shown to our wobbly moments.

As a recipient of a National Teaching Fellowship, Peter Ovens would like to thank the Higher Education Funding Council and the Higher Education Academy for their support. They provided helpful frameworks and personal encouragement as well as the resources, most crucially the time, which made all the difference.

Nottingham Trent University's School of Education supported the research leave taken by Frances Wells, with its focus on *'enhancing research-informed teaching'* which focused on her action research within the Inquiry Into Learning 1 module.

Chapter 1

Introduction

Is learning a taken-for-granted part of higher education? It just seems to happen on its own. Tutors who see learning as entirely students' responsibility can give all their attention to the subject matter and its presentation. But a tutor who wishes to share responsibility and control faces questions about how much and what kind. Is it a minimal responsibility to organise the syllabus, the explicit curriculum, using principles such as progression: from less difficult ideas to more difficult ones, or from smaller, contributory ideas to bigger, more general ones? Is it enough to vary teaching styles, inserting a tutorial or two, as a break from block lectures, to maintain interest? Are there parts of the syllabus/curriculum which are better learned through practical work than by being told? Or should tutors go further, making larger assumptions about students' learning and their needs, and plan in some depth and detail what learners are to do? Might this include planning learning tasks which determine a linear path of thought and cognitive development for students to follow? Or should there be open-ended activities, in which students' own initiatives set the direction? What are the implications for the provision of resources for learning, not least, time? Are there pedagogic principles or theories which should guide decisions? Finally, does a pragmatic consideration of formal feedback from students and external examiners direct some decisions about how much control over and responsibility for students' learning is taken by tutors?

At the time of writing, in the United Kingdom, undergraduate programmes are normally expected to address many of these sorts of questions. Every programme has practices and procedures which influence the students' learning, making it harder or easier for any individual student to learn how to learn, as part of studying for their qualification. Programmes vary in terms of the extent to which such practices are tacitly determined by custom and by explicit principles, values and theories to underpin them, or procedures for tutors to sustain inquiry into their effectiveness, for programme and professional development.

How a student learns and how well they do so depends on the personal repertoire of learning habits or approaches which they have on entry. It is likely to need expansion and enrichment to meet the challenges of the explicit curriculum of their programme of study. There is also the implicit, hidden curriculum, the 'rules of the game'. Like a stranger in a new cultural environment, students need to pick up the unspoken expectations, standards and procedures in order to be able to play the game. Also, there is a student's experience of the learning culture which emerges in their seminar group, contributing to the characteristic expectations and patterns of interaction which, for tutors, make each group unique to teach. Within this are the subcultures created by small groups of like-minded students with shared attitudes and beliefs about learning and subject matter. Many students are able to adapt and develop well, showing qualities of autonomous learners. Others may flounder and some are unsuccessful.

The original design of the BA in Childhood Studies at Nottingham Trent University gave extensive consideration to students' learning. With a cohort of about 100 students each year, it went so far as to decide to provide its students with ways of learning how to learn. This refers to the fostering of an amalgam of attitudes and abilities which enable a learner to improve themselves as learners as part of the process of doing their learning. A central core of the design is provided by a 'learning how to learn' component. There is one module in Year One and another in Year Two of the three-year programme, both called 'Inquiry Into Learning'. This book is about the particular way of addressing these questions about learning which is incorporated within the Inquiry Into Learning (IIL) approach. At its heart is a vision of just how good it would be for (ideally) all our students to be fired up, lively learners, thirsty to know more and do better, able to think and act independently and keen to go on improving, for themselves and each other. The vision held by the IIL tutors has values which cluster around autonomy as a personal, professional quality we aspire to nurture in our students. We want IIL to do nothing to impede students whose autonomy is already working well, merely to provide them with encouragement, support and the space and time for their practice to mature and, for others, to provide a personalised, self-directed and collaborative framework for fostering growth of their autonomy as learners.

The way of learning called 'action inquiry' has appropriate characteristics for such purposes. It is about improving practice, which is what we think learning is, fundamentally. It involves looking carefully at the experience of learning, thinking reflectively, using ideas and knowledge to think better, to practise more wisely and much discussion. We ask students to do action inquiry into their practice as learners as the main way in which they learn how to learn at university. We conduct our own, second-level action inquiry into the improvement of our practice, which includes our pedagogy, curriculum planning, organisation, assessment and evaluation. This requires us to develop our shared, tacit purposes surrounding what we think autonomy is, routinely to notice many things about events and interactions in IIL module sessions, and to discuss them with each other, to develop ourselves and the modules, so as to sustain and revise our vision of autonomy. We have not tried to produce one large, detached, external, summative evaluation of the IIL approach but, by cyclic inquiry, we repeatedly made formative evaluations which point to immediate practical and theoretical improvements, for evolutionary change. In both students' inquiry into learning and tutors' inquiry into teaching, the crucially important feature of action inquiry is that aims and values are thought about interactively with ways to achieve them more fully.

We were always aware of the disjunction between this process element of the IIL approach and the separation of ways, values and aims that has become a state-imposed norm in formal education in the United Kingdom, and is increasingly influential in many other countries. We found ways of complying creatively with the national standards and standardised ways of planning inherent in a technical rationalist way of thinking and doing. The 'target culture' sometimes stimulated but never confined us. We found value in our attitude of acceptance towards the difficulties which students presented in their abilities to learn. As we gathered more evidence of the characteristics of these difficulties, it has become clear to what extent they are manifestations of the excesses of technical rationalism in previous learning. We tolerate the paradox that a positively accepting stance towards the effects of technical rationalism on the learning of our students liberates the autonomy of most of them, but is not sufficient to enable others to ameliorate their difficulties as we would wish, provoking their resistance to being emancipated and rejection of the IIL approach. We believe the evidence and analyses provided here justify adding our voice to calls for a radical reform of state-organised education. Learning at all levels needs to be liberated from strait-jackets of targets and standardisation. What is learned should be subordinated to how it is learned, because this creates conditions for the learning and the learners to grow in self-actualisation. Teachers and tutors need to be trusted to internalise and creatively operationalise common educational purposes and goals which embrace imaginative, inquiry-based ways of achieving and developing them. Control and power have to be shared more and centralised less.

This book offers the Inquiry Into Learning approach. It is not a blueprint for helping all students everywhere to learn how to learn in higher education. It provides an account of *what* are the IIL ideas in action, which are coherent with the context and people involved in one situation. Consistent with its philosophy, it also provides an account of *how* those ideas and actions began, evolved and developed through organised coordination of experience and reflective thought. Both the what and the how are a resource for colleagues who wish to reconsider and improve their students' learning in any undergraduate programme. The book guides them through a process of development based on tutors' own values and vision, growth of their situational understanding and improving practice through inquiring into it.

The IIL approach is presented in Part I. Chapter 2 provides preliminary thinking about learning in higher education and what learning to learn is taken to mean, in theoretical and practical terms. Key concepts concerned with knowing are addressed, including our working definitions of autonomy, education compared with training and personal development. Also, a fundamental assumption of the approach is stated. Some of the complexities of learning touched upon here are examined in more detail later. In Chapter 3, the IIL approach is set out, emphasising its general ideas and key procedures, in a form which facilitates application to different academic and professional contexts. Autonomy is considered further, definitions are provided for the pedagogical principles of the IIL approach and the Patchwork Text assessment is outlined.

Part II of the book shows how this approach has developed in one particular context and how its various aspects can be understood as resources for pedagogical, curriculum and professional developments. Chapter 4 is about the Inquiry Into Learning 1 module, describing its detailed practical operation and showing key features of the teaching and assessment. Chapter 5 gives a similar account of the Inquiry Into Learning 2 module. Both chapters are concerned more with the tutors' perspectives than those of students, which come to the fore in Part III.

Part III provides evidence and analysis of the operation of IIL, focusing on three topics of wider interest. Chapter 6 is about the importance and power of student voice. This dimension of the IIL approach is considered with ample, rich evidence of students' struggle to learn how to learn. A method for eliciting and nurturing student voice (literally – through structured talk) called 'Intervision' is explored in depth. Chapter 7 is about setting expectations for learning through building a culture of informal formative assessment into learning processes. Chapter 8 is about how the processes and products of learning in IIL are progressively being enriched by using information technology.

Part IV examines some personal, theoretical and philosophical roots of the IIL approach. Chapter 9 is about general principles of curriculum design, within which is set the Patchwork Texts (PT) method of curriculum design and assessment used in IIL. The distinctive ideas and values of a process curriculum are presented and applied to IIL. Several virtues of a PT approach are considered, particularly its consistency with the process-oriented views of learning we espouse. These include educative kinds of instruction, communities of practice and sociocultural perspectives. Chapter 10 sets out the fundamentals of the action research we have used to develop IIL, with professional biographical statements by IIL team members to explain their involvement and distinctive contributions. Chapter 11 asks what is the point of IIL, to probe into those underlying beliefs which have become significant to us through our accumulated reflective experience of teaching students to learn how to learn in higher education and assessing their progress. It provides further and deeper thinking about conceptual frameworks which clarify and strengthen the theoretical basis of those aspects of the IIL approach which are most relevant to meeting the current challenges to students' learning in higher education.

Finally, Chapter 12 gives concluding reflections and summarised recommendations. It indicates current growth points in the further development of the IIL approach, and makes recommendations for students and tutors participating in other modules and programmes with similar aims to IIL.

The general approach of Inquiry Into Learning

Part 1

The general approach of
inquiry into learning

Chapter 2

Learning to learn in higher education

This chapter is about a particular vision for learning to learn in higher education which stimulated the educational explorations, professional developments and curriculum achievements presented in this book. A good place to start is the university classroom.

A new academic year is beginning. A new group of students are starting their course. Module Handbooks are distributed and teaching begins. After everyone's preparations and anticipations, the first moments have arrived. Here we all are, at the first session, looking at each other and weighing up what this new beginning is like. After some nervous, feverish introductions, things get under way. The tutor's head is full of practical concerns about resources, organisation and subject content. As well as endeavouring to make the first session an interesting and enjoyable start, the students need orientation. Meanwhile, they are feeling their way cautiously into many kinds of unknowns. Let's take a closer look at the different perspectives of tutors and of students.

Tutor's perspective

From the tutor's perspective, much preparation (but never enough) has taken place. Naturally, the tutor wants to build on past successes and avoid difficulties. So, feedback from previous participants (students and tutors) has been considered and, where appropriate, acted on, in an effort to improve the student experience. Each tutor carries a lumpy bag of vague concerns as well as clear practical questions and sharp educational dilemmas such as:

- Will things that wowed them last year work as well with this year's group?
- Might the new solutions to old problems work better?
- How to cover all content thoroughly and address key ideas deeply enough.
- How to prepare for the assignment without compromising the module content.

The tutor's aspiration of a smooth first session may be realised. However, sooner or later, depending on how much opportunity was given for students to respond, encouraging signs may mingle with worrying signals. Maybe this year's group reacts in unexpected ways. Disappointing attendance and negative body language seem to indicate that some students are becoming disaffected. Louder and/or more numerous voices suggest they know less than usual or that they find things more difficult. Some ask for more clarification of the module content or assignment or request closer guidance on the criteria of assessment; others seem to have settled quickly and to be happy with the new ideas. Vital questions that can get lost in all this: 'Are they learning?' and, if so, 'Are they learning well?'.

Stopping to reflect on the whole enterprise, a tutor may think about their role as a teacher: first, as a *teacher of their subject* and, second, as a *teacher of students*. The experience of teaching *this* group *now* may be a shared enjoyment of the subject matter or, in the face of difficulties, it may feel more like a battle for survival and credibility. Either way, it is the tutor's role to teach this module to these students. This may be seen as teaching the subject matter. Module aims normally specify mainly, if not exclusively, the knowledge to be taught. Students are obviously required to provide evidence of having learned what is necessary to progress. So, a tutor may, not unreasonably, take special care to *teach the knowledge* to be assessed, giving less attention to *teaching students*, whose learning is more or less their own responsibility. Module specifications may accentuate this priority by *what* is to be learned more than *how* it is to be learned.

This oversimplified picture of a teacher of a subject has the tutor transmitting clear, ordered subject knowledge by effective methods to their students by means of printed handouts, intranet documents and other sources plus the reading of set texts, as if knowledge were a commodity, either gift-wrapped or just dumped on students to take away and learn. A lesson plan may be like a timetable for coverage of the subject content and the planning of whole modules, and even the programme, may be similarly driven by delivery of the subject matter.

Detailed attention to curriculum planning is given in Chapter 9, where the following point is developed more fully. Higher education has come under growing central direction to use an objectives approach to curriculum planning with precise statements of what must be learned prespecified as objectives and/or outcomes. It encourages clear thinking about aims for specific skills and unambiguous items of knowledge. However, one of the several dangers of a dogmatic application of this model of planning is its failure to adequately guide the planning and assessment of aims that go further. Any tutor or programme which aspires to enable students to think and act critically and creatively with the knowledge and skills they gain needs to go beyond the objective/outcomes approach in the teaching and curriculum planning.

If this picture matches your experience as a tutor, it is worth considering questions which are explored later in this chapter, about where is the learning in this scenario? Educational thinking has developed ideas and practices which modify or supplant the approach caricatured above. Currently, the term 'student experience' is frequently used, implying the value of a student-centred view of teaching which encompasses more than a transmission of knowledge. Modules may aim to increase students' skills and enhance attitudes associated with 'knowing' a particular subject or professional field. Module aims may contribute to the achievement of overarching purposes of the entire programme, which are to do with induction into ways of thinking and acting as a specialist in that subject or field of professional practice, representing distinctive characteristics of worthwhile human achievement. A simple model of transmission teaching or delivery of content does not apply to more subtle aims such as these. To assist a search for ways of teaching, planning the curriculum and doing the assessments that have learning firmly at the centre, let's turn to the students' perspectives on becoming a learner in higher education.

Students' perspective

From students' points of view, just the idea of going to university or college can mean many different things, depending on personal interests, hopes, aspirations and current situations. It may mean following a passionate interest, or doing what is necessary to get a job. A student's immediate concerns during the early stages of the course may be about making many personal and social adjustments, wrestling with sometimes conflicting feelings of wanting to be independent and also wanting to belong, trying to adapt and to appear competent. When asked to say what feelings dominate their early experiences on entry to higher education, students routinely mention the fear of not being intelligent enough, fear of failing and of not fitting in with groups of strangers. Social acceptance by peers often seems to be an overwhelming priority. Students rarely refer to how they will learn, seeing it as something that is taken for granted, what you just do, more or less automatically. Students usually say that they don't need to know about what learning is, or how it happens. Their very presence at university is sufficient proof of their competence as learners. Or is it?

When talking to Year One undergraduates about previous experiences, they are aware of some areas in which they are successful learners and others in which they know they are not. Admitting, for example being 'rubbish' at exams is often just accepted without obvious questioning. Their approach to learning is to just get on with it, picking up any hints and tips that might work, but not treating it as a subject worthy of extended reflection or study in its own right. A picture emerges that this obvious yet invisible activity can be one of the most neglected aspects of being a student. No sustained attention or effort may be given explicitly to why or how to learn better. And yet success and enjoyment in studies may depend more than anything else on how a student thinks and feels about learning, about themselves as a learner and about how to develop their abilities to learn.

It is said, with increasing regularity and growing sadness, that students' attitudes to learning are shaped by a narrow instrumental priority of successful assignments. Passing assessments is believed to require abilities to remember or reproduce more and better knowledge of the subject, when these are the main learning outcomes that define success, plus skill in breaking knowledge into manageable bits to assimilate and practise recall. An assessment through performing a set task is again reduced to contributory parts. Students may believe they will be more successful at assignments if what must be done to succeed is clarified and simplified for them by the tutor. They may say, *'When the tutor tells me exactly what I must know and/or do, then I can learn effectively'*. The instrumentalism and dependence of this caricature of student learning are well-known and sometimes described as *'surface learning'*.

As if knowledge were a commodity to be delivered and taken possession of, some students 'clutch' onto transmissive learning, expressing satisfaction when receiving a handout, as if the tutor has 'given' them a piece of knowledge. A major characteristic of this kind of learning is the cultivation of attitudes of dependence and conformity. There is no need for a student to question, evaluate, hypothesise or criticise the learning outcomes – just get on and learn them! It is best to submit yourself to this externally imposed requirement now and leave until later, if ever, anything that you would like to understand better, probe into, link to something else, apply, disagree with or wonder about. This dependence is exacerbated if the criteria of assessment are not understood, deepening the difficulties caused by an impoverished view of learning. A student's judgement of how well they have performed an assessment may only be in terms of how closely it complies with the mechanical and technical formalities of presentational format and coverage. Having registered the all-important information – the mark or grade – students may ignore tutors' comments which explain and justify the assessment, because they deepen the mystery. Feedback on a student's qualities of learning is not valued as much as tutors would like. It seems as though learning to learn is little more than playing a game with unknown rules. If not knowing what you believe you are supposed to know has habitually been a shameful experience as a learner, then one coping strategy may be to conceal your doubt and ignorance from your teacher and pretend to know, asking no questions and hoping not to be asked any. Other students cope differently by declaring, in what can seem like an uncaring or almost aggressive tone, that they don't know X or can't understand Y, as if this is someone else's responsibility. They may expect the tutor to tell it again: *'my learning is dependent on the effectiveness of your transmission teaching – you must deliver it to me in better ways'*. Any move away from this mind set can seem like inviting even greater risks in an already vulnerable situation.

There may be a range of different aspects of learning such as these, which from the students' perspectives need attention. So tutors who regard themselves as teachers of students as well as teachers of subjects are interested in what can be done to enable their students to learn better, enjoy their learning more, persevere with their studies, gain higher grades and be better educated in their future lives. One way is to consider learning as a subject.

The 'subject' of learning

Recently, attempts to help students to learn have included publication of texts, online support and taught sessions. It is increasingly easy to access theoretical explanations of many aspects of the subject of learning, as well as practical advice and encouragement to improve learning, frequently emphasising skill development. Such resources may be provided by a programme and/or university learning support staff. A student interested in gaining knowledge of various explanations of learning which theorists have developed may find it a worthwhile subject of study. However, if treated like other subjects, with knowledge to be learned like acquiring a commodity, it may not become as meaningful or as usefully connected to practice. The fun of doing questionnaires about styles of learning, such as those in magazines, can produce an apparently authoritative categorisation, for example being a 'visual learner' which match self-perceptions of enjoying learning experiences that involve pictures, video and other visual material. But what then? Is a step to positive action sought or recognised? Or is the student frustrated that insufficient learning resources match their visual learning style and too much learning depends on listening and/or reading, which are perceived as relatively difficult? Knowing more of the subject of learning may not affect the practice of learning.

Following this example further, how can we help students to use the subject of learning as a resource for improving their practice of learning? Any theory can invite students to think about each others' similarities and differences as learners, provoking interest to explore practically. Having identified their learning style, some students may set themselves the challenge of what to do with learning material not presented in their 'preferred style'. There are potentially liberating effects of accepting individual differences, working out practical implications and developing collaborative encouragement and support for improvement. What can we do together about taking opportunities and overcoming difficulties that have become clearer to us? What makes the subject of learning a powerful resource for learning how to learn is students wanting to reach out to it and use it for their own purposes in their own ways.

Gaining study skills is a practical dimension of learning about learning. It can also be treated like a subject, with similar potential for improvement and danger of disappointment. Learning a physical skill, such as throwing a ball into a basket, can be helped by seeing a demonstration of more skilful performance, contrasting it with examples of less skilful performance, receiving tips on things to do and not to do, followed by repeated practice, with coaching on improvements in performance. The name 'study skill' implies a similar approach. This could be an appropriate way to learn how to take better lecture notes, for example. I could watch a demonstration and then have a go myself. I could compare my notes from the same lecture with notes by an experienced and more skilful taker of notes or, best of all, with the 'ideal' notes written for me by the lecturer. Using tips, I could analyse the errors and deficiencies in my notes and try to eliminate them next time. But then the question arises: if this is just a simple skill, like learning to throw a ball, how will it fit all of the different contexts in which I write notes and the various purposes I have? Is it more straightforward to apply this skill of note-taking to mainly factual and/or theoretical lectures that use transmission teaching than in discursive, awareness-arousing kinds of lectures? How do I develop judgement to apply the skill differently according to various learning needs? Seeing note-taking as a straightforward skill begins to wear thin if we consider sessions in which tutors are presenting contrasting theoretical perspectives as stimuli for reflection, for evaluation or application to new thinking and new practice. Is the same kind of note-taking needed here? Learning differentiation in note-taking skills and methods looks more like an ongoing inquiry. And what about improving my motivation to read? Is this a study skill? What counts as 'skilful motivation'? What excites one learner here, might scare another learner there. We are no longer in the realm of skills but complex combinations of dispositions, attitudes and values. What is needed is a spirit of personal inquiry.

An important meaning of the word 'subject' as it has been used so far now needs to be made explicit. It has been implied that a subject is the body of theoretical knowledge, with associated facts, principles and concepts, that are in the public domain as books, articles and other methods of communication. A subject is seen here as a convenient category of public knowledge (see also Chapter 11 under the heading *Rationalism*). The subject of learning can include public knowledge about many aspects including: remembering, understanding, analysing, styles or preferences, intelligence(s), internal and external personal conditions for learning, social conditions for learning, learning by habituation, by sensitisation, by conditioning, by association, learning through observation, play, enculturation, dialogue, problem solving, inquiry and so on. A traditional approach is that public knowledge is learned prior to, and in isolation from, its application and use: students need to know their stuff before they can be expected to think with it, do things with it and 'live' it. Following this, learning to learn could be a taught course: tutors presenting public knowledge of any or all of the topics suggested above to equip students to apply it and improve their learning in practice. Note that the assumed relationship between theory and practice is that theory is more important and determines good practice. An objectivist way of planning and rationalist assumptions about the pre-eminence of theory are both characteristics of current trends in education, which are important to recognise and be aware of. These themes are developed more fully in Chapter 9.

The Inquiry Into Learning approach does not see learning as a subject but as a social and moral practice. Learning how to learn is the refinement of this practice.

The practice of learning

The taken-for-granted quality about learning, which many students report, is understandable because we do it naturally as human organisms. Early years educators point out the complexity of learning to listen and speak, marvelling that it is a mostly natural and effortless process. They emphasise how much progress is made so early in life before formal instructional methods are used in school classrooms. It is achieved through basic ways of learning, such as noticing with all relevant senses, imitative and spontaneous actions, comparing, finding patterns in experience, testing tacitly held hypotheses and so on. Formal methods can consolidate learning by contriving situations with clearer purposes than natural ones and can also encourage self-knowledge as learners. Enjoyable, collaborative activities with optimistic, reflective attitudes can help a community to foster a culture of learning.

The meaning of 'practice' used here is not as a repetitive action that improves skill, such as, *'lots of practising recall helps you to remember facts in an examination'*. Nor does it mean practice in contrast to theory, such as, *'it's all very well in theory that a very quiet place helps your study to be more concentrated, but in practice I don't like quiet, I need music playing'*. Practice, as meant here, is not an unthinking physical action, however skilful, but an iterative blend of thinking and doing, with an element of personal involvement. The meaning is partly a *customary action*, as in, *'my usual practice when starting to study a text is to skim through all of it to find the parts that are most relevant to what I am most interested to learn in depth'*. There is also a sense of practice as the *ongoing pursuit of a craft or profession*, such as, *'in my learning practice I can give help (such as notes or references) to my fellow students who are my learning partners and ask for help from them when we talk about our work together'*. This example is intended to convey that, as in a craft or profession, practice implies what it is good to do. Not just in a technical, instrumental sense of what works best but also in a moral sense of *this is a good thing for me to do as a learning person, or this is the kind of good learner that I want to be* – something that is good in itself, not instrumental to another good. A summary of my practice as a learner could be a list of the actions I customarily take or procedures I follow together with indications of personal things that I think are good about my learning and important to me as a learner. For a science student, this might be:

> I want to learn things that relate to what I believe is important in life. For example, when we were being taught about DNA profiling, I wanted to understand how this knowledge is used by people in authority to do things like maintain a database, because it helped me think better about their justifications for doing this and enabled me to decide whether I agree with them.

This student is not merely acquiring knowledge or gaining skill, they are developing as a scientifically educated person by using their new knowledge and skill to think more deeply and act more wisely. The concepts are valuable, not merely to pass the assessment, but to make better personal sense of something perceived to be of human importance. A student teacher might refer to an aspect of their learning practice by saying when I was learning theories of children's development I wanted them to enable me, when I am on teaching practice, to observe pupils' behaviour more closely, talk to them more perceptively, understand them and teach them more skillfully and therefore become a better teacher.

Learning as a practice is not merely an individualised, taking possession of a cerebral commodity, it is mainly a social, whole-person-alised, process of reaching out.

Educating and training

Thinking about a learner's practice is illuminated by a distinction between education and training. According to Lawrence Stenhouse (1975), *training* is learning and teaching for acquiring and recalling informational kinds of knowledge and developing psychomotor kinds of skill. Successful learning is defined in detail beforehand and assessed as learning objectives and/or outcomes. Effective training would probably use formal instructional methods: clear, logically ordered presentation of information and a sequence of graded tasks to practise and shape skill development. *Education* subsumes Instruction and Skill *training* but goes further, to include *Induction* and *Initiation*. A teacher *inducts* a learner into a subject or professional activity by enabling them to gain an *understanding* type of knowledge (rather than only *informational* knowledge) and to use it to discipline their thinking. Since each person uses their knowledge differently, according to individual differences, such as what else they know, personal values, beliefs and individual creativity, induction yields different thinking in different students, not entirely predictable by the teacher, but nevertheless desirable educationally. *Initiation* is developing one's own values by testing them against the values and norms of the relevant culture of the subject or professional activity.

A science student may be *trained* to recall facts and informational kinds of explanation as well as develop skills to observe, describe, measure, record and report. To claim to have been *educated* in science, they must also (having been *inducted* into science knowledge) be able to think like a scientist, express a creative and critical appreciation of their science knowledge, discuss its applications and think about it from different perspectives. They must also (having been *initiated* into science) be able to demonstrate commitment to scientific values and attitudes, such as curiosity, questioning, skeptical ways of thinking and acting, endeavouring to be honest and objective with evidence and able to explore what different members of a scientific community might think about a controversial issue (see Ovens 2000).

A student teacher may be trained to recall facts and information about, for example, the National Curriculum, as well as develop skills to organise classroom materials, pupils and routine tasks. To claim to having been *educated* as a teacher, they must also (having been *inducted* into teaching) be able to think like a teacher, express a creative and critical appreciation of knowing what and how to teach and assess children, discuss methods and think about them from different perspectives. They must also (having been *initiated* into being a teacher) be able to demonstrate professional values and attitudes, such as inclusive and egalitarian ways of thinking and acting, endeavouring to be trustworthy, discreet and able to explore what different members of an educational community might think about a controversial issue.

A student of any higher education programme can be expected to develop as a learner those practices which are in harmony with being educated, not merely being trained. Their practice should engage them in learning as whole persons, drawing on emotional and social intelligences as well as powers of reasoning, their tacit knowledge and intuition as well as public knowledge, their individuality as well as collaboration, their contextualised experiences as well as abstract, generalised thinking. They should develop their confidence and decisiveness as well as doubt and ignorance as resources for directing and motivating questioning and deepening curiosity, their converging and critical dispositions as well as divergent and creative ones, their values, beliefs and commitments as well as information-processing techniques.

The practice of learning how to learn

At the inception of the BA in Childhood Studies programme at Nottingham Trent University, it was decided to design two core, compulsory modules called Inquiry Into Learning (IIL1 and IIL2) These two year-long modules underpin all other modules on the programme, providing a spine of important development: learning about learning, learning how to learn, learning how to inquire and learning to be a professional inquirer. In Year One, IIL1 refers to the subject of learning and its public knowledge, but does not teach it formally, taking an 'inquiry learning approach'. In Year Two, IIL2 continues the personal inquiry learning style, focusing attention on formal inquiry work for educational purposes and in professional, ethical ways.

The kind of inquiry used is 'action inquiry' into their practice, in order to improve it. Module organisation provides the frame for cycles of collaborative learning inquiries determined by students, with tutors' guidance.

A fundamental assumption is that the next step in a learner's learning can potentially take place under the influence of many different items of knowledge, many different skills and attitudes to develop and in relation to the learner's own values, beliefs and interests *at that moment*. A fundamental principle is that, having been appropriately prepared and receiving continuing support, it is the *student* who is the best person, in the best position, to take all of those things into account and take responsibility for deciding and taking the next step in the development of their learning.

This follows Julius Nyerere's principle that:

> People cannot be developed. They can only develop themselves.
>
> (Nyerere 1973: 5)

We are expecting students to embark on a journey of self-development and believe that they must take responsibility for it from the outset, while we co-create an environment that provides encouragement and support. Personal development is another human quality that everyone has at least the potential for, but which cannot be done to them or for them. It cannot be taught, but it can be learned.

An action inquiry begins with the student recognising what specific aspect of their learning practice they wish to improve. An information-gathering stage collects evidence of present practice, to notice more carefully what currently happens. Discussion with learning partners and the tutor helps to shape 'action steps': things to try, for the desired improvement, which are tested practically, gathering fresh evidence for critical reflection, discussion and further reading. Learning inquiries are discussed at Conferences with peers.

In both modules, the assessment method is in harmony with values and beliefs about learning. Called a 'Patchwork Texts' approach, students write a series of short pieces – patches – at set points across the module, culminating in an integrative final assignment – a Patchwork Text. Informal, formative peer feedback is built into the process to encourage collaborative, progressive learning. This is given extensive attention in Chapter 9.

In conclusion

This book is about how tutors can make a positive difference to student learning in higher education. It is intended to support tutors who wish to develop the *teaching students* aspect of their work as well as the teaching of a subject and/or vocational practice. It offers an approach that can be adapted to any higher education programme which trusts students to take increasing control over, and responsibility for, their own learning, becoming autonomous learners. The conditions which enable this are outlined next. They are underpinned by this chapter's coherent set of views of knowledge, education and, centrally, of learning as a socio-moral practice.

Chapter 3

The Inquiry Into Learning approach

During the design of a new undergraduate programme, the BA in Childhood Studies at Nottingham Trent University, much thought was given to the importance of students learning how to learn. It was decided to build into the programme a significant component, to complement the general support provided by the university for students' development of their learning abilities: two, year-long compulsory modules called Inquiry Into Learning (IIL), one in Year One and the other in Year Two. A straightforward, study skills based approach was rejected because, using distinctions detailed in Chapter 2, it would have had a *training* rather than an *educative* purpose. Neither is *learning* taught as a subject. Furthermore, IIL would not be a generic course in how to learn, which would be universally applicable to learning anything (as an MBA is said to be about *how to manage anything*). Inquiry Into Learning would help students on this programme to learn how to learn and also take a key role in achieving a central programme aim: the development of personal and professional autonomy enabling them to enter and contribute to professional worlds related to *Every Child Matters* (DfES 2003).

The IIL tutor team decided to conduct ongoing action research into their teaching, as a commitment to module development, and to be consistent with the IIL approach: engaging students in action research into improvement of their learning. Following traditions developed at the University of East Anglia, action research begins with an educational vision, containing central values, to guide improvements in practice. Adopting *autonomy* as a component of our vision, we refer to it during reflections on evidence of students' learning and to refine our practice. As IIL has progressed, our shared vision of autonomy has shifted, as the later parts of this book explain. As action researchers improve their practice towards achievement of their vision, their appreciation of its central values is modified and theorisation about its meanings in the current context deepens. Theory and practice relate to each other closely, improvements in one go hand in hand with developments in the other. There follows some of our thinking at the inception of IIL, starting with a clarification of the concept of autonomy, to sharpen future thinking, observation and reflection on autonomy in practice.

What is autonomy?

Teachers' intuitive sense of autonomy involves noticing a quality in things which learners say, write or do, which indicates their independence: asking an unusual question or presenting a distinctive line of thinking or taking an innovative course of action.

This type of behaviour was prized by John Holt (1991) when he reflected on learning characteristics in some children in his American elementary school class. He liked children who *'pleased themselves'*. He did not mean the self-indulgent, couldn't-care-less, *'I can please myself'* attitude of an immature person with no regard for others' views and he abhorred its opposite: a self-deprecatory, submissive desire to please teacher. He valued the sense that in doing their work, a child had wanted, more than anything else, to *'please themselves'*, to satisfy their internal locus of evaluation, that it was good, in their own estimation. The perceived good-ness may be in comparison with significant peers or norms (I want to read this book as well as my friend does), in comparison to set standards (I want to be able to read this book well enough to progress to the next level in the reading scheme) or in comparison with own previous achievements (I want to be able to read a more difficult book than the last one). Such achievements resulted less from *'compulsion'*, either externally by the teacher or internally to follow needs slavishly, but more by the child having a *'love of learning'*, free (relatively) from external or internal compulsions.

We have applied the idea of using knowledge for disciplining thinking not only to how we want students to learn how to learn, but also to our own thinking about developing our teaching. To understand an aspect of practice, we helped each other find others' knowledge, through talking, reading and participating in conferences, to discipline our thinking. We found that the philosophical writing of Richard Dearden helped us to think about the concept of autonomy:

> Autonomy is Independent judgment using criteria (which could be general rules, goals, principles, standards and values).
>
> (Dearden 1975: 7)

The independence of the judgements, in Dearden's view, is not equivalent to originality in the sense of novelty, but independence does imply *origination*, that is, how it came to be that the judgement is that individual's, *independent of external/internal compulsions*. Dearden's view requires that any education aimed at developing autonomy should specify at the start, the kinds of things it expects people to exercise independent judgment of, and what kinds of criteria it expects them to use. Any such course should have an inquiry dimension in which a person must reflect in *doubtful* terms, question the criteria of judgement and, in turn, doubt their reflection as a secure basis for proceeding, and so on. Autonomy is a *process* which is impossible to complete, and whose quality is judged as a matter of degree. Autonomy has its own inner logic of development, as it were, implying as an ideal its own growth towards completeness and integrity. It represents one out of many forms of the perfectibility of man.

(Dearden 1975: 10)

Developing autonomy is the same as practising it, involving an internal growth which cannot be measured against an absolute, external standard. Indeed, one of the qualifying characteristics of an autonomous judgement is its doubtfulness. However, if autonomy is not entirely 'out there' for all to see, amenable for objective measurement, neither is it entirely subjective, context dependent or arbitrary. In this sense, it is a quality that straddles objectivity and subjectivity, assessment requiring a blend of scientific and artistic approaches. Practising autonomy is something a student might claim to do (or a tutor might claim, on their behalf) when making a judgement which they believe to be their own. For this claim to be accepted in Dearden's terms as autonomous, the judgment would have to be a doubtful, reflective and tentative one, and it must be demonstrated to others to have originated not in external or internal compulsions but in a choice, made by reference to criteria related to the relevant personal, conceptual and contextual factors. This is a public test of autonomy.

The IIL approach expects students' action inquiry to reflect in doubtful terms on their developments. Qualities of autonomy should be recognisable in a student's learning inquiry by the *independence* of its aim, methods, evidence and improvements. They do not have to be novel, but the student must have originated them by referring to relevant personal learning needs, interests or aspirations, with critical use of evidence of their current practice and with relative freedom from external or internal compulsions. They should not choose things that are *false* or not authentic to them, for example, by guessing what the tutor wants or through fear of failure or ridicule. Nor should they choose inquiry focuses, etc. to please their peers or which seem to be a 'safe bet' for a 'successful' inquiry, anticipating the 'improvement'. Equally, tutors avoid saying things which are perceived as directing what to choose or how to do the inquiry, which inadvertently function as external compulsions. Autonomy is judged in these relative terms.

Planning IIL's place within the programme

Inquiry Into Learning occupies a spinal position in the design of the degree. It is the part of the programme which most intensely focuses on the development of qualities of learning and professionalism that underpin the whole degree.

Lawrence Stenhouse's (1975) distinction between training and education was set out in Chapter 2. He also argued that planning a training programme appropriately uses an objectives or outcomes model, but planning education cannot do so without distorting the educative process. Trainers legitimately define outcomes of successful training with SMART objectives of a technical kind, for the acquisition of informational knowledge or of psychomotor skills – SMART stands for Specific (specifying what is to be achieved by the learner) Measurable (the achievement must be capable of being measured) Achievable (the achievement must be attainable) Realistic (capable of being achieved with known resources) and Time (specifying when it is to be achieved) – This enables them to be assessed objectively or quantified in a quasi-scientific way. Educators, however, enable students to be initiated and inducted into understanding more than merely informational kinds of knowledge and wisdom of action. Successful outcomes of this process cannot be entirely predetermined. They have to be judged against broader criteria characterising qualities not capable of straight-forward quantification. This is because the person educated in a field, does not merely reproduce what has been trained into them, but demonstrates what comes from their independent thinking, personal understanding, justified choices and courses of action, within the field of study. Therefore, judgement of learning qualities takes into account the learner's own creativity, contextual variations and interpersonal differences. Assessment is more artistic in character, using different standards and procedures of judgement than purely scientific ones. Therefore, the centrally important quality of autonomy is not reduced to objective statements for quantitative measurement, but expressed as *learning qualities* which require intersubjective judgement.

Another vital feature of Stenhouse's model of curriculum planning is that deciding purposes of education should be simultaneous with considering ways of learning and teaching. Ends should not be separated from the means by which they are to be achieved. Students who are being educated engage in a process with educationally worthwhile qualities which are integral to what they think and do throughout the learning, not just at the end. This requires a particular kind of planning of the procedures used in the teaching, called 'pedagogic principles of procedure'. Finally, criteria by which successful learning is judged are aligned to learning qualities and pedagogic principles. Assessment of learning is not bolted on to the end of the curriculum plan, but is integral to it throughout the process.

The initial thinking about all these aspects for what was then an entirely new degree programme is presented below.

The meaning of the central aim of the programme

A central aim of the programme is professional autonomy. We want all graduates to possess the following aspects of this quality at the end, and therefore to practise them across the degree and continue to use them as lifelong learners:

I   Abilities to learn from such experiences as:

- observation of people, situations and interactions;
- involvement in practical experiences, including taking appropriate actions and initiatives;
- reading and discussion of significant texts;
- listening to and questioning others: peers, tutors, fellow professionals and 'clients';
- presenting one's own ideas to others, giving evidence, explanations and arguments.

2   Abilities to make connections and create patterns and relationships of meaning from the different learning opportunities provided and sought for oneself, in order to develop the personal understanding, values and abilities necessary to be able to act and interact appropriately.

3   Abilities to question, criticise, explore and make creative contributions to the development, particularly through discussion, of shared thinking about issues of importance, within both routine practice and high-level policy, tolerating ambiguity, complexity and uncertainty.

4   Abilities to reflect self-critically and constructively on one's own and on others' actions in order to understand and to negotiate control and responsibility for improvement.

5   Abilities to think, act and intervene constructively and reflectively in ways that aim to further one's own and shared ideals and values, while showing respect for evidence and respect for persons involved and while demonstrating an accurate appreciation of the context.

6   Abilities to clarify, develop and extend one's own personal, professional ideals and values as part of one's learning.

Students are encouraged to engage in these processes of learning throughout their degree course. Each module contributes to the students' growing range of skill, knowledge and understanding with obvious and explicit consistency in how they learn and how their learning is assessed.

Pedagogical principles for the processes of modules

1   Learning is *inquiry* based, encouraging students to adopt a questioning, doubting and critical stance towards the knowledge and the controversial issues in subject matter, involving them in self-initiated and self-directed inquiry. Suitable student inquiry outcomes would become study materials for the present and future groups.

2   Learning is *practice* based, through direct experience of the contexts in which knowledge can be gained and immediately applied, and through indirect experiences such as the study of multimedia resources, simulations, role play, case study, etc. as appropriate.

3   The teaching is planned so as to enable students to become more aware of their previous experience, initial thinking and action about the substantive areas and through inquiry, to *construct* personal meaning both from experience and also by disciplining their thinking and action with others' knowledge (not merely remembering others' knowledge).

4   Teaching enables students to *adapt* their own practice as well as *adopt* others' practices.

5   Teaching provokes students' personal and collaborative integration of theory and practice, encouraging *critical reflection* on their own and others' theories and values, testing them against practice and developing them by responding to contextualised problems in practice, and by carrying out practical problem solving and inquiry.

6   Each area of subject matter provides content, conceptual frameworks and contexts for the learning of know-how to be *integrated* with learning 'knowing-that' and 'knowing-why'.

These pedagogical principles are interpreted to match the distinctive aims and learning experiences of each module, while conferring coherence of learning approach across all modules, jointly working towards autonomy. This consistency applies also to assessment of learning, to convey the programme's central values.

Background ideas about the curriculum of the programme

Ronald Barnett (1997) proposed a schema for modern curricula in higher education with three curriculum domains, arguing that, particularly for professional degrees, they should be integrated with each other in the students' learning. The core concept is *critical being*, which embraces critical thinking and reasoning (hitherto a defining concept of the Western university, albeit in a narrow sense of criticising formal, public knowledge) to which is added *critical action* and *critical self-reflection* (broadening into the domains of the world and the self).

Barnett sees the meaning of the whole as more than the sum of its parts.

Barnett's three forms of criticality

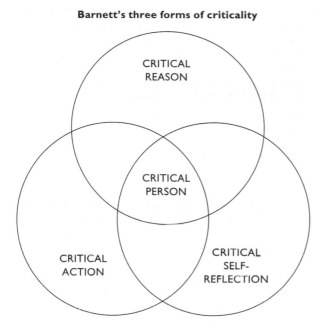

Figure 3.1 IIL1: How the organisation of the module matches the students' learning processes

Hitherto, conceptions of higher education have favoured either, first, the notion of critical thinking towards formalised knowledge or, second, a competence model of effective performance in the world or, third, a reflective practice model. The third alternative, according to Barnett (1997), seeks to unite action and self-reflection but downplays or disparages formal knowledge. His model is based on an amalgam of all three kinds of aims. Using these ideas, the IIL programme seeks to develop all three domains of critical being, which could include the kinds of qualities set out in Table 3.1 so as to indicate their interdependence (see Figure 3.2).

Table 3.1 Three qualities of critical being

Thinking and reasoning	Action	Personal self-reflection
Theoretical knowing and understanding theories, models and conceptual frameworks from a range of academic studies	Able to test theories in practice, apply theories to practice and develop one's own, new theories from practice	Being critical and self-critical towards theory and practice and ones' own thinking and action in practical professional contexts

Continued overleaf

Table 3.1 Continued

Thinking and reasoning	Action	Personal self-reflection
Procedural knowing and understanding: models and concepts of evidence and analysis	Able to answer questions and tackle problems through action inquiry in professional situations	Being curious, questioning, showing respect for accurate, relevant and significant evidence
Ability to think logically, make connections and tolerate uncertainty, ambiguity and complexity	Able to cope with stress and find appropriate forms of action or intervention to take manageable steps forwards	Being courageous, inventive, resourceful, tentative, playful, reflective
Understanding about diversity of needs and multiple interpretations and perspectives	Able to offer to and elicit from others, thoughts and actions of tolerance, openness, honesty and affirmation	Being aware and self-aware in personal professional relationships
Understanding about different forms/styles of communication, teaching and learning	Able to communicate and to facilitate others' communication as part of shared learning and development	Being empathic, lively, clear, stimulating and encouraging
Understanding of ideals, beliefs, and personal value systems	Able to elicit, explore and clarify values through dialogue and refinement of practice	Being respectful, aware and self-aware of the values dimension

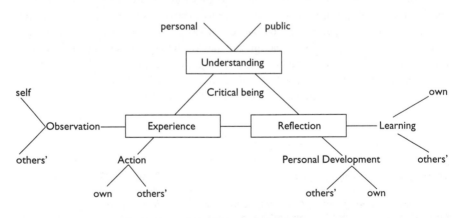

Dimensions of Becoming a Reflective Learner

Figure 3.2 Development of Barnett's critical person by the Inquiry Into Learning approach

An outline of the Inquiry Into Learning approach

The programme has two modules with the above title, one in each of the first two years. They are closely linked with a Year Three module, the Professional Research Project. They constitute a compulsory core to the programme in the sense that they are most fully dedicated to the development of students' professional autonomy and also because they link with all other modules to some extent and to certain modules particularly closely.

The title 'Inquiry Into Learning' has an intended ambiguity. The modules are about each student's own learning, how this proceeds, how it is enabled, managed, improved and assessed at the levels of the individual and of the group. The Inquiry Into learning modules use action inquiry methods, as applied to the improvement of students' learning. Therefore, the content of these modules can be a student's learning in any part of the programme.

1   The aim of the IIL modules is to learn how to learn, as part of becoming an autonomous professional person, developing capacities: to think critically about learning of many kinds and in many contexts; to improve the practices of one's own and others' learning; and to reflect on relevant personal, conceptual and contextual factors.

2   The practical experiences from which the students learn, are those involving themselves and others as learners across contexts in any modules and placements of the programme.

3   The learning through inquiry takes place in cycles. Each cycle typically starts with critical reflection on situations and experiences where students perceive a need, difficulty or opportunity to strengthen their learning, in relation to their own needs, ideals, aims and values about learning. This leads to the negotiation with tutors of a focus and methods to inquire into the practical and theoretical aspects of the problematic situations and experiences, with the purpose of improving their own and each others' learning practices. Improvements are tested and evaluated in practice through gathering and analysing evidence. Inquiry findings are reported to others at in-house conferences at which different groups of students critique the different inquiries. Then there is shared decision making about further collaborative inquiries into practical improvement and also the commissioning of theoretical presentations and workshops to deepen understanding, refine skills, and initiate new challenges to the collaborative learning about learning.

4   The encouragement of critical reflection on learning takes place through small group discussion and through short pieces of writing – patches – which each student discusses with their small group, makes available to the whole group, receives formative comment from tutors and accumulates in their portfolio of patches.

5   Improvements in the students' learning, as evidenced by their data gathering, are the practical outcomes of their inquiries. The pieces of writing indicate these personal gains and the wider insights into learning. Self and peer feedback is encouraged, to foster progressive improvements.

6   The conceptual content of the modules (which includes theories of learning and philosophies of knowledge, as well as methods of inquiry) are partly *emergent* and *developmental*, as students perform the theoretical parts of their inquiry work, and partly *imposed*, at the points when decisions are made about the commissioning of theoretical presentations and workshops, when some aspect of conceptual content is identified to be of a *challenging* kind, to initiate new lines of inquiry or prompt a step change in the level of inquiry.

7   The integration of thinking, action and self-reflection is facilitated by the keeping by each student of a Reflective Jotter. This is a routine task aimed at facilitating the formation of personal meaning and communications between students and with tutors, as well as building a record of progress.

8   Evaluation of students' engagement in these processes is monitored: by observing various aspects of students' inquiry work; by reading students' writing, including the Jotters; by noticing the extent and quality of their participation in discussion, including responses to tutors' challenges, and by regularly discussing students' evaluations of the processes and themselves.

9   The assessed assignment is a Patchwork Text. This is derived from each student reviewing their own portfolio of writing from which extracts of set pieces (the patches), together with extracts from the Jotter are selected and stitched together with an explanatory and critically reflective commentary. This creates a composite document which is an account of the student's learning processes and outcomes.

A Patchwork Texts format of coursework and assessment takes account of the variety of different ways in which individual students learn and are able to present their learning. Different kinds of writing allow a student to express their knowing in a range of ways, including as a personal process of self-exploration and self-questioning, in their learning 'journey' as a form of personal engagement with the course content. Sharing these pieces of writing encourages collaborative learning and formative feedback, to enrich the learning process, so that students can develop themselves into a *learning community*. The assignment is a composite text based on patches, extracts from the student's own set of pieces, with a reflective, unifying commentary which draws on further reading, including other students' patches, to produce a personal synthesis which addresses the main aims of the module. Refer to Chapters 7 and 9 for fuller accounts.

In IIL, students carry out a series of pieces of action inquiry into the improvement of a defined aspect of their learning. Each inquiry involves discussion, writing notes and taking practical action steps, culminating in the writing of an account, called a patch. Patches are shared electronically across the group. In parallel to the conduct of a series of individual and/or small group inquiries, a student is required to write reflectively about their experiences, ideas, deliberations, self-assessments and evaluations of progress. The format which is usually recommended, is a handwritten notebook or Jotter, but alternatively, blogs are increasingly used by a minority of students. The Patchwork Text assignment is produced at the end of the module as a composite document created mainly from the student's own patches but also their Jotter entries, with references to and use of ideas obtained from public knowledge, not only that of published authors but also of peers in their patch writing. The title of the Patchwork Text assignment in IIL1 is 'Becoming a reflective learner' and in IIL2 is 'Becoming a professional inquirer'. In preparing their Text, a student may present relevant extracts of their patches in the same sequence as they were done, using the structure of an unfolding story of their learning across the module. Other structures using different sequences of patches are encouraged, when a student wishes to address the title of the assignment differently, for example in a thematic way. Patch extracts are selected to fit with each other to create a coherent personal synthesis. Each student is expected to refer to their reflective writing in the choice of structure, patch extracts and sequences and encouraged, where appropriate, to insert extracts of their Jotter into their Text. In addition to the reading referred to in the patches, further reading about key concepts and central theories is carried out to strengthen the conceptual level of the Text.

The Inquiry Into Learning modules in action

The module process for IIL1 is summarised in Figure 3.3.

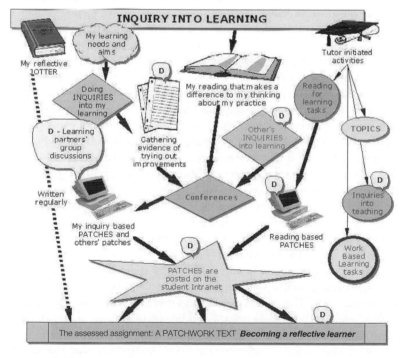

Figure 3.3 Module process for IIL1

Note: D signifies discussion of relevant issues at each of the points indicated in the process.

For Inquiry Into Learning 1, action inquiries incrementally improve specific aspects of the practice of learning. Each inquiry focus arises through reflection on perceived needs, difficulties, purposes and interests as learners, selecting what is judged to be the most significant at the current stage in learning and development as a learner. For example, a learning inquiry into *Improving my use of study time* could arise from a student's concern about or interest in this part of their learning practice, which would be the aspect of their learning which they would find most helpful to try to improve. The starting point is to gather evidence of relevant parts of current practice using simple inquiry techniques to generate evidence-based descriptions for each other and for tutors, which deepen understanding of what is actually happening now. In this example, evidence could include records of what was done, possibly in coded categories, for samples of time over a week as a database of how much time was used in which ways and in what kinds of patterns, etc., with self-evaluative notes on the quality of any learning that took place and reflections on the whole experience. Discussion of evidence follows, and making a personally empathic analysis of what happened leads to exploration of intuitions and reasons for events. Then the group's attention turns to considering ways to improve learning within each context, drawing ideas from public knowledge, as well as tacit knowledge and peer experiences. Each action step's potential for improvement is tested by putting it into action in a new, comparable context called 'fresh experience', gathering further evidence for reassessment. There is a parallel requirement to think reflectively about experiences, ideas, deliberations, self-assessments and evaluations of progress, and record thoughts in a handwritten notebook or Jotter, or voice recorder or a blog. At a meeting of the group called a 'conference' each student's learning story is discussed, with coaching by peers and the tutor for continuing improvements. There are explicit procedures for giving and receiving feedback to promote the quality of discussion. Relevant theoretical ideas and frameworks from public knowledge may enrich thinking, and may be applied to practice and tested.

Each inquiry enables a student to develop an evidenced, constructive expression of their intention to develop aspects of their learning, integrating practical improvements with personal theoretical insights. They are free to revisit, extend previous inquiries or start new ones emerging from their assessment of what is the next most important improvement in their practice. A cumulative, personal and collaborative approach to learning aims to contextualise learning rather than train students in skills through decontextualised exercises.

The final part of each action inquiry cycle is to write about the learning story as a patch, which is made available to students and tutors by appropriate electronic methods (see Chapter 8). Discussion of ideas and evidence with learning partners occurs at every stage. Other features of the module include structured, tutor-led inquiries into a series of conceptual frames for understanding learning.

At the end of the module, each student stitches together parts or whole patches, to create a composite document – a Patchwork Text, the module's assessed assignment. Extracts of significant material from their portfolio of patches are organised into a coherent sequence with short passages of linking, reflective commentary called the 'stitching'. Acknowledged extracts from other students' patches are admissible, as are references to further reading about key concepts and central theories to strengthen the conceptual level of the Text. Extracts from the Jotter about personal apprehensions, puzzles, questions and surprises arising from their learning journey are included to provide evidence of changes in perspective, deepening of awareness and gains in understanding, to link patches into a coherent whole.

The varying ways in which the presentation of patches may be made takes account of the variety of different ways in which individual students learn and are able to express their knowing, including as a personal process of *self-exploration* and *self-questioning*, when a learning 'journey' is a form of personal engagement with the course content. Regular sharing of writing encourages collaborative learning and formative feedback, so that students can develop themselves into a *learning community*. Refer to Chapters 7 and 9 for fuller accounts.

Concluding note

This chapter encapsulates our initial thinking about the IIL approach which provided the starting point for the subsequent developments presented in the rest of the book. In our action research project, we have met regularly to discuss our experiences, illuminate them with items of evidence such as notes of students' utterances, descriptions of their actions or samples of their writing, and to explore reflectively the relationship of these glimpses of each other's practice with each other's visions, theories and ideals. Some of these have been used to illustrate or exemplify points in the book to convey a similar amalgam of theory and practice. In Part II, some of the story of subsequent developments is presented. We invite readers to reflect with similar iterations in your own theory and practice, to explore the possible relevance of an IIL approach to another situation.

Using the Inquiry Into Learning approach in two modules of a Childhood Studies programme

Chapter 4

Inquiry Into Learning I
Becoming a reflective learner

This chapter provides the curriculum plan for this module together with evidence of its operation and some reflective, developmental analyses of practice. It is a snapshot of where this module is, at the time of writing. In trying to be clear, the account may give a greater impression of certainty, balance and stability in the operation of the module than we often experience. As teacher-researchers, seeing this module's curriculum in a dynamic way, we continue to try out new ideas, wrestle with dilemmas and maintain our action inquiries. Teaching the module feels more like watching a rather fuzzy, all-action film than looking at a pin-sharp snapshot. Several developmental issues concerning the module are addressed in the last part of this chapter and in greater depth in Parts III and IV. We hope this will convey how and why the module changes each year.

The chapter deals first with the process of establishing the IIL approach with each new group of students, which occupies the first few sessions. The cycles of students' action inquiry into the improvement of their learning, which is at the heart of the IIL approach (set out in Chapter 3) are presented in the middle of the chapter and the last section deals with the preparation of the Patchwork Text assignment and its assessment.

IIL I – the beginning

Pre-course preparation is provided for students on this degree programme. Prior to the first session at university, students receive a request to do a preliminary task while still at home, detailed in Box 4.1. It gives a common basis for initial discussions between students and also allows individual choice of reading to bring a diversity of experiences as a source for exchange of ideas in the first few seminar sessions of the module.

Box 4.1 Reading and thinking about children

We would like you to give some time to thinking about children and linking this with your own experiences and ideas about childhood. A good way to do this, which will also help you to prepare for your learning on the programme, is to choose a book about children that you:

- find interesting;
- can bring with you to the early stages of the course;
- would be willing to talk about and share with others.

You are free to choose ANY book.

This includes fiction, biography or other non-fiction books for adults or a book about children's lives specifically written for older children/teenagers.

Your choice includes books that you have already read, provided that you:

- really enjoyed reading it and that it developed your thinking about children's experiences;
- read it again before the start of the course.

This choice also includes selecting a book by one of the authors listed below, but we certainly don't want you to think that you *must* select from this list. We are also interested to hear about other books that you and other students know about and can share with all of us.

There is a huge range of authors to choose from but the following might give you some ideas:

Malorie Blackman   Melvyn Burgess   Torey Hayden   Mark Haddon
Phillipa Pearce   Doris Pilkington   Sue Townsend   Jacqueline Wilson

We ask you to write a short review of your book which summarises it and may also say what you found to be the most interesting things about it, what effects it had (and may still have) on your feelings and thoughts about children and childhood, and what you would like to find out more about, as a result of having read this book. The review can be about 500 words, but you can make it longer if you wish. There is no precise expectation of length but the 500 words is meant to be a rough guideline.

Do read more than one book if you want to! But just write one review.

During the Childhood Studies course, we value learning about children through thinking about ideas in books and also from videos, television, our own experiences and the experiences of others, so do take time to start on this learning journey by reading books that look interesting to you or are suggested by people you know.

We look forward to sharing the ideas from these books at the beginning of your course.

Students choose their 'Riveting Read' title from the wide range of topics to do with children's lives, about which we hope that students become more interested and knowledgeable. The activity aims for students to gain a wholehearted enjoyment from reading a *complete* book, to feel the interest and pleasure of a positive experience of oneself as a reader, to reflect and discuss. The greater importance of enjoyment over content is signalled by the large choice of titles of our full list of Riveting Reads – more than 60 titles – which is also sent to students. A shortened version of the list is reproduced in Box 4.2.

Box 4.2 List of Riveting Reads about children and their lives

Here is a short list of some of the books previous students have read and enjoyed.

Axline, Virginia *Dibs*
'moving story of a play therapist's work with Dibs – what the child and therapist learn together'

Blackman, Malorie
Noughts and Crosses, Knife Edge and Check-Mate
A trilogy of books about young people and the issues of racism where black people are in positions of power and privilege. 'You won't be able to put them down'

Browne, Anthony
The Visitors who Came to Stay, Changes, Look What I've Got and The Night Shimmy (co-written with Gat Strauss)

Books for children: *Look What I've Got* is about Jeremy who, it seems, has everything, a new bicycle, a pirate outfit and an enormous bag of lollipops, but he won't share anything with Sam. Selfishness gets its come-uppance in this modern morality tale that is packed with detail

Piggybook **and also** *The Tunnel*
Browne's books for young children that give adults insights into childhood similar to those by David MacKee In *Not Now Bernard* 'it's marvellous'

Dahl, Roald
Boy, Tales of Childhood
'the real life story of the author

Roald Dahl. It is funny and amazing. No wonder Roald Dahl could write such amazing fiction when his own life story was so full of rich and colourful stories'

Frank, Anne
The Diary of Anne Frank
Insightful diary of Anne Frank during the period when her Jewish family hid from the Nazis in Amsterdam in the Second World War. Reflections on growing up.

Haydn, Torey various titles including: *One Child, Ghost Girl, Tigers' Child, Twilight Children_*
Four books about an educational psychologist who becomes a special needs teacher and her work with children with emotional and behavioural concerns.

'I can't put them down'

'Gripping and insightful about children with behavioural difficulties and teaching responses. Inspirational at times'

Hill, Gredd and Gina
On The Run
'We were sent away, someplace we'd never been or even imagined, strangers in a strange place, to start over with nothing but fake names and everything to hide.'

Hosseini, Khaled
The Kite Runner
Twelve-year-old Amir is desperate to gain the approval of his father and resolves to win the local kite fighting tournament, to prove that he has the makings of a man. His loyal friend Hassan promises to help him, for he always helps Amir, but this is 1970s Afghanistan and Hassan is merely a low caste servant who is jeered at in the street, although Amir feels jealous of his natural courage and the place he holds in his father's heart. But neither of the boys could foresee what would happen to Hassan on the afternoon of the tournament, which was to shatter their lives. After the Russians invade and the family is forced to flee to America, Amir realises that one day he must return, to find the one thing that his new world cannot give him: redemption.

King, Clive
The Night the Water Came
A book for older children about a boy and his village surviving a flood caused by a cyclone hitting their island. 'It reminds me of the tsunami in SE Asia'

Munsch, R. and A. Lewis
Love You Forever
Story of a mother and her baby as he grows to adulthood: 'essentially about how love is passed through generations; a wonderful book that is still much loved by my children (now aged 22, 20 and 15!)'

Pearce, Phillipa
Goodnight Mr Tom
'a thought-provoking book, sometimes intensely sad and moving.

It traces the life of a boy evacuated during the Second World War and tells, in sometimes painful detail, the effect that war had on the lives of young children. This story has been made into a film with John Thaw in the lead role'

Pilkington, Dorris
Rabbit-proof Fence
A true aboriginal story about children's determination to escape the slavery of a white Christian mission and survive an 1800 km walk in search of freedom. 'Amazing – the courage of the children! Challenging in terms of the cultural context and racist attitudes'

The first session

The aim is to establish a positive emotional dimension for learning experiences, to develop an expectation of student initiative through inquiry and to encourage probing the idea of 'learning'. Key elements of the session are listed below.

A   At least one 'icebreaker' activity is used to help students to relax, meet other group members and find out about each other. There is an emphasis on learning each others' names and disclosing current thoughts and feelings about the experience of the first session.

B   IIL1 is presented as a major module in the programme with the centrally important aim of learning how to learn at university. Although some theoretical material will relate to children's learning, the purpose of the module is firmly about students' own learning. This causes surprise and a little frustration to a few students who immediately question the relevance of IIL to a Childhood Studies degree.

C   Next, there is tutor-led discussion about 'What have we/I achieved already at the university?'. Students describe what they have done to find their way (physically) to the room, how they completed registration and other tasks, started new relationships, formed initial expectations and so on. These are listed as gains made in awareness, new information and shifts in attitudes, which have happened naturally and effortlessly through what they have done. Using unconditional positive regard, tutors endorse these as learning achievements, explicitly using the word 'learn' in a broad sense, affirming the self-motivated, independent and collaborative aspects of the learning that is being celebrated. Students are asked individually to notice and note more examples of informal personal learning as they continue to adapt to being at university and begin their programme.

D   Having begun with *learning*, attention turns to the students as people. Activities are carried out to do with 'Who are we?', 'What are we/am I good at?', 'How do we/I learn well?'. The group assembles and sorts information about what proportion of its members live at home or on campus, what are the different reasons for choosing Childhood Studies, and for choosing this university, etc. This is pointed out to be fact finding for shared inquiry – a prominent, recurring activity of the module. The group is then asked to raise questions such as: 'What else (to do with X, Y or Z) would we like to know about each other?' and 'What would we like Year Two students to tell us about?'. The last question opens contact between Year groups of students: for the freshers to learn from more experienced counterparts. Small groups conduct fact finding inquiries for the second session.

E   The Riveting Read is discussed to gauge students' responses. The review writing task is clarified and students are asked to bring it to the second session.

F   Next, the tutor introduces concepts like 'learning partner' and 'critical friend', to refer to the kinds of mutual support and encouragement that students are expected to give and receive. Students talk, in groups of three, about becoming initial learning partners and start to share immediate personal concerns or questions about settling in to university life and becoming successful students.

G   In the final ten minutes of the two-hour session, the tutor asks students to reflect on what has taken place, identifying thoughts and feelings which characterise their experience of the session. Examples are elicited and responded to by the tutor in accepting terms. Reflection is stated to be an important part of learning how to learn at university. Students are asked to obtain a suitable notebook as their Reflective Jotter for one of the module activities.

The second session

This session is structured around developing continuity and progression from the first session.

A   Following C in the first session, more examples of informal learning about being a beginning student are discussed, from which features of self-directed learning are pointed out and valued by the tutor: using prior knowledge, asking questions, asking expert knowers, solving puzzles and problems, seeking and interpreting public information of various kinds, keeping records of key information, communicating new knowledge in a summarised form to others. Tutors model the analysis of naturalistic learning into named contributory skills, procedures and abilities. This helps to develop the shared use of a common language of learning and sets out different components for closer attention in the future.

B   Following D in the first session, small groups report answers to questions about adapting to life at university. This is pointed out to be the first of many collaborative student inquiries into subjects they identify and talking to Year

Two students is the first of several opportunities for formal contact between Year groups.

C   Printed copies of the Module Handbook are given out. Attention is drawn to recommended texts and a chapter from one of them is circulated for study. The focus of this chapter is on student responses to the transition in studying from school to higher education. Both documents are also provided in digitised form through the Virtual Learning Environment.

D   Riveting Read reviews are considered, first for their *content* about children and childhood and, second, as an experience (hopefully very positive) of being a reader, as an aspect of the *process* of becoming a better learner. Following IIL's process curriculum, the content of inquiries is open to alteration according to student interest, which the tutor facilitates, while the process (see Chapter 3) follows the pedagogical principles of procedure, that learning is:

- inquiry based;
- practice based;
- constructing personal meaning from experience and by disciplining thinking and action with others' knowledge;
- adapting own practice as well as adopting others' practices.

Each student describes and evaluates their experience as a reader, comparing it empathically with others' descriptions and evaluations, to understand their own and each others' personal strengths and needs as readers of books, on this occasion. Many aspects of the reading process are discussed: choosing times, places, situations, inhibiting and facilitating factors, kinds of concentration of thought, noticing faster and slower progress, habits of self-monitoring and recording, ways of responding to linguistic, stylistic, conceptual, ethical and emotional challenges, creation of links with previous experiences or with anticipated future experience, different kinds of interest and enjoyment, and so on. The tutor habitually ends sessions by stating outcomes in a generalised form for students to interpret as personally applicable, including an enthusiastic acceptance of the diversity of students' responses, citing examples, while also affirming the common purpose of improving learning, and prompting students' further reflection on self-development and collaborative support.

E   Following F in the first session, learning partner groups are convened to discuss students' experiences of work so far, establish areas that have been learning gains and raise questions or requests for support. The whole group discusses these and the tutor responds appropriately. Learning partners discuss G from the first session – starting to keep a reflective journal.

F   In preparation for the third session, students are asked to:

- make Jotter entries about what they feel are exciting, disappointing, satisfying, interesting, surprising, frustrating or worrying things in learning experiences;

- write a reflective addition to the Riveting Read review, summarising learning about how they read their book and how they see themselves as readers;
- read the chapter (provided at C) from a set text book and prepare to contribute to discussion about it and what was gained to help to improve learning;
- read the Module Handbook and bring comments and questions for discussion.

Tutor observations during the sessions, augmented by note taking, provide resources for our individual reflection afterwards and during discussion times at tutor team meetings. As well as dealing with immediate concerns about maintaining practical and organisational aspects, the primary focus is on our own inquiries into characteristics, needs, opportunities and challenges of a given group of students. We find it becomes apparent by this stage which students are more vocal in expressing ideas and suggestions, as well as doubts and uncertainties. We discuss questions and hypotheses about understanding the students' responses and consider choices of learning activities available for opportunistic use from a range we have accumulated; for example, exercises in reflective writing of various kinds.

Our intention over the next few sessions is to sustain sufficient pace, variety of task and level of student involvement to continue the purposeful and productive atmosphere in the session, while gradually withdrawing from continuously directive teacherly activity, for short spells of detached observation. The effectiveness of the IIL approach partly depends on tutors learning a lot about their students as learners. So when students are active, the tutor blends opportunistic teaching and on-the-spot support with unobtrusive watching, listening, eavesdropping and glancing at work in progress, to evaluate this group's learning here and now.

The Module Handbook introduces IIL1 as follows:

This module is intended to give you the space, support and encouragement to learn best from your experiences and study across all parts of the Programme. We want to develop your own and each others' abilities to learn reflectively, collaboratively and professionally. We want to enable you to become an increasingly successful learner in higher education in a way that lays good foundations for your continued learning and development after you have graduated, as a qualified professional person.

Learning may be something that you have already thought about and know a bit about. Or it may be that learning seems to be a new subject for you. How you learn may be something that you tend to take for granted, rather than regard as a practice that can be developed. You may have previous experience of taking some decisions for your self about what, when, where and how you learn, or these things may have been mainly decided for you by others. In this module, we will learn about what learning is like, in theory, in practice, by ourselves, by each other, and how we can make improvements in practice. You are invited to develop yourself as a learner by learning from the choices and decisions you make, the questions you ask, the improvements that you try out and the ideas you develop, in consultation with tutors. Your development is supported through collaborative learning within groups. The group work will include study which leads to a series of pieces of writing, called patches. You will also write about personal reflections on your own learning in a Jotter/Journal. By the end of the module, the whole collection of patches and your Jotter/Journal provide the main resources for your writing a Patchwork Text as the assessed assignment. It is intended that, through this way of working, you will increase your ability to learn professionally for yourself and increase your collaborative abilities, and have the confidence to go on learning and developing yourself professionally throughout your career.

The next few sessions

During the next few sessions, the Module Handbook is discussed, notably the requirements for the assignment and its assessment criteria, focusing attention on the meanings of 'reflection' and a 'reflective learner'. This can be a particularly difficult part of establishing the IIL approach. Inquiry-based teaching has an inherent tension between a tutor providing guidance, which is sufficiently specific to encourage apprehensive learners to make some kind of start, on the one hand and, on the other, saying enough unintentionally to sabotage any tentative qualities of autonomy (by being perceived to be *telling* students what to write or how to write it). Nevertheless, some students have enough of *something* (prior experience, or self-confidence or tolerance to running the risk of looking silly) to trust the tutor and the situation and have a go at writing reflectively. Once they have committed some thoughts to writing, the tutor can respond and the process can properly begin. Following Carl Rogers' language (1994) our guiding principles are *'unconditional positive regard, empathy and congruence'*. We assume that every student attempt is sincerely made and deserves our respect and appreciation, so we verbalise this immediately. We may need to clarify what has been offered, to empathise with it accurately enough to say back to the student what we think they mean and gently probe the thinking behind it. Then, with positive signs from the student, we may ask them to offer a self-evaluation of the reflectiveness of their writing. If that student's group seems to be sufficiently cohesive and supportive, we may invite them to comment on qualities of reflectiveness. Usually only then do we say to the student, honestly and tactfully, what we think is good and not so good, and suggest what and how to improve.

According to need, tutors lead tasks about characteristics of reflective learning and ways of practising it, such as comparing examples of less reflective and more reflective pieces about the same bit of experience, and applying the emergent list of features to examples from their own and each other's Jotters. We routinely encourage Jotter swaps between learning partners and occasionally invite discussion about selected passages which are read out to the whole group by a volunteer.

Ultimately, this is the only way to develop reflectiveness in learning. It cannot be taught. Like other human qualities, such as curiosity, it is part of us as human beings and cannot be inserted or trained in. This may be a harsh reality to face, for controlling kinds of teachers who expect to *cause* learning and for controlled kinds of learners, who expect to have learning done for them, or to them, somehow, by teachers. However, human qualities such as this can be learned, improved and developed, not primarily by what is done to or for the learner, but by what the learner does themselves, within enabling conditions. The incredibly fine tightrope walked by the tutor in this situation, trying to nurture growth of reflectiveness in students' writing, is to avoid falling off one side, into giving hints or clues to help, which are perceived as sustaining dependence, or, on the other side, being perceived as vague, unhelpful or uncaring. To Carl Rogers' three enabling conditions provided by the tutor, a fourth can be added:

1   *prizing* students' attempts, to show valuing and caring for what is done, not necessarily for its academic quality, not giving automatic praise, but acknowledging the courage to try;
2   *empathic understanding* of the reflections that are being attempted, the specific events or experiences, disentangling the thoughts and feelings involved;
3   *genuineness* in responding, saying and acting authentically, kindly and honestly.

Tutors practise these qualities, name them and act as role models for peers to do likewise. For some students, this is difficult to learn, because they are trapped in their dependence, from which escape is only possible by their own efforts, *plus*

4   *collaborative endeavour* – the ethos of a group growing in confidence and commitment, sharing examples of reflective thinking and its development.

To strengthen condition 4, there is value in extending opportunities to promote the social cohesion of the group and re-emphasise the importance of personal facets of learning. With these aims in mind, the tutor can take a few personal objects ('treasures') to pass round and talk about, as symbols of significant events or achievements in an individual's learning or development as a learner. Students are invited to do something similar in the subsequent session with their own small group and/or with the whole group. It can be surprising which students take this opportunity and what kinds of disclosures they make, some of which may be referred to by students in very positive terms a long time afterwards. Another technique is to ask each student to circulate and obtain the signature of a different student in each of the boxes of the grid shown in Table 4.1.

Table 4.1 Information gathering

From Nottingham	From north of Nottingham	From south of Nottingham	From a rural area	Living at home with family
Living at NTU Clifton site	Living at NTU site in City	Have worked with 0–3-year-olds	Have worked with 3–5-year-olds	Have worked with 5–11-year-olds
Speak at least two languages	Have lived abroad	Enjoy travelling	Enjoy clubbing	Play a musical instrument
Enjoy sports	Enjoy reading	*Have* to watch a certain soap on TV	Drive a car	Often ride a bicycle
Enjoy the countryside	Enjoy dramatics	Would like to work in a hospital environment	Enjoy using computers	Went to Goose Fair at the weekend
Wish I ate more healthily	Wish I did more exercise	Have studied Psychology	Love sending texts	Have worked with children with special needs

The small group inquiries into adapting to life as a student at university may be extended, with focuses moving from informal learning about student life to specific characteristics of learning at university. For example, information may be gathered about students' Information Technology skills using an audit, or about usage of the university library using an online questionnaire. Students are told to anticipate a change in the inquiry work from *gaining factual information* to *developing practice* and are asked to start thinking about an aspect of their learning which they would like to develop, paving the way for work described in the section below on 'IIL1 – the "middle" of the module'.

Students' attitudes to discussion as a way of learning are becoming clear by this stage and tutors judge how much and what kind of targeted teaching is needed to address this vital part of the IIL approach. Some students' feedback may already have shown that they value how their awareness has been expanded to learn useful lessons through purposeful talk with likeminded peers. Other students deride talk as pointlessly vague, tending not to speak or to make poor contributions or criticism of *discussion for learning*. We respond by managing discussions as skillfully as we can. We elicit many points of view and suggestions for action, try to facilitate clarification and decision making, drawing out important general points, without manufacturing a false consensus or imposing our own perspective. Some students follow this and understand how ideas expressed in their terms, about their concerns, can be usefully compared and developed into better expressed, more fully formed ideas and actions that the tutor clearly values. Other students tend to wish that the tutor would simply get to the point straight away and tell everyone what needs to be learned, saving a lot of time! Discussion is frequent, albeit in different forms, for a range of purposes, and is very important. So, according to the needs and abilities of their group, tutors may directly teach skills which contribute to *learning through discussion* and obtain feedback, such as students' notes from a discussion, to provide comments on their quality.

The concept of *learning as a subject* is presented to students. Many find it strange to apply knowledge about learning to their practice as learners. Those who have studied Psychology readily refer to concepts and theories of learning, but tend not to regard the subject knowledge as having much impact on how they learn in practice. Considering learning as a practice frequently elicits mild bewilderment because it is simply something they do 'naturally', without thinking, following intuitive methods or routines they have been trained to use. Tutor-led tasks explore kinds of learning and theory, acknowledging a possible gap between how abstract, general ideas about learning are presented authoritatively and their personal, contextualised application to improving learning practice. During the development of IIL1 this gap has been addressed by constructing the framework presented next.

The knowledge framework of the module

In IIL, we have found that students tend to regard learning as an activity that happens on its own, not worthy of reflection and not susceptible to improvement through considering academic theory. They use imprecise language and their understanding of learning is quite superficial. We wanted students to know technical terms and areas of study well enough to search efficiently for ideas and practical guidance for improvement. Initially, we taught them by stating and explaining a concept and/or theory opportunistically, in situations where it seemed to the tutor to be precisely relevant to students' immediate use. Monitoring showed disappointing improvements in students' accurate use of terminology or theoretical insight. We decided to supplement the *embedded* approach with direct teaching to all students. Having analysed IIL1 students' needs, we organised 27 components of subject knowledge into six topics, each presented by block lectures, spread across the first half of the module. The aim was to give theoretical resources for:

a   deeper reflection on their practice as learners;
b   disciplining their personal thinking and understanding; and
c   suggesting new learning inquiries.

Each topic is headed by a key question.

What is learning and what is my practice as a learner like?
1   Meanings of: 'information', 'knowledge', 'understanding', 'skill', 'intelligence';

2 *Processes* of learning versus *products* of learning: telling stories, fables, etc.;
3 The who, what, where, when, how and WHY of learning: motivation, aim, drive, desire, curiosity, passion;
4 Our nature and our differences as human beings and as learners: feelings, values, virtues (honesty, courage, openness, etc.), intentions, in relation to living and learning;
5 Understanding myself as a learner: self-assessment, attitudes, values (intrinsic and instrumental), beliefs, confidence;

What public knowledge about learning is relevant to me now?
6 Paulo Friere's banking model of learning (Friere 1996), behaviourist and constructivist models of learning: personal constructs, sociocultural, situated cognition;
7 Passive learning as in training (teaching as something done to you) and active learning as in education (teaching as empowering, transforming, liberating, etc.);
8 Learning from and through assessment: feedback, tests, examinations (the right answer syndrome), self-assessment, qualities, quantities, practical activity, locus of evaluation, IIL1 criteria of assessment;
9 Influences on learning/knowing of class, culture, gender, ethnic traditions, situation;
10 Experience: learning from and through describing, reflecting, discussing experience and gathering evidence;

How do we learn?
11 Learning through observing, listening, emoting, monitoring and (particularly) reading;
12 Learning through acting, role play, speaking, mind mapping, drawing and (particularly) writing (including technical support);
13 Learning from and through criticism and evaluation;
14 Theory and practice relationships: generality, singularity, particularity, situated, knowledge in action, practical knowledge;

How do my relationships affect my learning?
15 Relationships between teacher and learner: power, authority, roles, responsibilities;
16 Relationships between learners: power, role, responsibility, norms, competition, mutuality, collaboration, acceptance, belonging, security, learning partner, honest disclosure, trust, learning communities, interdependence, social intelligence, prizing, empathy, congruence;
17 Relationship with me, my self and I: knowing and understanding, self-experience, self-esteem, self-efficacy, fear of freedom/failure/shame/negative judgement, emotional intelligence, motivation, self-criticism and self-encouragement, prizing, honesty, openness, needs versus wants, personal

power, confidence, teaching myself, how others see me, how do I subvert or undermine or sabotage my own learning? Internal conditions for learning including calming 'chattering monkey' kinds of thought processes in my head;

How and how well do we and I learn?

18 Justifying learning claims: evidence, personal values and others' (including experts') ideas;
19 Ways of representing my knowing to myself and others: mind maps, notes, drawings, presentations, as an ongoing inquiry, reflective writing;
20 What is knowing for? Applying, answering, solving, creating, thinking, adapting, improving, being autonomous and independent, free from external and internal compulsions and inhibiting, constraining influences;
21 Personal (informal, tentative, disorganised, dynamic, three-dimensional, holistic, tacit, intuitive, implicit, usually acted, spoken or visual) versus public (formal, definite, organised, fixed, linear, authoritative, analytic, explicit, academic, usually written), knowing and knowledge – their respective characteristics, conventions and ways of thinking;

How can I understand learning and knowing better?

22 Certainty and doubt, ambiguity, clarity and confusion, order, chaos, multiple perspectives;
23 Objective versus subjective (reflective) versus intersubjective (discussing) ways of knowing;
24 Realist (single truth) versus interpretivist/multiple perspectivist views of knowing;
25 Scientific ways of understanding knowing: classifying, denoting and defining with conceptual clarity, logical thinking, being objective and rational, cause–effect relationships, learning styles, multiple intelligences, relationship between theory and practice from this perspective;
26 Artistic ways of understanding knowing: intuition, creativity, metaphor, analogy, connotation, relationship between theory and practice from this perspective;
27 Modernist and postmodernist ways of thinking and being.

Each lecture is preceded by the setting of preparatory tasks intended to sensitise thinking to the material and arouse curiosity and followed by discussion.

Summary of the processes of the module

The general expectations outlined in Box 4.3 are set out in the Module Handbook and referred to periodically during sessions.

Box 4.3 Expectations set out in Module Handbook

Students can expect tutors to:	Tutors expect students to:
Provide high-quality, research-led, challenging teaching	Take responsibility for their own learning, including writing reflectively in their Jotter/Journal/blog regularly
Provide well-prepared learning materials as part of the module's resources for learning	Read, think about and act on the materials provided, with a committed and conscientious approach
Give advice for students' own reading	Seek and act on this advice promptly and diligently
Provide a clear structure and guidance to module learning that is differentiated according to student need	Clarify, articulate and act on their own learning needs within the structure provided
Provide seminars, tutorials and lectures which are appropriately interesting and helpful, encouraging positive and critical interactions within the group	Attend punctually, bring all relevant materials, participate actively, contribute positively to discussion and to learning partner interactions
Provide an organisational framework for students to study and engage collaboratively in course work outside of contact time	Use this framework to organise themselves to study effectively, collaborate and complete patch writing punctually
Support and encourage students' individual interests and the development of their learning and their abilities to learn better	Reflect on and develop their own needs, interests and learning abilities, particularly through the thoughtful choice of inquiry focuses
Support and encourage students' collaborative learning	Be willing and increasingly skilful in engaging in shared tasks and projects to improve mutual learning
Organise and maintain the university's Virtual Learning Environment (VLE) as a learning resource for the module to which students contribute their work	Visit the VLE regularly to read material provided. Also visit the module wiki/ blog to read other students' contributions and make their own contributions and comments
Organise regular opportunities and provide support for students' reflection on experience and reflective decision making	Organise themselves to take advantage of support and opportunities so as to develop a reflective practitioner approach to professionalism

Continued overleaf

Students can expect tutors to:	Tutors expect students to:
Be responsive to students' comments on teaching	Be responsive to tutors' comments on learning and in giving and receiving peer comment
Respect differences, challenge discrimination and protect equality of opportunity for all	Respect differences, challenge discrimination and protect equality of opportunity for all
Be positive and express enjoyment in studies	Be positive and express enjoyment in studies

More specifically, the various kinds of activity in the module which have been presented above can be summarised as two main kinds of learning:

1   *Reflections on personal learning* You are expected to do this individually and with the support of small groups of peers called 'learning partners', meeting regularly and involving discussion and writing your own reflective Jotter/Journal/blog and using as resources the VLE, topics presented in block lectures and recommended texts.

2   *Inquiries into learning*   These are carried out individually or in small collaborative groups, as pieces of action inquiry to improve your practice as a learner and which result in short pieces of writing called patches.

Finally, the vital component of the IIL approach to be established and embedded into module processes is the regular giving and receiving of formative self and peer evaluative feedback. In the first few sessions, feedback is just indicating briefly the interest value of an idea or usefulness of a suggestion. By the time learning inquiries begin (see the following section on the 'middle' of the module), formal IIL1 assessment criteria have been presented and explained and their application has begun.

*   *Involvement* – which is about how well you show initiative, engagement, curiosity, perseverance and interdependence across a range of active involvements in your learning.
*   *Awareness of personal development* – which is about how well you make progress with being reflective, empathic, positively motivated, self aware and autonomous, in your learning.
*   *Credible, practical knowing* – which is about how well you use evidence, ideas from published work, critical interpretation and creativity, across a range of practical improvements in your learning and your ability to learn.

These criteria are consistent with a process curriculum. What is most important in students' learning is not what they learn but how they learn. They are not products of learning but qualities of mind that lay foundations for lifelong learning in professional contexts.

IIL I – the 'middle' of the module

The main part of the module consists of a series of cycles of action inquiry whose aims and methods are determined, with peer and tutor guidance, by each student independently, so as to contribute to a personally coherent journey of development. An account of each inquiry is written as a 'patch'. The accumulated series of patches, together with the associated reflective writing in the Jotter, will become the main resources for the compilation of the final assignment, a Patchwork Text.

Getting started with a learning inquiry

A gradual introductory preparation for doing a 'full' learning inquiry happens when students informally tell a *learning story* about the small practical things they found out as they adapted to being at university, with the tutor pointing out components of inquiry as part of the discussion. The tutor emphasises the importance of the inquirer's control over inquiry focus, choice of ways forward, assessment of the success or failure of tests carried out and the evaluation of improvement. By the time students select a focus for their first learning inquiry, there has been plenty of talk about what might be good to choose and why.

The following are positive suggestions:

- An aspect of your learning that you would like to improve.
- Something that you do quite regularly in your learning practice.
- A strength on which to build/a need to address/a difficulty to overcome.

The next three points are cautions about things to avoid:

- Something that you think will 'make a good inquiry, to please the tutor'.
- A focus that seems more 'safe' or 'easy' than really relevant to your learning.
- Something chosen by a student with whom you want to work.

There are innumerable factors that could help decide what aspect of learning a student would be best to focus on, at this time, in this situation, including thinking about:

- what the student sees as a particular skill or area of strength to be developed further, or a weakness to be overcome;

- what they have noticed in their own past learning practice which puzzles, astonishes or fascinates, and which needs to be understood more clearly;
- what situations or kinds of task have been experienced as creating an obstacle or a block to learning;
- what they know theoretically about learning, which sounds potentially good and that they would like to harness in practice more effectively;
- what is a recurring fear, doubt or sense of inadequacy in their learning ability which needs to be faced;
- what are becoming apparent from experiences since arriving at university as challenges to be addressed;
- what they have perceived to be admirable qualities of learning shown by other learners that would be good to emulate, and so on.

The belief is that:

> only the student can be aware of the influence of all these potential factors and only they can be enabled to take the personally significant into account in deciding the best focus for their learning inquiry in their current situation.

Working groups may form whose members choose distinct inquiry focuses, or work on a similar focus, to collaborate, in which case, there would be distinct personal justifications for choosing the focus and ways of gathering evidence of their own practice. For example, a group might wish to inquire into planning and use of time for private study and support each other's inquiries. This would enable collaborative searching of literature for insights and tips for improvement as well as giving and receiving particularly incisive comment on each other's inquiry work. Clear differences should become increasingly evident in how each student experiences their own practical difficulties with time, their personal habits, perceptions, working situations and past experiences of time management, to differentiate the inquiries.

Highly structured guidance is offered for the first few inquiries, while students gain experience. The selection of an inquiry focus is called Stage One. Stage Two is about gathering evidence of how the chosen aspect of current learning practice actually takes place.

What counts as evidence for inquiring into their learning differs from the factual, informational knowledge (e.g. gleaned from the web) for assignments. We call this 'other's facts' to teach students to understand that: for *my* action inquiry into the improvement of *my* learning, I need to gather evidence of *my* action, which includes things like descriptions of what *I* have done as well as my associated thoughts and feeling – *not* mere information. The inquirer at the heart of the inquiry, owns their practice as a learner, and therefore needs to include significant evidence about themselves, their dispositions, habits, assumptions, values and beliefs in developing an understanding of their own practice in order to improve it. This is evidence of *me* as a learner and what I do during my learning.

The first set of evidence to gather at Stage Two is from episodes of existing practice. This may at first seem odd, since the aim of the inquiry is improve practice and the inquirer may already have some potential improvements in mind that they want to try immediately. However, the inquirer must check their knowledge and deepen their understanding of what actually happens *now* by looking more closely at it in action. It is called gaining fresh experience of the chosen aspect of practice, without changing it yet. It is because what we think to ourselves, and tell others that we do, is not necessarily the same as what we actually do in practice. There are usually inconsistencies. Evidence substantiates a credible claim that we know what we do, without which there may be oversimplifications and misperceptions about present practice before improvement. Introducing changes to practice straightaway prevents development from being inquiry-based. Any improvements achieved would be simply random, like a process of intuitive trial and error. In Stage Two, evidence of present practice is gathered, reflected on and discussed with learning partners with continued use of the reflective Jotter.

Stage Three uses an evidence-based summary of present practice to justify possible action steps. Sometimes, Stage Two reveals unsuspected and surprising features of present practice that point clearly to improvement, making it easy to define action steps to test. Otherwise, justifications for action steps may not draw entirely on evidence and/or reasoning, but may be include some intuitive judgement as well.

The sheets reproduced as Figures 4.1–4.3 are students' records of their inquiry thinking at each of the Stages over the three module sessions.

Box 4.4 Summary of Stages and student tasks

Session	Stage in the learning inquiry	Students' tasks after each session
I	Stages I and 2. Write Sheet I	Implement the plan. Gather evidence of present practice. Read. Prepare to present to learning partners at Session 2.
2	Stages 3 and 4. Write Sheet 2	Try out action steps in practice. Gather evidence to test steps. Evaluate the evidence. Read. Summarise my learning story to present to the group at the learning inquiry conference.
3	The learning inquiry conference. Stage 5. Sheet 3	Reflect on peer feedback on my presentation. Write an account of my learning inquiry. Post my account on the Virtual Learning Environment. Read others' accounts.

Sheets 1 and 2 aim to structure the small group talk, providing stimuli to crystallise thinking. Each student completes a sheet individually. The tutor collects students' (double-sided) sheets and photocopies them for everyone's record of progress. Sheet 3 is not copied as it is a guide to preparing the patch written about each learning inquiry. The tutor prepares a list of current learning inquiry focuses. Reading these sheets helps the tutor to learn about students' characteristics as learners and give formative feedback comment. Many IIL sessions require the tutor to do less planning and preparation of the kind associated with more conventional teaching approaches, with presentation of tutor knowledge at the forefront. Instead of checking or updating one's grasp of the public knowledge content to be taught, or finding better ways to present it, an IIL tutor's preparation for the next session tends to be more about reflecting on the previous session, using evidence such as these sheets to check and update one's grasp of the students' learning. This is part of what is meant by:

> In IIL, students inquire into their content: improving a chosen aspect of their learning practice, while the tutor inquires into students' learning and how best to enable the processes – learning through inquiry means teaching through inquiry.

Weekly tutor team meetings provide a forum for discussion of this evidence, our self and peer monitoring of practice and reflective evaluation.

Sheet 1 for planning the inquiry is reproduced as Figure 4.1. It is printed as a single, two-sided sheet.

 MY LEARNING INQUIRY PLAN by _____ date _____ **Sheet 1**
complete up to Stage Two (other stages are shown for information) and give to your tutor

---

What I want to develop in my practice as a learner in higher education is . . .

I have tried to make this focus clearly defined, to involve practical improvements/developments that I can monitor and which will involve talking with my learning partners

---

This focus arose from my . . .

e.g. my reflections on a particular aspect of my practice as a learner (practice) and/or my ideas about learning that seem to be relevant to improvements I want to make (theory)

STAGE ONE   My plan

1. the specific aspect of my present learning practice I will work on during the next week is . . .

2. my *fresh experience* of this aspect that I am going to notice more closely, **when,** and **how** it happens is . . .

3. the **evidence** I will collect of my present practice will be . . .

e.g. careful notes to describe what happened and what I did, audio recordings of relevant talk, notes about what other significant people in the situation said about how they experienced it

---

STAGE TWO   Reflect and analyse my present practice
The evidence I select and organise of what happens in my present practice and share in discussion

My reflections openly and honestly on the overall experience and my **evidence** of what happened in my present practice

My reading about **key ideas** to **deepen my thinking** and **apply** them to my inquiry

Write my interpretation

STAGE THREE Evaluate the fresh experience and determine action steps
Discuss the **key ideas** from my reading plus significant evidence from Stage Two, to **deepen my thinking**, explore possible **action steps**: ideas for one or several changes to my current practice that are worth testing in practice

---

STAGE FOUR
Testing my **action steps** in my learning practice. Gathering new evidence of what happens. Reflecting on events and discussing them with learning partners. Writing my **re-evaluation** of what I have learned about improving my learning. What has surprised me; excited and/or pleased me; puzzled me?

STAGE FIVE
Prepare to tell others at a **conference** about my **learning story** of what I have learned about my learning

Figure 4.1 Sheet I

Making progress with the learning inquiry

In identifying topics for learning inquiries, students often include things like: concentration, organisation of study time, organisation of study materials, motivation to read, using the library.

Box 4.5 gives brief indications of how three learning inquiries might develop.

Box 4.5 Three possible learning inquiry paths

A learning inquiry focus	The relevant fresh experience monitored	Kinds of developments made
Improve my concentration so I don't get distracted so easily when working in my own room	Noted concentration every 20 minutes. Found worst distractions come from flat-mates encouraging me to postpone work	Try taking work to the library – its good to be in a better working space – gives me a reason to tell to flat-mates, and improves the status of my work for me
Improve my concentration during lectures, particularly ones covering familiar material, when I just make doodles instead of proper notes	Noticed that in my notes I tend to try to scribble down most things the tutor says and they don't make good enough sense later	Make the notes *mine*, to make more sense later, by trying to select the most important things at the time on a fresh page of A4, leaving room on opposite page for extra notes after
Improve my organisation – I often waste time looking for things in a mess and at the last minute so I end up being late	Realised that I was not getting my study things tidy but also not giving enough time to keep things well organised	Allocated little chunks of time, at the start of study (files on shelves, notebooks in drawer) and at the end of study time. Allow 21 days to make it a habit (made use of answerbag.com)

We are aware that some students might address their concerns without the involvement of a module like IIL and develop themselves as learners autonomously. Then we hope that, if nothing else, IIL does not impede such development. Even in these favourable cases, students benefit from having their positive values and attitudes affirmed and their abilities strengthened by organised access to support for making their learning to learn more explicit to each other.

Some students respond as though they have been given a key to unlock their self-development, quickly achieving important insights. One student said:

> I can see there is a common theme of me having a lack of confidence. A self-doubt in myself is visible now. I didn't seem to have any faith in myself that the Riveting Read would go well. Although I was hopeful I would find a book that interested me, prior experiences were clouding my judgement, as I was thinking that I had never enjoyed reading a book in the past. But reading *Goodnight Mr Tom* showed me what it was like to find a book that I enjoyed and I was actually reading for pleasure, and with a genuine interest in what was happening.

Most students readily acknowledge the need for IIL support, realising that they have been (in their words) *'over-dependent, mollycoddled, over-directed and spoon-fed'* as learners. They often say they gain considerable relief from finding out from peers that they are not alone or unique in experiencing difficulties in their learning, which hitherto had seemed to be a cause for shame or guilt. Widening their own viewpoints by listening to others' in discussion is a very common characteristic of students' appreciative comment.

In every group, a significant minority resists IIL expectations to do learning inquiries. They may say they don't see the point and don't know what to do, but will just do what tutors tell them. They tend to select a personally inauthentic focus and go through the motions of doing the inquiry, apparently gaining comparatively little.

A learning inquiry might seem to be about something very simple from an experienced tutor's perspective, making apparently rather trivial and obvious kinds of improvement. However, talking with the inquirer usually shows it is fairly easy to assess the authenticity of its purpose, the credibility of evidence obtained and the value of the progress claimed. The unusualness of some inquiry focuses strongly suggests their authenticity, such as *'trying not to let my learning be affected adversely by which students I am working with'*. This student had become aware that, in different social situations, she was more able or less able to engage with studies and her learning was affected accordingly. There may have been an assumption that learning is (or *should be*) more mechanical and less relational in character than the reality that was being experienced. By noticing what the working relationships with different students in various situations were like and how they influenced her learning experience, her learning inquiry developed ways to improve the management of her self, her work habits and organisation, as well as her peer interactions.

Another student asked *'Does opinion have a place in learning?'*. This arose from reflection on the growing experience at university that a valid part in learning can be played during discussion by what she classified as her *opinions*. She guiltily remembered a teacher's criticism that learners' opinions are not a respectable component of learning. Her learning inquiry scrutinised examples of her own and others' expressions of opinions, improving the awareness of differences in the extent to which they each had elements of testable information, personal whim, value positions, stereotyping or prejudice, tentative thinking, etc.

in varying combinations. The improvements in learning included a clarification of meanings of opinion as applied to students' use of them during discussion and a partial restoration of their status as a legitimate component in processes of learning; they may on occasion be even allowed to dominate thought, as long as they are well tested before being counted as academic knowledge.

A third example of the creativity of learning inquiry focus is 'daydreaming'. This student wanted to test an intuitive regard for doing what became evident as an apparently aimless, freewheeling kind of contemplation she called *'daydreaming'*. Her learning partners happily posed various challenges but, after investigating examples of practice, she concluded that she was *not* being idle or lazy when she did this, but was finding spaces to let ideas settle and be sorted out, however haphazardly.

Students' learning inquiry focuses such as these are unlikely to be predictable by tutors, either at all, or at the very moment when they would be most relevant to that student's development as a learner. This strongly indicates that any tutor-controlled or preplanned alternatives to IIL would limit students' learning, stifling the possibilities that open up when students are entrusted with freedom to learn for themselves. Lawrence Stenhouse (1975) was right: outcomes of education (as opposed to training) *are* unpredictable! Learning objectives *do* limit learning and put blinkers on educational achievement.

Connecting Stages Two and Three of the learning inquiry process can sometimes be challenging, so the format of Sheet 2 (one, double-sided sheet) has evolved to try to help (see Figure 4.2).

 MY LEARNING PROGRESS PLAN by _____ **date** _____ **Sheet 2**
complete up to Stage Four (the final stage is shown for information) and give to your tutor

---

A summary of what I am developing in my practice as a learner is . . .

Has this focus changed, shifted, become more clear, become less clear, deepened, become wider since I began?

STAGE TWO   A summary of how I have reflected and analysed my present practice
Having shared my evidence, ideas from reading and talked openly and honestly with my learning partners about what has happened in my fresh experience, here is a *Summary* of how I understand my inquiry focus more deeply

---

Figure 4.2 Sheet 2

STAGE THREE   Evaluate my present practice and determine action steps

Reflect on the overall experience in a calm and curious way

Present to learning partners my key **evidence** of what happened in my recent experience of present practice and key **ideas** that have come from my reading about this kind of learning

Discuss what I have learned from Stage Two, to deepen my thinking

Explore possible action steps: ideas for one or several changes to my current practice that are worth testing in practice

Decide which action step(s) to put into practice, to test their values as improvements or developments in learning

STAGE FOUR   Testing my action steps in my learning practice.
(gathering new evidence of what happens when I try out potential improvements in my practice as a learner)

My plan of how to monitor my implementation of the action step(s)

The kinds of evidence I will gather

Reflect on events and discuss them with learning partners

Write my **evaluation** of what I have learned about improving my learning

What has surprised me, excited and/or pleased me, puzzled me?

Continued overleaf

Continued

> **STAGE FIVE**
> Prepare to present my **learning story** of what I have learned about my learning, about improving my practice as a learner to others at a **conference**.
> Prepare a set of questions I would like peers to answer to help me learn more from my inquiry.
> Prepare to elicit their evaluations of my inquiry.

Many learning inquiries are about improving *motivation to learn*. Students can find it difficult to do the study they know is necessary, preferring to do something more enjoyable. They want to be more positive towards learning when attending sessions, and doing individual, private study (which some call *'homework'*) saying things like:

> even though I know that I have work to be handed in, I find it really hard to get myself to actually do it. I can promise myself that I will go and do it, but when it comes to it, I can't sit and work.

Monitoring a study session could include making brief notes of what is done to progress learning, interspersed with short comments about thoughts and feelings which arise. Descriptions of fresh experience of this difficulty often indicate that, when trying to study, there is little desire from within, such as curiosity or interest in the content. Reflections on past experience often suggest that the difficulty existed then, but was masked by external motivation. The fear of being told off or the threat of losing the regard of a significant other person, a parent or teacher, are frequently cited as the drivers that made them work. Although this is a popular issue, each inquiry has unique characteristics when brought to life by personal engagement. For example, a student who gathered fresh experience of her motivation while writing an essay that was due, decided to pause regularly to reflect on her feelings and note them. This proposal did not go to plan because she became so involved in the essay writing that she didn't want to be distracted by anything! She realised that she needed to study for long periods of time and exploit her ability to sustain her concentrated effort. Another student found that she learned better by using more conventional study skill advice: to divide a task into manageable chunks and have frequent breaks.

It often seems to be easier for a student to try to manufacture an artificial kind of self-motivation by recreating the missing external drive. Leaving a task until near the externally imposed deadline can cause sufficient anxiety to work. This creates for a tutor the dilemma between either setting deadlines to enforce more task completion while sacrificing the development of autonomous motivation, or tolerating variation in students' self-motivation but fostering a more authentic involvement in their learning. The tension is between conflicting aims: to teach the module content or enable students to learn how to learn. The solution to any professional and ethical dilemma like this is to find a context-dependent, responsive way of combining both. With groups which present this dilemma particularly strongly, an IIL tutor may carry out their own learning inquiry as part of their action research.

Learning inquiries can be conducted by a small group as well as by an individual, and they can be about improving learning in another module, such as a role play task in Multiple Disciplinary Studies (MDS). To paraphrase one student in this group writing in her patch:

> We split the task to make it easier for us to conduct. We all wanted to look at something we felt passionately about. One person looked on the Internet to find out what advice was already out there; one person asked the MDS tutor for guidance and one person asked some students for their opinions on the subject.

Advice from the internet was summarised as a PowerPoint presentation for other students. It included points such as:

- think about what type of language to use;
- listen to others' opinions;
- ask questions;
- practice within your group;
- try not to interrupt others;
- display professionalism.

Peer feedback about the presentation was gathered to address the need for credible, practical knowing. Peers said things like:

> 'This information was useful because it wasn't specific – I could apply it to any area I felt necessary.' 'I had not thought about the language I would use, I was too busy concentrating on what to say.' 'It was reassuring the three websites all gave the same advice so I felt it was advice I could trust.'

Students' opinions were found to be split as follows: 90 per cent of first years were worried about the role play, 90 per cent had not done a role play before, only 30 per cent felt confident speaking in front of a group of people. Many students reflected on these findings in their Jotters with entries such as:

> I found these statistics useful because they allowed us to know how our group was feeling. It was nice to hear that only 10 per cent of people had conducted a role play before, because I knew I wasn't the only person who was new to this experience.

The learning inquiry group concluded with a set of guidelines for peers doing role plays. Peer feedback included comments like:

I am more prepared for the role play. I felt the best advice I was given was to 'relax' and to 'be honest'. This is because I'd been feeling that I couldn't express my true feelings as someone may judge me and may not agree with my opinion.

The growing sense of confidence was shared across the whole group, one student commenting: *'The inquiry has allowed the group to pull together because many people were worried about the role-play'*.

The usual duration of each learning inquiry in IIL1 is three weeks. The third module session is mainly devoted to the conference. Its organisation is negotiated with each group, sharing decisions such as whether each learning inquiry is presented to a small group or to the whole group. As the module progresses, discussion increasingly makes explicit reference to module assessment criteria to emphasise the desirable learning qualities:

- *involvement* – an amalgam of initiative, autonomy, engagement, curiosity, perseverance, collaboration and interdependence;
- *awareness of my personal development* – being empathic, positively motivated, self-aware and reflective; and
- *credible, practical knowing* – using evidence, ideas from published work, critical interpretation and creativity.

The process of writing a patch

While conducting a learning inquiry, each student is expected to:

- keep written notes and other evidence of practice before and during the implementation of action steps;
- talk with peers in learning inquiry groups, a learning partner and the tutor;
- make regular reflective Jotter entries about the personal dimensions of the experiences;
- read public knowledge about relevant skills and theories that deepen thinking and potentially improve practice;
- give a mainly spoken presentation called a 'learning story' at the learning inquiry Conference and elicit evaluative feedback.

After the conference, an account of the inquiry is prepared, usually written, with a blend of 'report format' (stating ideas and evidence in a clear and coherent way) and personal, tentative, reflective, exploratory writing that could be called 'story format'. With an indicative length of about 1,000 words, it is made available to all students in the Year group using the Virtual Learning Environment (VLE). Students are expected to read the cumulative store of learning inquiry accounts to improve their learning and think about future learning inquiry focuses. The VLE is also used to facilitate giving and receiving student feedback. Formal guidance is given by Sheet 3 shown in Figure 4.3.

WRITING MY LEARNING INQUIRY PATCH **Sheet 3**

Guidance on what to include

My aim: what I have tried to develop in my practice as a learner
Why this was important to me to work on in my learning inquiry
Did my focus change, shift, become more clear, become less clear?

What this aspect of my practice was like at the start of the inquiry
Key evidence of my actions during my fresh experience, with my reflections on how the actions, and how I thought and felt about them, formed part of my practice as a learner then
Key ideas from my reading and from discussions with my learning partners about what happened.
A summary of how I understood my inquiry focus more deeply

My evaluation of that practice and what were the action steps which might bring improvement
Reflections on what is most important to me to improve
Ideas for action steps to try out as potential improvements in this aspect of my practice.
My key evidence and key *ideas* that justify choosing these action steps
What my learning partners and peers at the conference said about my inquiry at this stage

Testing my action steps in my learning practice
Key evidence of what happened when I tried out potential improvements in my practice as a learner
What it was like to implement the action steps
How I and my learning partners evaluated my practice and the effects of taking the action steps

What I have learned about improving my practice and about myself as a learner
Ways in which my practice has changed
Things that have surprised/excited/ pleased/ puzzled me in my experience as a learner
What I have come to think about the key ideas I found in my reading about learning
How my image of what I was trying to improve in my learning has changed, deepened, or widened
How my image of myself as a learner has developed
Learning partners' and peers' ideas and evaluations of my inquiry
Things that I might do, read or find out about, to build on this inquiry and continue my development

Figure 4.3 Sheet 3

This account is called a learning inquiry patch. It contributes to each student's portfolio of writing which also includes the account of the Riveting Read and to which will be added further learning inquiry patches and other set pieces of writing. One of these is a patch written for a Reading4Learning Project. This was devised after tutors' reflection on the disappointing amount and quality of students' reading for IIL. Students are required to identify a book or chapter about an aspect of learning of relevance to the improvement of their practice as learners. Having read it, they prepare an account of the main ideas they gained, relevance to learning and how they intend to use it, as well as the bibliographical information that would facilitate access for other students. Together with the reflective Jotter, this portfolio is used as the resource for writing the Patchwork Text assignment.

Each separate learning inquiry is one cycle of action research. The next cycle can begin where the previous one ended, or take a different focus, according to each student's priorities and interests, following the principle stated above under *Getting started with a learning inquiry*. Sometimes, a student may propose to do a learning inquiry again, having realised what needs to be different, such as better action steps which could lead to further or greater improvement. Alternatively, they may have noticed (or the tutor may have pointed out) in others' work a need to look really hard at fresh experience of a difficulty to understand it well enough to take sufficiently well-informed action steps.

IIL1 – the Patchwork Texts assignment

The IIL module's assessed assignment is presented in the Module Handbook as follows.

The assessed assignment is a *Patchwork Text* of 2,000 words, derived from your Jotter/Journal writing and patches, entitled:

Becoming a reflective learner

The assignment is made up of an edited selection of patches, or extracts from them, with an interpretive, reflective and critical commentary, or *stitching*, which draw on material in your Jotter/Journal. The Patchwork Text (PT) brings out and explores theme(s) across the separate pieces of writing. The patches are chosen for their significance to your main learning achievements. They are linked by the *stitching*, which introduces and explains each patch, and links them, to bring out themes, trends, developments or patterns in your learning across the module. For example, any such theme(s) in the PT may be one(s) relating to your personal questions or problems as they have arisen through the processes of writing your Jotter/Journal, and reflection linked to critical friends group discussion. However, you are not expected to arrive at simple, clear answers to these questions but to give an honest exploration of the issues which you have or have not resolved, indicating any new questions which may have been raised, and so on. Overall, the PT should convey significant ways in which your learning has achieved the qualities indicated by the assessment criteria as appropriate to a reflective learner, across your learning outcomes.

The IIL module is likely to be the first one in which a PT assignment is set, therefore students need help in understanding it. So, about halfway through the module, they do a PT assignment with similar expectations but just using patches written thus far. The procedure for peer and tutor feedback is presented in Chapter 7. The printed task guidance is given in Figure 4.4.

 WRITING MY PATCHWORK TEXT

This is intended to give encouragement and guidance to your preparation of the Patchwork Text assignment which is the formal basis on which your learning achievements in this module are assessed.

The assignment is the **Patchwork Text** with one **appendix** containing **all of your own patches**.

Resources

You need to have: your patches, your Jotter, other students' patches, text books, articles and/or web sourced material and enough time to make positive progress which will encourage you to persevere.

Suggested procedure

Read your own and others' patches, making **notes** about points and issues that seem to be most interesting, significant, surprising, puzzling etc. in relation to the focus of the assignment, which is, of course: **Becoming a reflective learner** and is the title of your Patchwork Text.

The implied bit of the title is that it is about **YOU becoming a reflective learner**, so it is about your own learning, not anyone else's, except where their learning helps you to understand and improve your own. You are meant to put yourself and your learning at the centre of the Text. *Continued overleaf*

Figure 4.4 Guidance for completing the Patchwork Text

Another important bit of the title is the word **becoming**, which is meant to convey that, like all important kinds of personal development, it is a never ending process which is being written about just one particular student, over this particular period of time, in this particular context.

The Handbook guidance says that the **Patchwork Text, of 2,500 words, is derived from your *Jotter* writing and *patches*** so you probably ought to start by choosing **which** patches or parts of the patches and **which** bits of the Jotter are worth including in the Patchwork Text and deciding **why** they are worth including. Having done this, and reflecting on your **notes** (see above), work out a way of organising these contributory parts for the Patchwork Text into a coherent whole.

Your structure could be either (or a combination) of the following:

- simply a kind of **unfolding story of your learning**, where the **patches** would be in the same sequence as when they were written, and so the organisational structure would be to pick out a prominent feature of your learning at each of the different stages of the story
- an **account** of one or several **themes** to do with the title, where you would organise the patches or extracts of patches around the theme(s) in such a way as to help the themes to be clear and say worthwhile things.

If you feel that the basic structure you used in writing your Course Work Assignment, part way through this module, was good enough, and if the feedback from peers and from the tutor agrees with this view, then you may decide to use it again for this assignment. It would, of course, be important to read the feedback carefully, to gain as much from it as you can. So your starting point could be that text, to which you add the further work that you have done since. If you decide to do this, you need to be satisfied that your own assessment of your learning achievements in this module would not be better conveyed by a different structure. This decision would be one you could discuss with your learning partners in the group. Make sure that the concluding reflections review all your progress across the year.

Having decided on a workable, and interesting structure to organise the main things you want to say about your learning, the next things would probably be to think about how to **stitch** the relevant patches and extracts of the Jotter together. To do this it may be helpful to imagine yourself doing the following (or you might do it for real!):

Pretend that you have a chunk of quality time to share with a learning partner who is a good critical friend, someone who may know enough about you and your work to be supportive, and who wants you to do well, but is also willing and able to ask questions or make suggestions which are constructively critical, to help you to improve. Pretend that the purpose of your uninterrupted time together is to communicate to your learning partner what you know about **Becoming a reflective learner** and to do this, you have prepared paper copies of the patches and Jotter extracts to show them. Pretend that you start by talking to her/him by very briefly saying what are the most important things about your learning that you want them to be ready to understand and explaining to her/him how each of the pieces of paper you will ask them to read will contribute to their understanding. After giving them this friendly introduction, you give them the first piece to read (an extract of a patch or the whole patch or an extract from your Jotter) saying why it has been chosen for this stage in the process. When they have finished reading it, pretend that you need to say to them at that point some things about what is most important, interesting or puzzling about it and how it is linked to the next piece of reading you have prepared for them. Continue like this, working your way through the patches, and making sure that they are building up an understanding as they go. Then finish the meeting by saying things at the end about what you hope your critical friend has by then come to appreciate about your learning so far, what questions and difficulties you are still working on and what possibilities there seem to be for your further improvement of your learning in the future. **The things that you think you would SAY in this imaginary meeting are a good guide to what you need to WRITE in your stitching.** (Naturally, your writing would not be exactly the same as the things you might say because it has to be more formal and must be grammatically correct and so on.) You might imagine what questions and suggestions your critical friend could put to you, and then incorporate into what you write in your stitching some things that will anticipate and deal helpfully with such points.

Now re-read the Module Handbook **guidance** on the assessed assignment, to check how this suggestion fits with the ideas there. In particular, read the **assessment criteria** carefully and think hard about how your planned Patchwork Text will provide evidence that your learning has these three qualities.

Next, let's imagine, very roughly, just what the Patchwork Text might actually look like. The wording used in the following pretend assignment is deliberately vague, because the main idea is to get a rough glimpse of what the layout and structure might be like.

Continued overleaf

Continued

Becoming a reflective learner by Gertrude Corncrake

Introduction

This assignment is about the main things that I believe I have learned and about some of the ways in which I have learned them, as part of becoming a reflective learner on my course. In this Patchwork Text, I will include various pieces of my writing for the Inquiry Into Learning module, using Arial font and I will continue to use this font (Times) for the 'stitching'. The way I will convey my development is to begin with . . . . . . and then turn to . . . . and then move on to deal with . . . . Then attention turns to my . . . . and finally I will draw things together by . . . .

When I started this module, my learning about . . . . . was . . . . . As an example of what I was working on and thinking about, here is an extract of the patch that I wrote at the time:

The thing that I am trying to improve in my practice as a learner is . . . .
. . . .
. . . . When I was trying to understand this, I found it important to bear in mind a point made by Bloggs:

. . . .
Bloggs, J. (2002, page 9)

Bloggs' idea was relevant to what I was thinking in relation to . . . .
. . . . because . . . .
. . . . .Although this Inquiry has helped me to learn better in the sense that I . . . . it has raised new questions about how best to deal with . . . . which may become the focus of a future Inquiry. (My patch on X, of 23.10.2006).

The concern I had then for X was mainly because of Y, which linked to the improvement of Z in my learning. As an illustration of how I was thinking at that time and how this affected my development, here is an extract form my Jotter dated 3.11.04.

I hadn't seen it in this way before, but what I think is happening here is that I have been assuming that . . . . and this may be why . . . .

It was then an important and helpful development to try to improve Z further, by doing an inquiry into Q. The aim and method of this Inquiry is summarised as follows:
Having a difficulty to do with . . . .
I feel sure that it would be worth trying to . . . . So I decided to . . . . (Extract of my patch on Q, written 18.1.2007).

Important advice about your writing, with criterion 3 particularly in mind (credible, practical knowing)

When you make a **general** statement, particularly an important one, make sure that it follows from, or leads in to **specific** descriptions of **examples** and/or **illustrations** of the general idea happening in your **experience** in a **particular** context. Without this, a general idea can seem to be vague, because it is not easy to see what it means in a real situation or it can seem to be too theoretical or idealistic, because the lack of a practical example prevents you from showing that it has been evident in things that you have seen and/or done and reflected on.

When you see the importance of a particular idea in your writing and are aware that you need to show that you have thought hard about it, get help from books, journals or the Internet from writers who have developed a helpful or powerful way of understanding the idea.

It is good to write in a personal way, using the first person singular (I), as indicated above. But avoid writing in a way that is too informal, like conversation. Personal writing can also be highly professional in the way that it says things clearly, concisely and with purpose, with careful use of correct language, just like a formal document.

Unless you are an exceptionally gifted writer, who can attain high quality very fast, the only way to produce a polished piece of writing is to just keep on polishing it! I know a Professor who is a very experienced writer, but who, unlike some, has a good reputation for writing difficult and complex ideas in a clear and lively way, and who routinely expects to redraft a piece of writing (on the computer) at least thirty of forty times before it is good enough! You do get better as you practice, but even highly practised writers usually have to redraft many times.

When your first draft of the complete Text is finished, put it away and forget about it. You are still too familiar with it to be able to see what needs to be improved. About two or three days should be long enough to enable you, when you read it again, to read it with a more critical and creative attitude with which to redraft. This would also be a good point at which to go through the Text and ask yourself, as the tutor who will mark it has to ask: where is there evidence of this Text meeting the assessment criteria?

Does the Text show **Involvement, which is about how well I show initiative, autonomy, engagement, curiosity, perseverance, collaboration and interdependence across a range of active involvements in my**

Continued overleaf

Continued

learning? Is there an appropriate kind of **Awareness of my personal development, which is about how well I make progress with** *being empathic, positively motivated, self-aware and reflective,* **in my learning** ? Does it deal with its subject matter in a way that shows **Credible, practical knowing, which is about how well I use** *evidence, ideas from published work, critical interpretation and creativity,* **across a range of practical improvements in my learning achievements and in my ability to learn?**

Last, but by no means least, remember all the technical bits to do with spelling, punctuation, grammar, pagination, referencing and so on must be spot-on. Put references to other students' patches in the same way as for published authors: name, date and title of patch, with the source being the VLE.

Finally bind the assignment: the Patchwork Text with one simple Appendix containing each of your own patches, included in the order that you wrote them.

This printed advice is supplemented by time in sessions for planning and discussion. Occasionally, all this is somehow ignored, and an assignment is submitted which has been written conventionally, like an essay, about 'Becoming a reflective learner'. However, nearly all Patchwork Texts are successful in using a theme or developmental thread (often found retrospectively) which gives personal meaning to the year's achievements in learning how to learn, by which the extracts of patches and Jotter can be organised. This confers on many of the assignments a striking individuality. They are interestingly varied to read because they display each person's unique learning journey. Students who have been unable to overcome a detached, task-oriented, instrumental attitude to the module, and simply go through the motions, are unlikely to meet the 'Involvement' criterion above pass level. Similarly, those who neglect to reflect deeply enough on themselves and their progress as learners are unlikely to meet the 'Awareness of personal development' criterion. The commonest failures tend to be the excessive use of bland descriptions and vague claims, which do not meet the criterion of 'Credible practical knowing'.

The following extract is from a successful IIL1 assignment which was assessed as meeting the criteria well. Tutor comments have been added in the column on the right.

Assignments like this one have been made available to students during PT preparation, but only for a short period of shared study and discussion, as numbered printed copies which are collected in at the end of the session. This is to minimise the unwanted effect on some students of seeing what they perceive to be hints, tips or formulae for passing the assignment.

Becoming a Reflective Learner

I believe a reflective learner is a person who continually evaluates their learning by criticising and thinking about how they study and identifying their strengths and weakness. They use a combination of their strengths, reflection and advice to improve and to overcome their weaknesses, therefore becoming a better learner. This Patchwork Text uses extracts from my patches to describe how I have started to become a reflective learner. I have chosen only to include extracts from three of my patches as I feel I have learnt the most from these patches.

Starts with a helpful personal definition.

In my opinion my reflective Jotter has been the most important tool in helping me to become a reflective learner. At first I struggled when writing in my Jotter but by reading material on how to write reflectively I became more at ease with it. The main piece that helped me was 'Writing and keeping a journal (infed [online])' as it explains what information to include in each entry. I included the following information in my entries:

Ownership of achievements and methods is immediately apparent.

- Description of situation/encounter/experience – include some attention to feelings at time.
- Additional material – information that comes to our notice after the event.
- Reflection – going back to the experience, attending to feelings and evaluating experiences.
- Things to do – reflection may lead to looking at the situation again or to exploring something deeper. (infed [online])

At first I referred to this list whenever I wrote in my Jotter but as I have become more confident I only refer to it to refresh my memory.

It would have been an advantage to read a Jotter extract which is seen as deeper reflection.

I have used my Jotter to deepen my thinking. Having studied an issue I now dwell on the issue longer and think about it more in-depth. This also helps me to find solutions to problems as I reflect on them for longer, an example of this can be seen in my Jotter entry 29/10 (see appendix F).

Many of my patches have concentrated on how the environment I am in affects how I learn and I have identified several factors that affect my learning. My third patch on motivation helped me to identify the distractions in my environment.

> After talking to my learning partners about the sort of distractions that could affect my motivation levels I experimented working in different environments. I found that switching off my mobile phone and the TV greatly increased my motivation to start work as I wasn't tempted to watch another programme or to text somebody. However the main factor affecting my motivation levels was whether I was reading a book. This affects my learning because I find books very hard to put down and this decreases my motivation levels as I would prefer to be reading. I also find that during periods when I am reading a book my mind tends to wander to the plot while doing an uninteresting or difficult activity and this causes me to feel less enthusiastic about my work as I would rather be discovering the plot. I now believe that it might be a good idea not to read books for pleasure when working on assignments.
>
> (Patch 3, appendix C)

A reasonably credible and clear gain is made with reducing distractions.

Since working on this patch I have chosen to read these books while travelling, as from my first inquiry I know I find it unproductive to work at this time, and this has meant when I get home I am more likely to work as I have been able to spend some time reading.

My third patch also highlighted to me how sleep can affect my motivation.

> From reading student patches (Coe, [online]) it was obvious that many of them thought that sleep was a major factor that affects motivation levels. From recording the number of hours I sleep and the amount of work I complete I have discovered that I am most motivated when I have slept between 8 and 9 hours, as the table below shows.

A well evidenced, if technicist test of the effect of varying sleep time.

Day	Work Completed	Time Taken	Other Activities	Number of hours of sleep	No. of tasks done	Feelings/ environment
Tuesday	Start inquiry into motivation. Course reading on gender Reflective Jotter	1 Hour (10:15– 11:15) 50 mins (11:30–1:00 with break for lunch) 30 mins (5:00–5:30)	Physio- therapy Shopping	8 hours	3/4	In the house by myself – environ- ment quiet. Happy with the amount of work I got completed especially as I was out for a while.
Saturday	Finding material to compliment my gender leaflet Social relationship reading Social justice reading.	1½ hours (5.30–7.00)	Shopping	10 hours	1/3	Was slightly tired and didn't feel like working.

After reflecting on this I have come to believe that if I sleep longer than 8–9 hours my motivation levels will decrease because I do not feel that I have the same amount of energy and therefore am more likely to put off work or get distracted. In future on days when I want to work I need to ensure that I get the correct amount of sleep.

(Patch 3, appendix C)

Whilst reading my Jotter entries and the comments from my lecturer I realised that allocating equal amounts of time to different modules is very important. I realised this when I became so preoccupied with completing an assignment that

A more reflective study of the value of setting goals for learning is linked to improving perceptions of own motivation to learn and self esteem as a learner.

I allowed little time to write in my Jotter. As a result the entries around this time were rushed and brief, and offered little reflection. I now try to allocate equal amounts of time to work but still struggle as I find some modules more interesting and I find myself allocating more time to these modules.

From reading The Study Skills Handbook (Cottrell 2003: 90–94) I realised that to increase my motivation I should set myself clear goals.

> Using my table and my reflective Jotter I have realised that I am more motivated when I have clear focused goals to concentrate on. I believe this is because clear goals make a task seem less daunting as they seem more achievable. I feel that this has a very important effect on me because at the end of the day if I feel I have achieved something which increases my self esteem and confidence, allowing me to remain motivated. If I don't feel I have achieved something it severely affects my motivation because I feel like I have wasted my time, which depresses me as I know I will have even more to do next time I sit down to work. Therefore I feel less enthusiastic when I next face my work as it feels more daunting.
>
> (Patch 3, appendix C)

It would have been good to know more about the reasons for using this sequence of topics in the learning journey.

Since working on this patch I have seen how clear goals help my motivation. On the week beginning 30/04, I set myself these tasks

- read through handouts for each lecture
- read The Great Outdoors
- read the first two chapters of Early Childhood Services
  – complete second riveting read inquiry
- complete game cards for children interacting with the environment.

An internal locus of evaluation is increasingly prominent in the identification of learning gains.

Earlier in the year I would not have expected to complete this list, especially the reading, but by setting myself clear goals instead of just stating 'Multi-disciplinary services reading' I felt more motivated and completed everything on the list. This has greatly improved how I feel about my learning as I had begun to feel like a poor student who did little work and I now feel more studious.

While working on my riveting read inquiry I realised that learning can happen at anytime not just whilst studying at university.

> Even though I read these books for pleasure while writing in my reflective Jotter I realised that I can actually learn and develop skills by reading them. The main skill these books help me to develop is empathy. As I read I find myself thinking about the different characters, how they are feeling and how I would react in their situation. This is an important skill to develop, especially when working with children because to help a child develop you need to be able to understand how they feel.
>
> (Patch 2, appendix B)

Valuable qualities in own learning are identified, probed and finer discriminations are made so as to improve practice.

This discovery was later reinforced when I saw an article on the VLE about research by Mar et al. (2006) which indicates that there is a link between reading novels and empathy levels.

My riveting read inquiry also highlighted to me how I read and how this can aid and hinder my learning.

> The main thing I learnt from my riveting read was the fact that I am a fast reader who tends to skim read. After reflecting in my journal I can see that this has both advantages and disadvantages. The main advantage of being a fast reader is that it allows me to complete course reading quickly. It also means I can quickly find relevant information without wasting time reading information which will not be useful to me. However being a fast reader also has a major disadvantage as I have a tendency to miss pieces of information. This has little consequence when reading for pleasure but when studying I could miss out vital information which could cause me to either misinterpret or misunderstand facts. This has made me realise that when reading course material I need to make sure I re-read passages to ensure I have clearly understood all the information.
>
> (Patch 2, appendix B)

Impressive levels of involvement in learning as well as in learning to learn.

The significant origins of this learning inquiry are stated as inspirations. The link to using mind maps is unclear, but the benefits are vividly conveyed.

Knowing this has helped me with my assignments especially the foundations of social relationships assignment as I had to read about theories I had never heard of before which were quite confusing. However instead of thinking I did not understand the theory I made sure I read it several times and each time the meaning became clearer. Realising this has helped me to become a more independent learner because instead of needing my lecturer to help me solve my problem I was able to solve it myself.

This inquiry also helped me to . . .

Assignments like this one have been made available to students during PT preparation, but only for a short period of shared study and discussion, as numbered printed copies which are collected in at the end of the session. This is to minimise the unwanted effect on some students of seeing what they perceive to be hints, tips or formulae for passing the assignment.

Chapter 5

Inquiry Into Learning 2
Becoming a professional inquirer

This chapter details the curriculum planning for the Inquiry Into Learning 2 module (IIL2) which takes place in Year Two of the degree programme, together with evidence of its operation and reflective, developmental analyses of practice.

Having the same title for both modules is intended to signal a continuity of approach. We want students to continue to learn through inquiry and improve their ability to do so. The IIL1 aim of becoming more reflective as learners feeds into the IIL2 aim of becoming inquirers in wider and more professional contexts. Interest moves from *me and my peers* as learners, to *our professional clients, colleagues and situations in which we are becoming reflective practitioners and taking professional action.*

Therefore, it is intended that students continue to nurture their powers of learning reflectively from fresh experience and from public knowledge, aiming to improve practice, using a similar structure of collaborative inquiry work, reflective journal writing, presentations at conferences, patch writing and posting electronically, all through discussion with learning partners. Grafted on to this stem is the challenge of learning how to understand more deeply about the improvement of professional practice by inquiring into it collaboratively. By the end of IIL2, students will have completed a fairly extensive action inquiry, in a small group, and be ready to take the Professional Research Project module in Year Three of the programme in which their inquiry is entirely their own. The aims of IIL2 are consequently intermediate ones in the progress represented by these three modules together, which form a central spine of a BA in Childhood Studies programme.

As in IIL1, the process of learning is to work collaboratively on a series of different inquiry projects, sharing findings and developments in various ways. The projects are about professional inquiry methods and carrying out real inquiry work to practise becoming a reflective professional inquirer.

The module Learning Outcomes are that students will be able to demonstrate abilities:

*   to question, analyse, criticise, explore and make creative contributions, particularly through discussion, to the development of shared thinking about

issues of importance, within both details of practice and high-level policy, tolerating ambiguity, complexity and uncertainty;

- to monitor and reflect self-critically and constructively on one's own and on others' actions in order to understand and to negotiate control and responsibility for improvement;
- to conduct full inquiries using appropriate inquiry methods from the following types: participant and non-participant observation, questionnaires, structured, unstructured and instance interviews, case studies of various kinds, action research.

This chapter is organised into four parts which deal with the four phases of IIL2:

1   learning about professional inquiry;
2   the Commissioned Inquiry;
3   reflective professional practice; and
4   the Patchwork Text assignment.

Learning about professional inquiry

Inquiry in everyday life

As in IIL1, we use the general pedagogical principle that learning can start from where learners are, whatever that means and however it is discerned. IIL2 has tried several ways of doing this. We assume that students have prior experience of inquiry in everyday contexts (although they may not see it as such) and have an elementary awareness, at least, of some qualities of inquiry which enable them to examine examples critically.

For instance, national media attention was recently being given to drunken behaviour of young people in city centres. We collected newspaper and website material about this as a general social issue, with particular news media attention, including a BBC *Panorama* programme, being focused on events in Nottingham. The material contained claims about the behaviour of people involved and comment about causes and consequences. The coverage included factual information, direct observational and interview evidence, interpretation, speculation and moral judgement. It was chosen as a focus for study because it was likely to be within the direct or indirect experience of the predominantly young people taking the module. The local connection was an added bonus. Material was initially presented in a neutral way, as being of interest to students, and as a kind of inquiry activity which could be scrutinised closely.

In Session One, after completing the usual preliminaries to do with introducing the module, the first task for students was to examine and discuss the collected material, which included serious newspaper coverage as well as tabloid reports with sensationalist headlines.

A group debate was led by students' concerns, dominated by critical views of the accuracy and fairness of the portrayal of young people. The tutor asked questions like: 'What do you believe actually happened?' 'Why were these events written about in these ways?' 'What effects do the writers intend their writing to have on readers?'. This led to discussion of any characteristics of the accounts which could be called 'features of inquiry': what they are and how good they are, how independent of bias, and so on. From this experience, a list of inquiry-related qualities was elicited. This established a set of inquiry techniques used in the accounts. Each media piece was evaluated as an inquiry, considering qualities of accuracy, independence, credibility, reliability, fairness and bias, using students' own current meanings of those qualities.

This kind of task, based on current material from the 'real' world out there, is usually successful in providing a basis for the kinds of concepts and procedures to be applied, practised and refined. A personal perspective on inquiry activity is also discussed, including curiosity, interest, purpose, respect for evidence and for persons, social justice and objectivity as ideals. Inquiry for enlarging knowledge or deepening understanding is contrasted with inquiry for improving professional practice.

The concepts which students are expected increasingly to incorporate into their talk and writing include: breadth of inquiry purpose, degree of structure of inquiry, evidence, type of sampling and selection of evidence, interpretation, analysis, conclusion, recommendations for action, awareness of bias, the validity and reliability of the evidence and its use.

Inquiry techniques and methods

Having distinguished methods of inquiry (case study, action research) from inquiry techniques (ways of obtaining evidence) students undertake Learning Inquiry 1 (LI1) and write the first patch for a Patchwork Text assignment entitled 'Becoming a professional inquirer'.

Students choose an inquiry theme from the following list of artificial exercises:

a   Observing children in an educational setting
b   Observing each other during university sessions
c   Observing students in the campus dining room
d   Observing students using the fruit and vegetable stall on campus
e   Discovering students' reasons for choosing their university course
f   Discovering students' reasons for choosing their present temporary home in Nottingham
g   Analysing our IIL1 patches.

Each student selects a theme for Learning Inquiry 1. In Chapter 4, under 'IIL1 – the "middle" of the module', a principle of inquiry learning is stated, concerning the primacy of student choice and taking responsibility for their learning. The principle is applied to IIL2 at this point by asking students to choose inquiry themes and techniques to try out. Their decision could include thinking about which aspects of inquiry they;

- see as a personal strength to be developed further;
- see as an area of ignorance or a weakness to be overcome;
- have noticed in the past as puzzling or fascinating and which needs to be better understood and/or practised;
- know about theoretically and would like to put into practice;
- perceive as admirable when used in other inquiries and which it would be good to emulate.

The twelve techniques/contexts listed below are explored through discussion:

1   Observation

   1.1 Non-participant observation of interaction in a social situation
   1.2 Non-participant observation of an individual's actions
   1.3 Participant observation/peer observation
   1.4 Phenomenological/ethnographic observation

2   Interview

   2.1 Formal, structured interview
   2.2 Semi-formal, semi-structured interview
   2.3 Informal unstructured interview
   2.4 Instance interview following observation of action
   2.5 Group interview/focus group

3   Questionnaire

   3.1 Structured questionnaire
   3.2 Unstructured questionnaire
   3.3 Survey

Groups of 4 students are organised to carry out Learning Inquiry 1 so that each group selects one of the themes from the list and then generates a list of possible inquiry questions that fit within the broad theme selected. They decide which technique to use for each question and then divide into two subgroups, each group taking one of the two questions, which use different techniques. Choices are recorded on the sheet shown in Figure 5.1 so as to ensuring a good spread of themes and techniques across the group. Some techniques are not suitable for some themes and have been blocked out.

Instance interviews about observed action

This is one of the distinctive ways in which evidence can be gathered in action research (technique 2.4 in the above list). The inquirer interviews participants in a situation where there is a recurring action or utterance which seems to be relevant to an aspect of practice which the inquiry is trying to improve. For example,

Inquiry theme	Inquiry techniques											
	1 Observation				2 Interview					3 Questionnaire		
	1	2	3	4	1	2	3	4	5	1	2	3
a												
b												
c												
d												
e												
f												
g												

Figure 5.1 Record sheet

a teacher who is trying to improve students' discussion will say various things to try to establish what the learners think. After one learner has said something, the teacher often says to the others, 'Do you all agree?'. Then the other members of the group usually say nothing, or maybe just 'Yes' and the teacher feels disappointed. The teacher is signalling a revised expectation of the learners' role that is desired. It does not work and the teacher doesn't understand why. Having observed the utterance, 'Do you all agree?' several times, and recognised it as a potentially significant instance of teacher talk, a visitor to the classroom as an action inquiry assistant can interview the teacher and the learners to probe into this instance of action which they have shared socially.

Whereas an ordinary interview might ask a person about their individual opinions or general thoughts, an instance interview presents the instance of a recurring social action and elicits the thoughts and feelings about its meaning and purpose, its effects on the situation and subsequent action, from various actors. Every actor taking part in the action could be interviewed in this way to generate multiple perspectives.

In this example, the teacher claimed in an instance interview that the question 'Do you all agree?' was intended to get the learners to say what they freely thought. To represent the perspective of the learners, a few of them were instance interviewed. They said they thought the teacher had wanted them to agree with what had already been said. Their previous experience of this teacher's teaching had been that right answers were valued much more than what learners freely thought for themselves. They had not been sufficiently helped to revise their expectations of the teacher's role by utterances such as 'Do you all agree?'.

Observations and instance interviews help to develop professional practice by providing evidence for reflection. One person's intentions underpinning their practice (in this case, the teacher's desire for free, open discussion) are translated into actions which can be experienced by others in the social situation as if they were expressions of quite different intentions. Progress can be made by uncovering the different ways in which intentions are perceived to be linked to actions, through observation, instance interviewing and reflection on the evidence. The interviews can be made either by the practitioner, doing action research to improve their own practice, or with the help of *inquiry assistants* who are visitors to the context of the action in support of the practitioner's action research.

Instance interviewing originated in the Ford Teaching Project based at the Cambridge Institute of Education under the direction of Clem Adelman and John Elliott (see Elliott 1975) from which this example is taken.

Students who practised technique 2.4 in their Learning Inquiry 1 are given the following summarised guidance:

When inquiring into practice, in which action has been observed and/or recorded, notice instances of action and/or speech which seem to be significant to the inquiry question or, in action research, which seem important to intended improvement.

Identify these instances and describe them clearly, so as to be able to refer to evidence of them during an interview.

Conduct instance interviews with the various participants in the practice observed. Present to them the observational evidence of the instances. Invite them to give comments from their own perspectives, on what the instances of actions or of the speech meant to them at the time, what they seemed to mean, what were the effects on them, how they reacted in response and their other reflections. Record this interview for further analysis.

Tutors need to give closer attention to groups using this technique in Learning Inquiry 1, because of its complexity and unfamiliarity and the care needed in certain contexts.

Professional characteristics of inquiry

During the introduction to inquiry in everyday life, (see above) students examine evidence of city centre, drunken behaviour, which is associated with themselves as members of a group known as 'students'. Some IIL2 students identify themselves with the situation, responding defensively to negative comments in the media while others agree and add further criticisms. Student debate about the fairness of such comment is fertile ground for tutors to help students to examine their working concepts of: inquiry aims of various kinds, respect for evidence and for persons and sources of bias and characteristics of prejudice in the way that evidence is obtained and selectively used. Comparing the range of ways in which the same phenomena are presented across as many media sources as reasonably possible can help to increase students' understanding of the academic and professional characteristics of inquiry.

As Year Two students of Childhood Studies, their awareness of professionalism has begun to grow. Tutors of IIL2 draw explicitly on this developing awareness to introduce ethical and professional standards of conducting inquiry in the workplace, which are the focus of intensive study later in the academic year, presented in below under the heading *Reflective professional practice*. Starting with extracts from the European Declaration of Human Rights, tutors present questions and challenges to students about how to perceive and relate to people involved in inquiry, particularly those from whom evidence is collected, which will not, on this occasion, include children, but will in the future. Attention is given to issues such as confidentiality towards people, evidence and the protection of freedom of participation and expression. Reference is made to the British Educational Research Association's (2004) *Revised Ethical Guidelines for Educational Research*.

IIL2 criteria for the assessment of learning

The patterns, processes and procedures established in IIL1 for students' learning are continued in IIL2. This includes the use of a reflective Jotter, meetings in small groups for inquiry work and with learning partners to review progress. Cycles of activity culminate in a conference, after which a patch is written. At such points in the learning, and occasionally also at other times, small groups will be allocated the task of giving feedback about a piece of course work indicating the extent to which it has the following qualities:

- *Inquiry-mindedness* refers to the extent to which the work shows professional curiosity, open-mindedness, an awareness of the limitations of views expressed, alternatives to choices made and different perspectives on the same events.
- *Credible, practical knowing* refers to the extent to which the work shows credible relationships between inquiry purposes, processes, evidence, interpretation and critical evaluation, coherence, clarity and conceptual depth.
- *Professional engagement* refers to the extent to which the work shows your ability to reflect ethically, critically and constructively on your own and others' autonomy, involvement, perseverance, collaboration and the negotiation of control and responsibility for improvement.

These are the same as the module assignment assessment criteria. The intention is that students should develop a fuller understanding of their meaning, improve their ability to apply these criteria to their own and others' work and therefore internalise them in the self-assessment of their learning.

The Commissioned Inquiry

The first part of the IIL2 module presented above occupies the first six sessions of the module. In preparation for the Commissioned Inquiry (CI) work, students complete two learning inquiries into the development of inquiry techniques to be used in a limited range of simple inquiry methods. The other kind of preparatory study is of published sources about inquiry methods. Students are provided with a list of selected reference texts and websites from which to locate material for writing about the theoretical ideas underpinning one of the inquiry techniques they have been practising which enables them to write a patch with the trendy title of 'Reading4Learning'. Tutors provide headings for writing this patch, including: the bibliographic details of the source used; information about how others can most easily access it; the student's personal evaluation of the text; a summary of the main things it provides; a list of the new questions raised for further reading, possible links with other ideas to learn about or things to try out in practice. As resources for the CI, postings on the VLE include all of the learning inquiry and Reading4Learning patches as well as a matrix document which is a directory to all the patches. The whole year group meets in a lecture theatre to hear a talk by a professional researcher, receive general training on the use of digital voice recorders, still cameras and video cameras for collecting evidence, a role play of Stanley Milgram's (1974) experiment on obedience and authority as a stimulus for revisiting ethical issues, and an introduction to the progress schedule for the CI itself.

The planning of a Commissioned Inquiry

By this time in the module, students are expected to be ready to be actively involved in a genuine inquiry; not determining its aims, but offering suggestions for what evidence to gather, how to obtain it, under what conditions and how to use it to further the inquiry purpose. They act as 'inquiry assistants' to a tutor's action inquiry into the improvement or development of an area of her or his teaching or curriculum development at the university. A group of about 25 'commissioning tutors', colleagues in the School of Education, have previously identified an inquiry of personal, professional interests and agreed to guide their inquiry assistants, IIL2 students, through the inquiry over a period of about ten weeks.

The checklist given in Box 5.1 is intended to guide students' preparation for the CI.

Box 5.1 Things to consider when planning a Commissioned Inquiry

Before the first meeting with the commissioning tutor check:

1 Am I really clear about what are the inquiry *purposes*?

2 What does the commissioning tutor say are *key concepts* of my inquiry?

3 Do I know and understand enough about the professional *context*?

4 Am I clear about what *evidence* I need to collect, from *whom* (including *when* and *where* this is to be done) and by which *method*?

5 What *permissions* and *agreements* do I need to negotiate?

Things to consider before starting the inquiry:

6 How will I *record* the most important evidence?

7 What is the most important thing I need to *learn* from this evidence?

8 How will I *categorise, structure, interpret* and *analyse* my evidence?

9 Should the evidence be *categorised* before it is gathered or afterwards?

10 How will I *clear* the evidence for analysis and for publication?

11 How well does the analysis meet the *purposes* of the inquiry?

12 What *suggestions* and *advice* does the commissioning tutor give me about my *inquiry plan*?

13 How will I *organise* all of the practical tasks in the *time* available?

During the final stages

14 How well does my *report* convey the significant aspects of the inquiry?

15 How are the inquiry findings best *summarised* and *presented*?

16 What *other research* do I need to know about, to link with this inquiry?

17 What *new* ideas, questions, limitations or surprises appear at this stage?

18 Have I got *clearance* from all relevant people to *release* the report?

19 What is the most important *feedback* from the commissioning tutor on the draft of my report?

20 What have I as an inquiry assistant *learned* about professional inquiry?

21 How would I like my inquiry to be *assessed* by others?

It has been crucial to the success of this initiative that many colleagues have been willing to be involved in this part of the IIL2 module, as tutor-researchers. There was already a well-established tradition of small, local action research projects carried out by tutors with technical and administrative support staff, to promote developments in pedagogic practice and curriculum development. Many colleagues are able to nominate with relative ease an aspect of their current work about which they would like to gather evidence, if only time would permit, to be able to reflect more deeply and to advance an intention for change. We ask them to choose any aspect of their teaching and/or the students' learning that they see as in some way problematic, puzzling or interesting for either theoretical or practical reasons. They commission an inquiry to examine a small, simple, clear aspect of one of the following kinds of focus:

1   an aspect of the tutor's role, such as the choice of aims for the session, the tutor's questioning, the tasks allocated, the group work or the resources provided;
2   an aspect of the students' responses, such as the discussion which takes place, the quality of engagement or the kind of activity and/or learning which results;
3   an aspect of assessments made, to do with the processes or products of the learning.

The focus is expressed as a question to be answered or a hypothesis to be tested but is essentially about a practical professional problem. The tutor is allocated about five IIL2 students as inquiry assistants, meeting regularly to oversee progress, discuss evidence, guide analysis and check the report before 'publication'. Methods could include observations and/or recordings of particular aspects of interactions between:

•   the tutor and the tutor's students or between the students;
•   observations of and/or interviews with the tutor's students concerning, for example, an aspect of their activity or their discussion during the session and/or their perception of the purposes of the session;
•   *instance interviews* such as interviewing chosen students about their views of a specific example of a recurring event in the session, of which they select an instance, on which to base their interview;
•   other methods;
•   a combination of methods.

Table 5.1 opposite provides a list of some Commissioned Inquiries.

Table 5.1 Examples of Commissioned Inquiries

The inquiry focus: a practical professional problem	Context: programme and module	Relevant techniques/ evidence
Difficulties encountered by first generation entrants to universities	Any	Interview '1st generation' female students
Matching Directed Learning Tasks more closely to student needs	BA Primary Education Year One Music	Interview and/or questionnaire
Understanding students' use of mind maps: what they record, how, why, what value?	BA Primary Education Year Three Maths education	Observation and instance interview
Redesign and apply an online evaluation of ICT services in placement colleges	PGCE for HE	Electronic evaluation and report to tutors
Review electronic survey tools. Select appropriate tool. Set up survey and pilot	All Year One undergraduates	Electronic evaluation
Students' use of digitised reading material	BA Primary Education Year Two Geography	Questionnaire
Compare student support during School Based Training	BA Primary Education Years Two and Three	Interview
Mentor's motivations and expectations for working with student teachers	BA Primary Education Year Three	Interview
Students' perceptions of the relevance of university sessions to professional applications	BA Primary Education Year Three Inclusion	Instance interview
Students' understanding of the research process	BA Childhood Studies Year Three Professional Research Project module	Document analysis, interview
Students' Directed Learning Task process	BA Primary Education Year One	Instance interview
Students' evaluations of Values Week	BA Primary Education and BA Childhood Studies – all years	Interview
Factors influencing students' choice of Early Years strand	BA Primary Education Year Three	Interviews/questionnaire
Improving tutors' practice of putting questions to students during sessions	A range of contexts	Participant observation and instance interview

Most importantly, IIL2 students are challenged by experiences of doing a real inquiry. The commissioning tutor genuinely wants to know things that can only be learned by obtaining evidence and analysing it, to make their students' learning better in some way. Students are expected to gain competence and professionalism as inquirers, developing qualities defined in the assessment criteria. Unlike the slightly unreal exercises in Learning Inquiry 1 and 2, students who show an indifferent *inquiry mindedness*, poor *professional engagement* or weak commitment to *credible, practical knowing*, let down not only themselves but also their peers and tutors, and may compromise the value of the inquiry to the students who are intended to benefit. For some, the immediacy and significance of the CI seem to be a stimulus to more dependable involvement; for others, it exposes their difficulties still further.

Students and commissioning tutors are given a schedule for inquiry progress like that shown in Box 5.2.

Box 5.2 Schedule for Commissioned Inquiry progress

Stage A

All members of the team of inquiry assistants *meet* your commissioning tutor during Week 16 and not later than 16/11.

   You must contact them to fix a time to meet and discuss the next level of detail of your commission.

1   Please check that you understand the exact *purpose* of your inquiry.
2   You need you to gain enough *contextual* information to appreciate how your inquiry arises.
3   You need to fully understand the *key concepts* of the *inquiry focus*.
4   You may need the tutor's *advice* on making the *methods* for evidence *gathering* and *analysis* tightly *focused* on your inquiry purpose and *manageable* in the short time available.

Stage B

1   Send the inquiry plan to your commissioning tutor, and ask them to check it and offer feedback. Do this in Week 17 and not later than 23/11.
2   Ask the tutor to contact you if there are any aspects which need adjustment or for which you may need additional information or advice.

Stage C

You gather *evidence* during Weeks 18 and/or 19, and complete this not later than 7/12.

Depending on what you agreed in the plan, this may necessitate you attending a university session to observe or to meet the relevant students during that week.

Stage D
You may need to agree to meet your commissioning tutor to *discuss* your evidence and its analysis, your *progress* with drawing out relevant *findings* and the *scope* of the forthcoming report during Week 25.

Stage E
Send your *draft report* to your commissioning tutor during Week 27 and not later than 1/2. **22/2/07**
   Ask your tutor to

1   check the report to protect their students' rights to confidentiality, and any other relevant ethical considerations;
2   advise you on redrafting the report of the inquiry so as to be suitable for 'publication' on the VLE;
3   give feedback on:

   • the credibility of your findings against the evidence you have gathered
   • the inquiry qualities you recognise in your work and
   • their suggestions for further improvement of your inquiry abilities;

4   authorise you to release your redrafted report.

Stage F
Send your *report* to your IIL2 tutor during Week 28 and not later than 15/2, together with a self-assessment of the Professional Qualities evident in your conduct of the inquiry.

Bring two (printed) copies of both documents to the session in Week 29.

Students are expected to adopt appropriate terminology of inquiry in their talk and writing.

The Commissioned Inquiry in action

The last thing before work begins is to organise student membership of groups of inquiry assistants. One year, we followed the principle of giving students free choice, with clear tutor advice that personal interest in the inquiry focus or context should precede choosing to work with a friend. The resulting groups were almost always determined by friendship and most worked well. A few which did not do so well had included or were entirely composed of students who were regarded by tutors as weak, in the sense that either

- there had been a pattern of disappointing engagement with IIL1 and/or IIL2, or
- there was evidence of negative or indifferent attitudes or conduct towards learning and/or professionalism, or
- both.

Problematic groups and group members tend to miss deadlines and meetings, appear to be vague and muddled, give spoken commitments which they did not act upon promptly, if at all, gather evidence incompetently. Furthermore, they communicated with each other and with tutors ineffectively, if at all, and, worst, tended either to give breathtakingly trivial excuses or deny responsibility for their actions outright.

As 'good teachers', we looked critically at ourselves, taking responsibility to rectify these 'faults'. We considered actions to force errant students to conform, to minimise difficulties for the commissioning tutor, to whom we felt a debt of gratitude, and to sustain some sort of fairness. Hard-working students whose group was not functioning well showed greatest concern about fairness concerning the group writing of the report – 'How could student X claim joint authorship of a patch about an inquiry to which they had contributed so little?'. Tutor meetings and module evaluation reports contained some linguistic hand-wringing about these difficulties! What had seemed a straightforward part of the organisation became a difficulty for the learning, development and fair assessment of a sizeable minority of students, not to mention a disappointment for some commissioning tutors, whose valued goodwill might be threatened. As action researchers, we analysed the old dilemma in a new form, between too much and too little control.

The process employed to decide the composition of groups in the following year used a rough categorisation of students' expected disposition to respond positively to the commissioned inquiry – 'Does this student show positive attitudes and commitment to study?'. Group membership included a mixture of this roughly assessed disposition within each group. When the groups were announced, about half of the students were critical. At one end of the spectrum of responses were students who saw the task as one which it would be nice to do with friends but, if that were not an option, it would be more important to get on and do a good job, taking opportunities to work with people they didn't know very well and/or hadn't worked with before. Next, there were similarly positive comments qualified by reservations about the inclusion of a student who was not regarded by the other students as being good at shared work. At the other end of the spectrum were opinions that it would (almost) not be possible for the group to work together *'because they did not know each other well enough'*!

We had decided to control group membership, believing that alongside a threat posed by the less well-disposed students within a mixed group to the success of an inquiry, is an opportunity for important learning by all group members about how to collaborate professionally. We increased the emphasis on keeping the reflective Jotter to note significant events, talk, action, personal thoughts and feelings, related to the professionalism part of the module aim: becoming a professional inquirer.

Our action step slightly increased the proportion of groups whose work was affected adversely by students who contributed less than necessary. We found courage and confidence to press on with the strategy. In tutorials with such a group, we took an explicitly neutral and accepting stance towards reports that X had not turned up at the meeting with the commissioning tutor or that Y had not sent everyone the draft of interview questions which had been agreed by all. Without condoning or condemning these actions, we tried to be role models, leading talk about what would be constructive steps forward, not only for the progress of the inquiry but also for the strengthening of working relationships between everyone involved. We explored what could count as more professional or less professional action, and how to seek improvement. We encouraged each student to write reflectively about their own perspective on events and their own conduct, in relation to tutors and the students who were intended to benefit from the success of the inquiry. We said that this was important material for the module assignment, because it would contribute to understanding the professional dimension of learning to be a professional inquirer. It is not easy to pursue a path which could be seen in terms of *'You will gain good things from your suffering, so I will not intervene in the way you might like'* when students are justifiably angry and frustrated by being let down by peers.

The weekly IIL2 sessions during the several weeks of CI work are designed to sustain the inquiry progress. We provide a series of sheets for inquiry groups to complete and hand in to tutors, intended to prompt clearer thinking and action about that stage of the work and contribute to our records of progress. For example, the sheet for the planning stage is reproduced over page as Figure 5.2.

COMMISSIONED INQUIRY PLANNING I | Group

Commissioning tutor   Date_____

Title of Commissioned Inquiry

Names of students in this Commissioned Inquiry TEAM of Inquiry Assistants

Name and contact information of the agreed COORDINATOR of this team of Inquiry Assistants

What the team needs, to clarify the Inquiry *List of questions*	How the team plans to obtain clarifications

Plan for organising the first meeting with the Commissioning Tutor

Plan for organising the preparation of the COMMISSIONED INQUIRY PLAN

Figure 5.2 Commissioned Inquiry planning stage

III L   **COMMISSIONED INQUIRY PROGRESS 2** | Group |

Commissioning tutor _____ Date of meeting _____

Names of Inquiry Assistants who **met the Commissioning Tutor** to discuss the Plan

Agreed **purpose(s)** of the Inquiry?	What kinds of **evidence** are needed?

Agreed **Key Concepts** of the Inquiry?	What **reading** is needed?

Agreed **methods** and **techniques** of gathering and **recording** evidence which are to be used	Where and when the evidence will be **obtained**

Agreed list of the **ethical considerations** of the Inquiry	How these are to be addressed in doing the Inquiry

Agreed plan for **organising** and **analysing** the evidence

Plan for **organising** the **collaboration** of Inquiry Assistants to complete these tasks

Figure 5.2 Continued

Session time is also given to regular short tutorials with each group. Tutors' monitoring of progress is facilitated by the use of record sheets such as that reproduced as Figure 5.3.

COMMISSIONED INQUIRY
RECORD OF TEAMWORK COLLABORATION

IIL INQUIRY INTO LEARNING

Group

Commissioning tutor _____ Write into each cell of the table below a note of what each student did at each stage and (in the bottom row) the proportion of the total team effort that has been agreed by all members of the team to have been contributed by each team member

Stage of the Inquiry	Names of the students (Inquiry Assistants) in this team (up to 6) Underline the name of the Coordinator					
	I	2	3	4	5	6
Coordination, communication & participation						
A. Meet Commissioning Tutor						
B. Planning the inquiry						
Background reading						
C. Gathering & analysing evidence						
D. Discuss evidence with Commissioning tutor						
E. Prepare Draft report						
F. Clear Draft with Commissioning Tutor						
G. Prepare Final report						
H. Conference preparation						
Agreed proportion of total team effort contributed by each team member						

Signatures of all students in the group to show that they agree that the above record is accurate and fair

I	2	3	4	5	6

Figure 5.3 Commissioning tutor's record sheet

INQUIRY PROGRESS RECORD SHEET

Commissioning Tutor(s) (CT)	Commissioned inquiry title	Inquiry assistants (IA) incl. contact

Stages	Tutorials with IIL tutor
A All IAs **meet** CT before 16/11 *Check understanding of inquiry* **purpose**, *gain* **contextual** *information,* **key concepts** *of the* **inquiry focus** *and* **methods** *for evidence* **gathering** *and* **analysis focused** *on inquiry purpose &* **manageable** Date of meeting _____ Attendance Progress	Date and time Attendance Purposes Issues Agreements
B Send **plan** to your CT, request **checking** and **feedback** before 23/11 IA's plan sent to CT on _____ CT's response to plan received on _____ CT's requests for adjustments IA's additional information needs	Date and time Attendance Purposes Issues Agreements
C Complete **evidence gathering** and **recording** by 7/12 IA's meeting at session on _____ Attendance Types of evidence presented Records of evidence available Participation of all IAs	Date and time Attendance Purposes Issues Agreements
D Meet CT to **discuss** evidence and analysis, **progress**, **findings** and **scope** of **report**, during **Week 25** Date of meeting _____ Attendance Progress CT's advice Write draft report	Date and time Attendance Purposes Issues Agreements
E Send **draft report** to CT by 22/2 *CT to* **check** *report and* **ethical** *aspects,* **advise** *on redrafting report for 'publication'* CT to give **feedback** on **credibility** of **findings** against **evidence** provided, the **inquiry qualities** and suggested **improvements** **CT to authorise release** of redrafted report	Date and time Attendance Purposes Issues Agreements

Stage F

Send your **report** to your IIL2 Tutor during **Week 28** and not later than **Friday 15th February**, together with a **self assessment** of the **Professional Qualities** evident in your conduct of the inquiry.

Bring two (printed) copies of both documents to the session in Week 29 (19th February).

A Commissioned Inquiry conference of the whole Year group takes place at the end of this part of the IIL2 module. A conference organising group of tutors with students plan times and groupings for CI presentations and a printed programme with Inquiry Abstracts. Presentation rooms equipped with IT facilitate and record the presentations, questions and discussion. Group organisation maximises the sharing across seminar groups in Year Two. Commissioning tutors and other colleagues teaching the programme, not least the Programme Leader, are invited to attend and contribute to the conference. We aim for students to gain a realistic experience and develop confidence, skill to perform well and a deeper sense of collegiate communication of knowledge in professional dialogue. A cleared report on each Commissioned Inquiry, coauthored by the inquiry assistants, is posted on the VLE. Students are encouraged to use their participation in the conference to reflect on events from different perspectives (see Box 5.3).

Box 5.3 Learning from the conference experience

Suggestions for personal reflections to write about in the Jotter

As I participate in the conference:
- What are the opportunities to learn, that an event like this offers me?
- What do I need to do to maximise my own learning at a conference?
- What do I need to do to facilitate others' learning at a conference?
- What counts as professional behaviour at a conference?

As I and my group give our presentation and share in discussion:
- Does the audience show understanding and interest in our inquiry?
- How might I/we present our work differently/better?
- What have I/we learned from our experience, others' feedback and the discussion?

As I listen to and discuss each presentation:
- What would I do if I were in the situation of these inquirers?
- What can I learn about the conduct of an inquiry like theirs?
- What did they do or think about, that might have made my inquiry better?
- What have I done or thought about, that might help these inquirers evaluate their inquiry better?
- What contributions to discussion can I make from my own perspective?

Consider joining in discussion about:

1   my understanding of the inquiry aim and *what* was found out;

2   my understanding of the inquiry method and *how* it was found out.

Does the inquiry show these IIL2 module qualities?

- *Inquiry-mindedness* which refers to the extent to which the work shows professional curiosity, open-mindedness, an awareness of the limitations of views expressed, alternatives to choices made, different perspectives on the same events.

- *Credible, practical knowing* which refers to the extent to which the work shows credible relationships between inquiry purposes, processes, evidence, interpretation and critical evaluation, coherence, clarity and conceptual depth.

- *Professional engagement* which refers to the extent to which the work shows an ability to reflect ethically, critically and constructively on one's own and others': autonomy, involvement, perseverance, collaboration, and the negotiation of control and responsibility for improvement.

The CI project has become well-established as a valuable resource for School of Education colleagues' small scale professional and curriculum development projects, at the same time as challenging IIL2 students to contribute to worthwhile professional, educational inquiry.

Commissioned Inquiry achievements

The following are summaries of a few Inquiries, illustrating the range, depth and value of work done.

- The distinctive perspective of mature student members in sessions for mixed age group undergraduates was found to support team development.
- A tutor with responsibility for timetabling obtained helpful insights into ways in which the timing and frequency of study days and other features of the timetable are perceived to assist learning.
- An evaluation of the IIL1 and IIL2 modules was elicited from Final Year students in the Childhood Studies programme to discover more about the longer term learning outcomes of these modules.
- Students' perceptions of the sustainability of conventional practices in teaching and learning, such as printed handout learning material, were obtained and used to inform tutors' planning.

- A tutor with a staff development role gained comparative evidence of students' perspectives of tutors' main ways of asking questions during sessions.
- Tutors' allocation of set reading in preparation for students' participation in class discussion was investigated to improve the quality of learning.

Table 5.2 presents a scheme for the self and peer assessment of the processes of a group assignment adapted from Sue Bloxham and Peter Boyd's book about assessment in higher education, to match the CI situation.

Table 5.2 Scheme for the assessment of a group assignment

A contribution worth 10/10	A contribution worth 0/10	Mark /10 allocated	Justifications for the mark allocated
attended all meetings, well-prepared, participated helpfully, followed up thoroughly	no/low attendance at meetings, inadequate preparation, minor/no participation, little/no follow up		
contributed plenty of ideas and good ideas, built on others' ideas, made valuable suggestions for improvement	contributed few/weak/ no ideas, little/no building on others' ideas or suggestions for improvement		
addressed personal differences constructively, tolerated/healed conflict, sustained momentum	made personal differences into obstacles, provoked conflict, hindered/ blocked progress		
communicated reliably, listened carefully, encouraged others, showed appreciation	hard to keep in touch, ignored or talked over others, passive/ indifferent to others		
willing to try new things, took initiative, was reliable, made contributions of a high standard	unwilling to join in, avoided responsibilities, was unreliable, made little/poor contribution		

Source: Bloxham and Boyd 2007: 101.

Reflective professional practice

The final third of the IIL2 module is about professionalism. Students have met terms and concepts about being professional in other modules as well as in IIL, and have been expected to conduct themselves in professional ways during placements and visits. Most students do part-time work, which may involve an element of professionalism. Doing the CI raised questions, problems and opportunities to observe and enact professionalism. Now we examine meanings and practices more closely and critically, starting with past experiences, current perceptions and interests, moving into formal and informed ways of thinking and acting.

Here are some of the points of departure for discussing meanings of professionalism that we have used, in combination with each other:

- Students' descriptions of a critical/controversial incident in a professional setting, from their own experience of acting as, for example, a helper or assistant to a teacher, child minder, care centre, official visitor, etc. in a placement or as paid work.
- Students' descriptions of a critical/controversial incident in a paid work setting of an ordinary kind, from their own experience of, for example, serving in a shop or café or behind a bar, being a receptionist, etc.
- Students' or family members' descriptions of experience of a critical/controversial incident in dealings with a professional person, notably a doctor, solicitor, police officer, teacher, etc.
- Critical/controversial incidents reported in the media about the conduct of social workers, teachers, child support staff and so on.

From discussions of these experiences, the dominant images of professionalism which emerge, coloured by popular usage, are quite superficial. The glaring omission in most of what students believe to be examples of professionalism is an ethical or moral dimension. High value is placed on clean, smart appearance, polite interactions with 'clients', a deferential attitude to authority figures and being technically competent in performing tasks rigorously, as prescribed by others. In discussions of critical/controversial incidents, it is usually quite difficult to find students recognising what we would call a moral dilemma or a conflict of interest between participants. Their mind set is one of needing to have artificial clarity imposed on any *'messy but important problems'* in the *'swampy lowlands of practice'* by a clear view of what should happen. Readers of Donald Schön (1983) will recognise two of his phrases. These meanings of professionalism contain a weak desire to please 'clients', but without a strong sense of putting the good of a client over one's own, should the need arise. There is little differentiation between (for example) serving a meal to a customer and advising a parent about the development of their child in terms of professional significance. After having been told that they have served meals professionally, it may be difficult for a proud student to accept that this is not what professionalism is really about, or less significant than giving advice to parents. All this should be unsurprising in a world where the language of professionalism has been degraded by such extensive commercial misuse. We have noticed that mature students are less likely to hold such a restricted image, presumably having reflected more deeply on experiences of personal and social difficulties, not least those which may have needed the involvement of professional people.

Having reached the halfway stage of their degree, students have probably heard the phrase 'reflective practitioner' and seen it in their reading. We decided that studying the book by Donald Schön, which originated the concept and locates it in an influential theoretical and philosophical frame, would offer advantages that outweighed the difficulties. *The Reflective Practitioner: How Professionals Think in Action* (Schön 1983) frequently appears in the Bibliographies of writing in the fields of education, some using the term as an epithet for a professional person who reflects. The underlying juxtaposition of reflective practice with 'technical rationality' is not often apparent, even though it is a powerful resource for deconstructing many phenomena. We want our students to realise, both intellectually and practically, fuller meanings of these concepts. We feel we are trying to open up a reflective practitioner perspective within students, many of whom would otherwise assume an *infallible expert* style of professionalism. Our teaching tries to enable students to link the challenge of understanding Donald Schön's book with several pieces of experience, and develop theoretical ideas interdependently with reflections on practice.

Donald Schön's *Reflective Practitioner* (1983) begins with what he calls the 'crisis of confidence' in professional knowledge that was taking place during the 1970s. The field of Childhood Studies has many recent examples, which our students know about, of crises of confidence in professionals and conflicting implied notions of professionalism. We present our summary of this to students and teach them about the content of Chapter 2 of the book, which is entitled 'From technical rationality to reflection in action'. It explains a shift in ways of understanding professional knowledge from mainly positivist separations of theory from practice to views of the professional person addressing complex, ambiguous practical problems by initiating a *conversation with the situation* and generating responses in which the *knowing is the action*. The dilemma for a professional person is between *rigour*: the traditionally expert application of certain, research based theory and technique to clearly defined problems, and *relevance*: inquiring reflectively and doubtfully into the client's messy, ambiguous practical problems which are often of greater human importance.

In subsequent chapters, Schön provides case studies of practice in five professions: engineering, architecture, management, psychotherapy and town planning, with close observations of professionals in action, solving particular problems. Tutors allocate the study of each of these chapters to five groups of students to address these questions:

1   What practical professional problem(s) is/are being considered in this study?
2   How do the professional people depicted in each case study perceive the problem(s)?
3   How do they interact during the course of developing possible solutions to the problem(s)?
4   What do the people in the study actually say and do that seems to be what Schön calls *reflection in action*?
5   Does (and, if so, how does) the reflection in action contribute to progress in solving the problem(s)?
6   Does the process depicted in each study show any (and, if so, which) characteristics of a *technical rational* approach to problem solving?

Each group presents an account of 'their' profession, its case study and an analysis using the above questions. Students may find difficulty in relating to areas of work so removed from their experience, but give helpful material for general discussion. As Childhood Studies students, this expands their sense of professional practice to enable them to more readily appreciate its reflective qualities.

The concluding chapter of Schön's book summarises the implications of the contrasting approaches for the professional–client relationship. A summary is provided in Box 5.4 overleaf.

Students then examine critical incidents from their experience of doing the Commissioned Inquiry using Schön's concepts and frames, drawing on reflective writing in their Jotters about what happened, how they reacted at the time and subsequently. We expect them to discover manifestations of the infallible expert as well as the reflective practitioner kinds of practice in events they have experienced and make constructively self-critical comments on relevant aspects of their own development. A short piece of writing about this is discussed with learning partners and posted as a patch on the VLE. Figure 5.4 gives an example of the kind of mind map which, through structured discussion, an IIL2 tutor may develop with their group as a way of representing the shared ideas and experiences.

Students returning from a block of Work Based Learning, on placement in a professional setting, are often more aware of a wider range of issues involved in professional contexts, such as:

- How do you deal with staff shortages due to illness?
- How can you maintain staff enthusiasm and motivation?
- How can staff make themselves available for parents to talk to at any time even if they are feeling pressured?
- How can staff working with children be so positive all the time?
- How do staff cope under the pressure of working with severely disabled children?
- How can we communicate with people who speak other languages?

Box 5.4 **Summary of contrasting approaches for the professional–client relationship**

Traditional practice

The professional
- delivers services to the limits of special competences
- respects confidences
- promises not to misuse special powers of status
- *may* show sympathy with the client's problems, understand the situation, reveal some special knowledge
- is directly *accountable to the client*, but this is not normally tested, except legally, in cases of misconduct
- is also *accountable to peers*, but the privacy which normally applies to the relationship with clients prevents routine access to it by peers
- *is presumed to know*, and must claim to do so, *regardless of their own uncertainty*
- keeps a *distance* from the client, to sustain the expert's role (and mystique?)
- looks for *deference* and status in the client's responses.

Reflective practice

The professional
- recognises that their technical expertise is *embedded in a context of meanings*
- tries to discover what the client's meanings are
- is obliged to make own understandings accessible to the client (and thus will often *reflect anew* on what they know)
- tries to discover the *limits* of their own expertise through *reflective conversation* with the client
- tries to help the client understand the professional's advice and the rationale for their actions
- presumes to know, but regards their own *uncertainties as a possible source of learning* by both professional and client
- does not regard themselves as the only person in the situation to have relevant and important knowledge.

Traditional practice

The client
- accepts the professional's authority and may gain a sense of security based on a faith that all will be well
- submits to the professional's ministrations
- pays for services
- may show deference and compliance, or may challenge the professional's advice
- has limited ability to determine whether or not their own legitimate expectations have been met

Reflective practice

The client
- does not agree to accept the professional's authority but 'to suspend disbelief in it'
- agrees to join the professional in enquiring into the situation for which the client seeks help, and may thereby gain a sense of increased involvement and action
- tries to understand what the professional is experiencing, and to make their own perspective accessible to the professional within a relationship of interdependence
- confronts the professional when they do not understand or agree

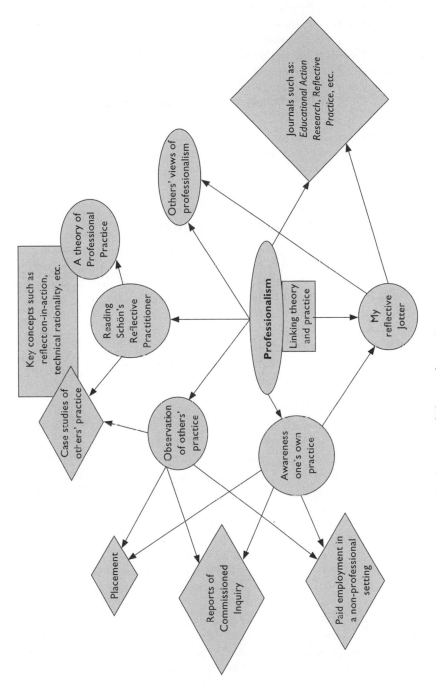

Figure 5.4 Mind map representing development of ideas and experiences

These questions give tutors insight into students' beliefs about professional attitudes. We explore both the positive sense of self-actualisation and appropriate professional values such as commitment, effort and valuing others. These links between the IIL module and the Work Based Learning module appear to support students in explicitly integrating ideas from various professional contexts with work at university, such as developing reflective practice and professional behaviour and values. For instance, during a discussion using the Intervision strategy (see Chapter 6) about 'How do you deal with staff shortages due to illness?', students contributed a wide range of issues about illness and motivation. Whether to fulfil professional responsibilities at work or take a 'sickie' were seen for the first time as having a parallel in choices about attendance and commitment to group responsibilities in university sessions.

IIL2 – the Patchwork Text assignment

Unless they have transferred into the degree programme since Year One, all students will have learned during IIL1 about this approach to assessed work. In comparison with IIL1, students have written fewer patches for IIL2, but one (the Commissioned Inquiry Report) is larger and collaboratively written. The assignment is presented in the Module Handbook as follows:

The assessed assignment is a *Patchwork Text* of 2,500 words, derived from your Jotter writing and patches, entitled:

Becoming a professional inquirer

The assignment is made up of an edited selection of patches, or extracts from them, with an interpretive, reflective and critical commentary, or *stitches*, which draw on material in your Jotter/Journal. The Patchwork Text (PT) brings out and explores theme(s) across the separate pieces of writing. The patches are chosen for their significance to your main learning achievements. They are linked by the *stitching*, which introduces and explains each *patch*, and links them, to bring out themes, trends, developments or patterns in your learning across the module. For example, any such theme(s) in the PT may be one(s) relating to your personal questions or problems as they have arisen through the processes of writing your Jotter/Journal, and reflection linked to critical friends group discussion. However, you are not expected to arrive at simple, clear answers to these questions but to give an honest exploration of the issues which you have or have not resolved, indicating any new questions which may have been raised, and so on. Overall, the PT should convey significant ways in which your learning has achieved the qualities indicated by the assessment criteria which are appropriate to a reflective professional inquirer, across the module learning outcomes.

Module sessions, together with small group and individual tutorials, are allocated to students' preparation of the assignment. As a Level Two assignment, the IIL2 Patchwork Text expects increased usage of theoretical resources to deepen thinking.

An edited extract from an IIL2 assignment which was assessed as meeting the criteria well is reproduced below. Tutor comments have been added in the column on the right. The assessment criteria are reproduced here, with numbers to which the tutor comments refer:

1   *Inquiry-mindedness* refers to the extent to which the work shows professional curiosity, open-mindedness, an awareness of the limitations of views expressed, alternatives to choices made and different perspectives on the same events.
2   *Credible, practical knowing* refers to the extent to which the work shows credible relationships between inquiry purposes, processes, evidence, interpretation and critical evaluation, coherence, clarity and conceptual depth.
3   *Professional engagement* refers to the extent to which the work shows your ability to reflect ethically, critically and constructively on your own and others' autonomy, involvement, perseverance, collaboration, and the negotiation of control and responsibility for improvement.

Becoming a Professional Inquirer

This Patchwork Text uses patches, Jotter entries, and readings to evaluate how I have started to become a professional inquirer.

Ethics play an important role in research ...
The first research method I looked at was action research. I chose this research method because even though I had heard of the method, I was unsure about what it involved. I had also read that it is used by professionals working in education and therefore I thought that it would be beneficial to learn about action research, as I may need to use it in my career.

When professionals undertake action research they are looking at their own practice in order to improve it (Costello, 2003). This may because they want to introduce a change in the setting, i.e. a policy, or because they want to gain more knowledge in a particular area (Roberts-Holmes, 2006).

(Patch 1)

Tutor's commentary

These are helpful indicators of qualities in Criterion 2: the credible examples of understanding in action; and 3: in relation to the awareness of the ethical dimension of inquiry and of own developmental progress.

After reading about action research I realised that I had used this method in Inquiry Into Learning I and therefore did have some experience with it. I also found out how effective this method could be when working on the commissioned inquiry.

> Our commissioned inquiry is a piece of action research looking at how mature students view their course, especially the communication methods used ... Our commissioning tutor was surprised to find that many of the students found it hard to use the VLE.
>
> (Journal entry [15/12/2007])

This made me realise that this type of research is useful for highlighting areas of improvement professionals may not have thought about. After seeing action research in practice I now feel it may be a valuable tool for me to use in the future to improve my own practice.

After reading a section of Donald Schön's book about the meaning of reflection in action, I have realised that reflection in action and action research are very similar, as they both involve reflecting, criticising and modifying practice.

> Reflection in action means when a professional encounters a problem they reflect on the situation and act upon their reflection. They constantly criticise, evaluate and reflect on their implementations until they find a solution (Schön, 1983).
>
> (Patch 3)

Schön believed that professionals should be able to reflect in action and this has highlighted to me that in order to be a professional inquirer I need to be able to be reflective and criticise my own work in order to improve my practice. The view that professionals are able to reflect in action was further emphasised when I was investigating the early years professional status, as part of the assessment requires students to show that they are able to reflect on, evaluate and modify their practice (CWDC, 2006 [online]). As the early years professional status is a status I wish to achieve, I feel that my first inquiry and the commissioned inquiry has helped me to see important elements of professional practice that will help me achieve this qualification.

The choices of author and definition about action research are a little disappointing, but the explicit link to own learning in IIL1 is valuable in suggesting a reasonable grasp.

Starting action research with a practical professional problem is implied rather than stated explicitly.

Links between action research and Schön's ideas about reflective practice, which are in turn linked to consideration of the Early Years professional status, are impressive.

The next research method I chose to investigate was questionnaires. Even though I have used and created questionnaires in the past I wanted to find out about how to design an effective questionnaire and when in research is the most appropriate place to use them. This information is important to me as I might use questionnaires for my final research project and therefore I need to know how to use them correctly. After reading about the advantages and disadvantages of questionnaires I decided I wanted to see whether email questionnaires were effective.

> As the text highlights that it is important to have at least 30 questionnaires to ensure the results are reliable, I am interested in finding out whether sending questionnaires via email or handing them out produce a higher return rate.
>
> (R4L Patch)

The inquiry into Questionnaires shows credibility in the way that relevant questions are raised and attended to, concerning what is of personal significance and general importance.

In order to investigate this I worked with my critical friends. We decided not to base the questionnaire on our course, as this would mean that the people handing out the questionnaires would be limited to using the people in our classes. Instead we chose to base it on university life, as this is something everyone on the campus has in common.

> I decided to send the questionnaires out by e-mail because this is the first technique the Higher Education Funding Council for England uses to send out their National Student Satisfaction Survey (Macleod, 2004 [online]). We also thought that people would be more likely to respond to a questionnaire sent by email because when the recipient reads them they are likely to have the time to complete them, compared to someone asking them to fill them out as they are going around the university campus. As they are more likely to be on their way somewhere and therefore are more likely to say no.
>
> (Patch 1)

Other decisions are reasonably well justified in terms of a sense of the inquiry mindedness shown towards practical choices, valid comparisons, learning from experience, and the accurate use of inquiry concepts.

I personally thought that more people would respond to an email questionnaire, as they could fill it out when they had time. However when discussing the methods in our critical friends groups we realised that the traditional method, of handing out questionnaires, received the most replies, even though a smaller sample was used.

A low return rate is one of the disadvantages of email questionnaires and it is not only small scale research like our inquiry that suffers this problem. The HEFCE National Student Satisfaction Survey also recognises this problem only expecting a 60% return rate, when using a combination of email, postal and telephone questionnaires (Macloed, 2004 [online]).

(Patch 2)

After completing this research I realised it may have been useful to send out a pilot questionnaire, as this would have shown us straight away that sending questionnaires by email in a word document form was ineffective and we could have tried sending a survey email using the software available at university.

Another disadvantage of questionnaires was that even though we included open ended questions, the answers we received contained little detail, meaning we could not make many in-depth conclusions. Although there were some disadvantages of questionnaires there were also some advantages. Firstly questionnaires mainly produce quantitative data and this made the data easy to collect and easy to compare, as it could be made into graphs. This made comparison and spotting trends easy. Email questionnaires were also less time consuming, taking only a few minutes to send compared to the two hours taken to hand out questionnaires. This highlighted to me that all research methods have advantages and disadvantages and in order to choose the appropriate method, researchers have to decide what their priorities are. For example if time is limited email questionnaires may be more appropriate.

The final research method I have used is interviews ...
Even though the interviews were more structured than we originally imagined, they allowed us to go more in-depth than a questionnaire, as we could encourage the students to elaborate on certain topics. Unlike questionnaires, interviews gave us qualitative data which was more time consuming to collect and analyse. This in-depth information we collected made it easier to draw a range of in-depth conclusions than it was with the questionnaires. However a disadvantage of using interviews is that it takes a longer time to collect a large sample to ensure the results are valid.

The middle sections of the Text indicate good qualities in all three criteria for asserting that this student is *becoming a professional inquirer.*

It would have added a little more to the sense of inquiry mindedness if the data-gathering methods had been linked more fully to the inquiry purposes, to demonstrate their relevance, as well as their practical suitability.

I have conducted interviews in the past and have always found it difficult to keep track of what was being said, as well as accurately recording the information. The commissioned inquiry allowed me to experiment with using a Dictaphone and writing transcripts.

> Using a Dictaphone allowed me to pay more attention to what the participant was saying and think of more appropriate questions to encourage them to expand on their points ... This inquiry also allowed me to see how time-consuming writing transcripts are, we were only required to write up the main points from each interview and this took me around half an hour to do each interview. If I had been required to write a full transcript it would have been much more time consuming.
>
> (Journal entry [15/12/2007])

...

After reflecting on the interviews I did not feel very professional.

> I feel very unprofessional about how I handled the interviews, they were too structured when we were specifically asked to do unstructured interviews. I think part of the reason for this was because I did not feel very confident asking the students just to explain how they felt and I found it easier to ask certain questions in order to ensure we got the information we needed. This has highlighted to me that I need to improve my confidence and interview technique, as I am likely to use interviews in my research project next year. One way of doing this would be running through my interview with a critical friend in order to ensure I am following the correct method and that the interviews provide me with relevant information.
>
> (Journal entry [18/12/2007])

Even though I should have paid more attention to making sure I kept the interviews unstructured, the fact that the students seemed to prefer the structured interview format was also influential. A reason for this could have been that the students had been at work all day then had come into university and they may have wanted the interview to take as little time as

Similarly, including some brief items of the evidence which had been gathered, would have strengthened by xemplification the points being made about the limitations of the analysis.

Inquiry mindedness is better developed in relation to detailed comparisons of a good range of data-gathering techniques, practical considerations and competence than in relation to some broader aspects of a whole inquiry.

possible, so preferred us to run through our questions. Even though the students seemed to prefer this method it does mean we may not have gained views that truly reflected their opinions, as our questions may not have covered something they may have had strong views about.

Another important part of being a professional inquirer is professional practice ...

References

CHILDREN'S WORKFORCE DEVELOPMENT COUNCIL, 2006. *A Head Start for All: Early Years Professional Status* [online]. Available at http://www.bcftcs.ac.uk/pdf/EYPS Head.pdf [accessed 6/6/2008]

HUGHES, T., 2003. *Being a Professional* [online]. Word Constructions. Available at http://www.wordconstructions.com/articles/business/professional.html [accessed 7/6/2008]

MACLEOD, D., 2004. 'How was it for you?' [online]. *The Guardian*. Available at http://education.guardian.co.uk/students/news/story/0,12891,1228520,00.html [accessed 7/6/2008]

ROBERTS-HOLMES, G., 2006. *Doing your Early Years Research Project*. London: Paul Chapman Publishing

SCHÖN, D., 1983. *The Reflective Practitioner: How Professionals Think In Action*. London: Temple Smith

Using experience of the Inquiry Into Learning approach to address topics related to developments in higher education

The importance and power of student voice for promoting informal, formative assessment

Frances Wells

This chapter is an exploration of some aspects of student responses to the Inquiry Into Learning 1 module that have been examined in depth as part of my contribution to the teaching team's action research. Our module development has been through weekly team meetings to which tutors brought issues arising from their observations of their seminar sessions. Often our meetings had a primary school staffroom feeling to me, in that discussion was focused on students' contributions and our personal responses. It might begin with comments like *'I was amazed by ...'* or *'What can I do to help move this student's issue forward?'* or *'I can't believe it – they've said ... what could I try next?'*. This mutual, collegial support was crucial since we were opening ourselves up to shared observations of the student experience, listening to their views and problems. We were often faced with the very unexpected. We had to *hear* their *authentic* student voice in order to support them to be reflective and assess themselves; opening up this dialogue provided great insights and great challenges. This chapter explores how we responded as part of our ongoing research into strategies that might support students in developing growing intrapersonal awareness of their learning. It begins by focusing on students' interpersonal and intrapersonal kinds of reflective activity and the use of the *Intervision* method. Through examples of students' mutual support in learning how to learn, attention is given to learning-oriented goals rather than performance-oriented goals, and how students decide whether to attribute a difficulty they experience in a task to either the hard effort needed to complete it or to their own limited ability as a learner. The chapter concludes with ways in which the person-centred principles which underpin our relationships with students apply to spoken as well as written contexts for reflective learning.

Learning to learn reflectively

As we developed students' use of Reflective Jotters, we noticed that many students were hesitant about this expectation and some developed a strong sense of their inability to respond confidently. When working with the same group of students on a different module, a different perception of them as learners emerged. It was Interacting with the Environment, a module largely based on active experiences of learning in and about different environments and their value for children's learning. I noticed a real student confidence and motivation in tasks such as designing a den to go on a dragon hunt or creating a large dragon mask and developing a dramatic reconstruction of a dragon adventure. This prompted my reflection on student strengths and how to build on these to develop independent, confident reflection on themselves as learners. Most of these students appeared to be very confident learners in the interpersonal context but less so in the intrapersonal domain. There was a strong interpersonal dimension to group work on learning inquiries, sharing ideas with learning partners in discussion, electronically and in Conferences. We explicitly recognised the broad potential cognitive and social value of these activities. The question I now raised was, *'How can I enrich the cognitive challenge of personal reflection in interpersonal situations?'*. The importance of reflecting with others is well-documented (see, for example, Jasper 2003) and we had incorporated this element in our sessions in a broad way. My concern was over the lack of structure to these sessions, in which some students seem to find it difficult to contribute, perhaps because of demotivation or lack of confidence, so that many groups did not seem to achieve the potential to support individual members in the way that had been envisaged.

Peer review and peer assist approaches, as explained on a video by the University of Ottawa (www.saea.uottawa.ca) are embedded in many professional and business organisations. We considered them as models to support students in their growth towards professional approaches. In many approaches, the assistee shared an issue and then the group interacted to clarify and support. An approach was sought with more structure than such a free discussion, to assist analysis and reflection but with a less problem-solving orientation. The 'Intervisie' (Intervision) approach, documented in German by Jeroen Hendriksen (2002), is used extensively in teacher education in Dutch universities and in a range of European community organisations such as the Council of European Judges (www.coe.int), The Nodes Committee of the Global Diversity Information Facility (www.gbif.org), the International Association of Facilitators (www.iaf-methods.org), the Faculty of Arts at the University of Groningen, Netherlands (www.imaginal.nl) and the Teacher Education department at Masaryk University, Czech Republic (www.muni.cz/research/publications/230086). It appears to facilitate collegial consultation in a structured way. Although not yet well-documented in English, an adaptation of the approach used in the Utrecht Hogeschool (CARN 2006) in teacher education, was incorporated into our programme. The interpretation of the process of Intervision used within IIL involves both individual and group processes in succession as set out in Table 6.1.

This approach is known to have been used in the United Kingdom by the Social Care Association (www.socialcareassociation.co.uk) working with health care professionals to facilitate supervision of a group of experienced staff by each other. It is called *Intervision* in Dutch because no one is 'super' or 'above' the group.

Table 6.1 The application of Intervision to IIL

Individual		Group as individuals	
1	Explain the problem/issue	2	Write the questions you'd like to ask the individual about their issue
		3	Pose the questions one at a time
4	Answer the question	5	Write a further question based on the response to the initial questions
		6	Pose the questions
7	Answer the question	8	Analyse the problem in preparation to share it and write it down formally as stage 10
9	Additional information you'd like the group to offer or that you want to provide	10	Write up: 'I think the problem of the problem bringer is ... If I were him/her ... I would do ...'
		11	Read out the ideas

This method was presented to students as being about them developing insights through interaction – to get a deeper sense of vision or insight into an issue through 'inter' approaches to be complementary to the 'intra' approach of personal Jotter reflective writing. The intention was for it to be a tool to support reflection and analysis rather than to look for solutions to problems and it therefore had the potential to provide social network analysis; some organisations might use it as a problem-orientated approach but our intention was to develop generative insights in a context of equal peers so that knowledge became distributative rather than tutor/student orientated.

Initial findings from the use of this technique suggest it has supported students in expressing a voice and improving their analysis of issues. Also, it promoted confidence for some students, through the requirement to contribute. Students' end-of-year evaluations commented that a strict routine of Intervision helped them to contribute, and to feel that their suggestions had been listened to. They also comment on how, initially, it is daunting to have peers focusing on your issues, but that the structure gives permission for everyone to be given and to take the necessary time, avoiding the need to negotiate with other students for time and attention.

During Intervision sessions, interactions were very focused, students remaining on task; the requirement to participate and keep notes gave a clear sense of purpose to the interactions. Students demonstrated commitment to supporting each other and valuing the insights that others contributed. It would appear that, by giving time to focused reflection, we raised the profile of the reflective process, so that it became more open and not just a personal matter, providing opportunities to consider and then analyse other perspectives. For example: 'I seem to *find it difficult to allocate time to working on my academic work and feel that I socialise too much'*. This time-management issue is a recurrent theme in student personal reflection and many select a learning inquiry about it. During an Intervision session, fellow students asked questions such as, *'Do you have a set time for studying?'* and *'Do you get distracted and so don't study even after you have tried to start?'*. These questions prompted the students to consider a wide range of aspects of the issue so that the initial focus broadened, to raise a range of general issues about strategies to manage time, motivation and distraction. One student raised a very different perspective: *'Do you think of your time at Uni as for study or for socialising? Could you think of it as being for studying with socialising needing timetabling rather than trying to fit work into the socialising?'* This reversed perception of time really challenged the student concerned and other students, so that they then discussed such issues as, *'Why do we think of Uni as for fun rather than work; when we go out to work we will have the work time allocated and then fit in other activities around that'* and *'Maybe we should see our time at Uni as for work with socialising fitting around that'*. This complete shift shows a willingness to change motivation and a valuing of study, prompted by one student's radical alternative, to which other students were open.

Developing the use of *Intervision*

Observation of Intervision sessions is ongoing but further preliminary analysis suggests that students do open up about issues, often of a very personal and sensitive nature, in an effective way. One student voiced her feelings of lack of confidence in group sessions, having chosen to do an inquiry to develop her learning for a role-play assessed task in another module. Her focus for the Intervision was *'I'm trying to be more confident in participating in seminar group discussions in sessions'*. As other students raised questions, it emerged that her lack of confidence was not apparent in small group situations; she perceived that other students had responded negatively to her ideas early on in the year, making her less confident in large group situations. Students discovering these kinds of things for themselves seem empowered to manage themselves during challenging situations in a more honest and insightfully reflective way. As suggested by John Dewey (1910 in O'Connor and Diggins 2002) students can show a very refreshing sense of open-mindness to consider other perspectives and wholeheartedness in seeking informed decisions based on responsibility.

Students also found a voice to probe issues that, individually, they found caused anxiety but were willing to express in a supportive context. They said that *'Reflection ... is a challenge, which can be daunting, especially allowing yourself to think about negative areas, which, in most cases, I would generally choose not to have to think so deeply about'*. Perhaps writing in a Jotter about challenging situations can be a negative experience that provokes more anxiety because it appears in an isolated and apparently unsupported learning context; whereas raising an issue with a group has its own set of challenges, but with the sense of an opportunity to receive support from a group of peers who can empathise with you. So, perhaps the Intervision strategy opens up a wider range of important issues for students, that they might otherwise ignore or deny as a self-protective strategy, as worth further investigation. Providing this openness is not easy. Students' comments to peers such as *'Do not feel ashamed to ask for help'* are crucial. They help to generate a sense of learning as being about facing challenges and responding positively, in which asking for help can be viewed as a constructive step towards a sense of well-being in a working context.

Reflecting on the role of a tutor during these sessions, it is noticeable that a leadership role does not appear in the documentation about Intervision. Emphasis is placed on the peer nature of the collaborative learning context in which personal decisions are to be made. For my action research, I initially decided to observe and make notes of selected interactions. Structured observations have been proposed by researchers on Intervision at Onderzoek Institute (Meijer) as well as video-recording of group sessions, but we felt that naturalistic observation was appropriate to the use of the Intervision strategy in our situation. During sessions in Dutch universities, the tutor observed but did not interact with students so as not directly to influence students' use and content of collaborative structures, which would develop fuller ownership and independence of tutors. We too rejected a directive role of a transmission-oriented tutor, giving a structured opportunity in which students recognised the changes in respective responsibilities. They said things like, *'I feel it makes a change from just having a tutor speaking at the front of the class, as it can be easier to relate to other people your age, and to empathise with what they are saying'.* The integrated elements within this approach are that students learn to *'collaborate to learn'* and *'learn to collaborate'* (Black *et al.* 2006: 125). Both aspects appear to be enriched by the Intervision strategy. We hope that students take their collaborative skills and a positive attitude about the value of learning from and with others, into future studies and employment, building on these experiences of interpersonal collaboration and intrapersonal, reflective learning.

Considering when to introduce the Intervision strategy, an advantage of doing so at the stage of groups formation is that they can subsequently make an informed choice about using it permanently or selectively. During their first year at university, this strategy may support students' identification and analysis of transition issues, giving and receiving empathic support to address them in their own way. Peers who understand the person and their situation may have already addressed a similar issue, or feel less emotionally involved, and can bring different perspectives. We explicitly acknowledge to students the importance of a wide range of study and life skills, plus the establishment of a group identity and peer support, in their successful transition to university, seeing it as a key aspect of retention (Foster 2008).

Having introduced a way of supporting both intrapersonal and interpersonal reflection, students' initial responses to Intervision were very positive. How and when to continue its use is part of our ongoing research. For many students, the clear structure felt unusually precise compared to 'discussion' or 'brainstorming' sessions, giving a prescriptiveness that felt uncomfortable at times. However, they valued the principle of equal participation. There was also a strong sense of their confidence growing in their ability to make suggestions through personal analysis of the situations being raised; they realised that they could really make a difference to other students by drawing on their own experiences. At times they were amazed that ideas they'd previously thought were widely recognised or 'easy' were actually new to other students and greatly valued by them. This appears to enhance the emotional dimension and the visibility of a student's personal knowledge, to develop their self-image as a supportive colleague who draws on personal experiences analytically, identifies relevant ideas, shares them with respect and empathy; all developing what one student called, *'a faith in myself'*. This mirrors the process towards self-regulation and metacognition developed by Askell-Williams *et al.* (2007) with student teachers. The early identification of possible mismatches between perceptions of student and tutor roles is a very important aspect to unravel early on in a degree programme.

Nurturing student voice

Developing this confidence in themselves as learners is crucial for students to foster their self-regulation. Its association with a stronger sense of learning-orientated goals rather than performance goals has been recognised as important by Carol Dweck (2000). We try to prevent students from become self-handicapping by employing strategies of defensiveness, limiting their effort and developing a risk aversion. These self-defeating strategies are consistent with the personal view held by many students that they have a fixed level of intelligence, which appear to be grounded in many of their experiences of learning in school. We try to encourage them to take a more positive view of themselves as learners with mastery-orientated qualities (Dweck 2000) which include a *positive vulnerability* in the recognition of personal learning needs. Most students on the BA Childhood Studies degree are women who, through having gained entry into university, can be characterised as 'bright girls'. Some may have developed the belief that if they have to try hard at a task, the difficulty they experience is attributable to them not having high ability, even if it is a hard task which simply requires a lot of effort, even from an able person. Consequently, they need *'attribution retraining'* (Dweck 2000) to encourage the recognition that experiencing difficulty, or even failure, should not necessarily be interpreted in relation to ability but in relation to effort. These students might gain support within an Intervision context by being challenged to acknowledge that many issues concerning transition from school to university are normal and can be seen as challenges, rather than inadequacies. Otherwise, students appear unintentionally to collude with a self-image of inadequacy and yield to an unconscious resistance to trying harder. They tend to reinterpret a difficult task into a less challenging version, to be able to complete it within a personal comfort zone which places a self-imposed limit on their achievement.

When speaking with students in situations like these, we try to nurture Carl Rogers' (1969) conditions for educative relationships: combining an unconditional positive regard, valuing or prizing of the student's perspective on their experience, with our own congruence and empathy. In other words: while showing that we feel as accurately as we can what a student is experiencing about a difficulty, and demonstrating our default assumption that they are doing their best with it, we will also say honestly what we think about possible ways of improvement. We are relentlessly positive, avoiding the dangers of routinely praising easy success, and giving honest praise only for clear effort and achievement.

This is also relevant to tutors' responses to a *deficit-based* approach taken by some students towards their learning inquiries, which was found by Christine Morley (2007: 67) in studies of the reflective practice of school nurses. She advocates an *appreciative inquiry* way of emphasising deeper understanding, different perceptions and deeper analysis rather than a more negative view of learning associated with problem-solving. Of the various approaches to reflection and coaching, many stress the value of identifying the positive as a basis for change (O'Connor and Diggins 2002) to avoid *'scapegoat'* (Morley 2007: 67) attitudes. It is not easy to avoid perceiving as 'a problem to be solved' such difficulties as: poor time management; lack of concentration in sessions; not feeling confident in presentations; not knowing what to read and how incorporate this into writing. A student may easily say that self-criticism is a major challenge of reflection and is not easy for someone who can not accept negativity. As tutors, we encourage learning inquiry language like: *'How can I improve ... '* or *'How can I learn ... '* or *'What do I already know about ... that I need to extend?'* or *'Which parts of my good organisation do I need to adapt or strengthen to match the demands of university learning, as the workload increases?'*.

IIL started from a premise that writing a reflective Jotter was a key tool to promoting reflective learning, aware of a strong body of evidence for the view that written reflection is a key to professional development (Bolton 2010). Our observation of students' hesitancy has led us to refine this demand. Many found it initially to be a negative experience, reporting things like: *'At the moment I don't understand the importance of reflecting, neither do I understand how to reflect properly in the Jotter'* or *'I have been asked to write in this Jotter reflectively, but I am not entirely sure about what I need to write'* and *'I'm finding it very hard to write in my Jotter, as I'm very confused if I'm doing it right'*. *'I think many people from our course are still unsure of how to reflect'*. The paradigm of education of which reflective writing is part, can provoke feelings of alienation from which it could be hard to emerge. Therefore our research led us to take steps which focus on the generally better developed interpersonal skills that have led these students to seek a degree about working with children and families, using predominantly face-to-face interactions. Some students find verbal reflection a particularly powerful feature of their style of learning. For others, the verbal interaction created by Intervision can be a learning space in which they feel more confident, subsequently using notes from such interactions to build individual reflections. Some students have said things like, *'I'm sure I reflect more by speaking than I do writing'*. Having noticed a personal preference for verbal reflection rather than in the Jotter, some began to make digital voice recordings of their reflections, which they replay and add more. Having found that it was easier to record, but harder to refer back to what had been said, they decided to buy a Dictaphone; this is also an approach of particular interest to students with dyslexic characteristics of learning. We are still exploring the developmental use of different media for reflection. This mirrors work at the University of Surrey (2007) in the use of video for reflection by midwives during their professional training. We are investigating other ways of using technology to support reflection such as wikis and blogs (developed in Chapter 8) which could feel more accessible to students than a written Jotter. We encourage an increasingly wider diversity of approaches to reflection, supporting students' choices between verbal and written methods. Some students personalise their approach to reflection by making it the focus of a learning inquiry. We still currently retain a written Patchwork Text assignment entitled 'Becoming a reflective learner'. It is our hope that students' growing confidence with the use of different media for reflection will improve their learning further as they recognise and value their own voice and that of their peers.

Questions for reflection on developing student voice for advancing *learning how to learn* in other contexts

These questions provide starting points for thinking, talking and writing about designing a new module or programme or adapting an existing one.

1   Does the programme or module already provide contexts in which students can express their thoughts and feelings about their learning experiences, perceptions, questions and concerns?
2   If not, are there other existing situations or tasks which could be adapted or extended to create opportunities for student voice to be expressed?
3   If so, when and how is the student voice expressed and what are the gains for students and tutors?
4   How well do students express their thoughts and feelings about their learning experiences, perceptions, questions and concerns?
5   Could the conditions and stimuli for promoting this activity be improved?
6   Does students' sharing of perspectives on their learning help to develop a Community of Learning?
7   Do students' perspectives on their learning link with the programme/ module monitoring and evaluation processes, to influence pedagogy and/or assessment of learning?

Chapter 7

Setting expectations through assessment for learning

This chapter explains our strengthening belief that tutors' choice of wording of the criteria for the summative assessment of students' learning achievements is a critically important decision. During the development of formative assessment, using peer and tutor feedback as a routine element of our teaching and learning, we have encouraged students explicitly to use the same criteria as for summative assessment. We want students to become more fully aware of qualities in their learning related to these criteria, think about their own and each other's talk and writing to discuss how well they demonstrate such qualities. We want this to empower students' use of such qualities in their learning and integrate them into their own *internal locus of evaluation*. The crowning glory would be a student who can prepare their Patchwork Text assignment, knowing where and how it displays these qualities, and submit it with confidence of success.

Expectations of learning

Running like a thread through a student's subjective experience of learning is their *expectation* about what learning is, what they have to do and how it will be seen by others. By expectation we mean:

> a student's state of mind, as they anticipate what is going to happen, including thoughts (whether firm ideas or vague guesses) and feelings (from fear, through apprehension, to curious excitement) about the good (or not-so-good) things which events may bring for them, what they might do or say which could affect the situation and what significant others may think and feel, particularly in a judgemental way.

We attend closely to the particular expectations we find in each student and every group, because we see them as powerful influences on their learning. They are manifestations of each student's situational understanding. This account starts at the beginning of the IIL1 module.

Tutors naturally like to teach students who show a love of learning and curiosity about the subject, often referred to as a 'deep approach', because they are likely to do well and if they don't, it is easy to respond supportively to their requests for assistance. And, naturally, we are disappointed by manifestations of a 'surface approach' because these are students who may not do so well, and are less likely to share our subject-matter fascinations and commitments. As tutors of the Inquiry Into Learning 1 module, we put it to new students at the beginning of the programme that we regard them as successful learners, to the extent that they have gained qualifications necessary for this programme at the university. We challenge them to name qualities of learning they believe to be strengths on which to build, and what they regard as needs for development. They say this is a difficult task, in the ways indicated in Chapter 3. A picture emerging from discussion often shows a tendency for students to have instrumental attitudes towards learning, and beliefs that their success depends on knowing what the tutor wants. At this early stage in IIL1, we explicitly notice these expectations, name them and explore their characteristics. Also, we draw out what some students may initially deny: an underlying fear of failure. This is cited as a major obstacle to learning, not only by such perceptive naturalistic observers of learning as John Holt, but also by behaviourist theorists such as B F Skinner (although they might not have meant it in exactly the same way).

Having revisited the guiding principles of *behaviourism*, to compare them with what students say about their learning hitherto, we infer it has directly or implicitly shaped much of our students' learning practice. After some reflection and discussion, many students realise that they had been *'spoon-fed'* (as they often put it) by their teachers. They had been warned to expect learning at university to be much more independent than at school. Nevertheless, they still expect set tasks to break learning into small steps for them, with clear and detailed teacher directions, as well as frequent positive reinforcement. They have been used to doing a lot of short, closed, targeted assignments which are teacher-assessed. As well as promoting these characteristics, Skinner's theory advocates that the teacher's directions should be repeated as many times as possible, and that teaching should progress from the most simple to the most complex tasks. We acknowledge the value of this approach to training (as opposed to education – see Chapter 2), where clear objectives are set beforehand. We endorse it for students whose learning inquiry sets a sharply defined aim, such as acquiring particular factual knowledge and/or developing a specific skill. We say that ideas about behaviourist approaches are worth finding out about and testing in their practice as learners. Learning inquiries like this, through which students *programme themselves* with more knowledge and/or greater technical proficiency, may feel familiar – like a process of learning they are used to, except that, now, it is the students themselves who are determining aims, carrying responsibility for finding methods and applying the findings. We are content with this kind of learning inquiry, particularly in the early stages of the IIL1 module as students gain confidence in taking increasing control over their own learning while staying within a personal comfort zone.

However, we reject a behaviourist approach as a basis for how students learn how to do inquiry learning in IIL. By the time a student has begun to do a personal inquiry into an aspect of their learning, they have learned (or are in the process of learning) to identify a specific learning need and work out a way of addressing it. We believe students need to be educated to do this, not trained. Their learning should be thought about with constructivist ideas and values rather than behaviourist ones. This is because doing inquiry into learning involves *induction* into public knowledge about learning and the personally reflective understanding of relevant parts of the knowledge to one's own development and oneself as a learner. It also engages students with processes of valuing their learning in relation to norms of the culture of childhood-related professional work, into which they are being *initiated*. A learning inquiry cannot be broken into small, logically developing steps with close, detailed teacher direction. Any attempt to do so would distort the nature of the inquiry beyond recognition and reduce the meaning of higher education in this context to training. Each inquiry is a whole thing that is more than the sum of its parts. Neither is this task one which can be controlled by the teacher to progress from simpler to more complex content, unless the fundamental principle of student control over their learning is to be contradicted. We do not tell students to begin with simple inquiries such as how to take better lecture notes and move on from there, we ask for what is personally significant and we find that some students happily and successfully choose complex and worthwhile subjects from the start, if they are about practical concerns which genuinely arise from self-awareness. Evidence for this is available in the learning inquiry titles cited in Chapter 4, in the section on *Making progress with the learning inquiry*.

The following two anecdotes show the idiosyncratic ways in which students' learning inquiries can progress when they have personal authenticity and follow personally intuitive as well as rational influences on progress.

One student found it *'very interesting'* to hear discussion of research about which side of the brain is used most and why. It made her think a lot about what this meant to her and how she could use it to help her learn. She said,

> I often find group work frustrating, I am quite impatient and want to just get on with it. Some students like to discuss the task and take it apart before putting it together and getting on with it. But maybe I could learn from this approach?

She tested the idea of *'taking things slower'* and found that it helped her gain a better understanding of set tasks and what was being expected. Later she claimed that, *'This has benefits for my learning as an individual and the understanding I could offer in a group situation'*. There is no sense of this student continuing to learn as at school, by being spoon-fed, or of her using a 'theory applied to practice' approach. She found that hearing about brain research triggered reflection about an aspect of her learning which was causing concern, in such as way as to make her feel empowered to try an unpredictable action step – *'taking things slower – which turned out to be helpful'*.

Another student declared a dislike for group work. She preferred to work alone because she just wanted to *'get on with it'* and *'others take too long'*. She complained that they *'over-analyse the situation and read too much into things'*. At the same time, she was aware of a need to address this aspect of her learning. Her action step was to hold back, verbally and physically. In practical activities she distanced herself from any artifact so that she could not *'bulldoze the group'*. In "non-practical' situations she offered to make notes for the group, so that others had more time to talk and express their opinions. At first it was frustrating, but she explained: *'I know I am going to have to learn to be a team player so I need to practise this'* and concluded her inquiry: *'I learned that others have just as valid a response as I do'*. Once again, the student is the *agent* of their learning and *owns* their development as a learner.

A constructivist approach to inquiry learning challenges a student to start the process off and just have a go! Looking at a student's initial attempt enables a constructivist teacher to see the extent to which initiation and induction into becoming a learner in higher education are already evident, and respond with suggestions and guidelines for improvement. This sequence puts learning experience first. Assessment, evaluation and analysis come second. Having been set a loose, open task, selected what you most want to improve in your practice as a learner, each student defines their own inquiry aim and has a go. As initial evidence is gathered, and the original aim is examined in action, more specific learning objectives *emerge* from an assessment of one attempt at improvement of learning practice to shape expectations for the next. This could be called 'feed back' or 'feed forward' (Torrance and Pryor 1998). As a kind of formative assessment, feedback on each inquiry is intended to be timely, understandable and immediately applicable to improving learning. Tutors exert close control over the *process* of the IIL curriculum, which is a sequence of cycles of action inquiry that progressively improve the student's ability to learn. Within the broad parameters provided by the module, students determine the *content* of the IIL curriculum by matching inquiry aims to their learning needs and collaboratively constructing their own meaning.

To summarise, IIL1 sets challenges to many students' expectations about what and how we expect them to learn. The development of IIL1, intertwined with our own professional development through doing action research, has seen progressive use of various ways to accommodate some of students' starting expectations while gradually changing them. For example, we have increased the use of what appear to be highly directive response sheets as stimuli, not to compel students to follow our trains of thought, but to create their own, through brainstorming, choice making, interpretation, discussion, decision making, assessment and evaluation. These kinds of response sheets are intended to elicit students' situational understanding of specific aspects of themselves as learners on this programme, now. The way in which we have used formative assessment to shape students' expectations is examined below.

The criteria are key

Asking ourselves over and again: *'How do we really want our students to learn?'*, we developed a series of qualities grouped into three clusters. They are content-free indicators of processes of learning that we value. The wording gradually changed, partly through reflective discussion of evidence of the criteria in use, and partly through reading others' theoretical understanding of the kind of learning we value (see Table 7.1). We justify these criteria to ourselves, our colleagues and authorities as representing what we intend our students will become, which is *good in itself*, as well as of *instrumental good* to their learning in other modules, the programme and in life-long learning. We justify them to our students in similar terms, with an additional point that employers expect such qualities.

Table 7.1 How the assessment criteria relate to the educative process aims of the module

Assessment criteria	Initiation	Induction
The definitions currently used in Inquiry Into Learning I	into the norms and values of the professional culture of learning about *Childhood Studies*	into public knowledge for disciplining thinking about one's personal knowledge
Involvement: how well I show initiative, autonomy, engagement, curiosity, perseverance, collaboration and interdependence across a range of active involvements in my learning	becoming autonomous in the demonstration of these qualities as a learner for advancing my personal and professional learning	understanding about how the personal and social characteristics of learning, particularly of collaborative kinds, are expected and practised in professional work contexts
Awareness of my personal development: how well I make progress with *being empathic, positively motivated, self-aware and reflective*, in my learning	showing responsibility for promoting, monitoring and evaluating my own development and sustained growth in awareness	understanding about how people (including clients and their families) develop and what kinds of context may enhance or inhibit development and growth
Credible, practical knowing: how well I use *evidence, ideas from published work, critical interpretation and creativity*, across a range of practical improvements in my learning achievements and in my ability to learn	awareness of others' expectation of my accountability for my actions and ideas as a practitioner both of learning and of the care of children	understanding how we know about professional practice through gathering and interpreting evidence of events using personal and public knowledge to explain and justify coherently

In IIL1, early in the first term, at the stage described in Chapter 4 under *Summary of the processes of the module*, these criteria are presented to students for the first time (preceding work having given attention to constituent ideas within the criteria). A list of *tutors' expectations of students* is also presented (see the same section in Chapter 4), which gives detailed practical elaboration of the criteria. The first occasion when they are used is near the end of the first cycle of learning inquiries. At conferences, when students are discussing each other's attempts to improve an aspect of their practice as learners, the worksheet shown in Figure 7.1 is presented to encourage discussion.

HOW ARE WE GETTING ON?

This is intended to encourage your group to think about the learning inquiry work being discussed, help to clarify the qualities in it and explore ideas about how to develop them further.

Qualities	A note of things in this inquiry which are examples of this quality being achieved	Ideas for what could be done to help the inquiry to show this quality more fully
Involvement, which is about how well you show *initiative, autonomy, engagement, curiosity, perseverance, collaboration and interdependence across a range of active involvements* in your learning.		
Awareness of personal development, which is about how well you make progress with *being empathic, positively motivated, self-aware and reflective* in your learning.		
Credible, practical knowing, which is about how well you use *evidence, ideas from published work, critical interpretation and creativity*, across a range of practical improvements in your learning achievements and in your ability to learn.		

Figure 7.1 Assessment worksheet

We find that students are so used to being given response sheets that they almost never react negatively; on the contrary, they are an expected component of any session, regardless of content. Students' demeanour often changes markedly when one is distributed, creating a studious atmosphere, giving increased attention to the task and reducing social talk. When less structure to discussion is provided, its quality can seem to suffer and some students complain that the task is aimless. So we have, reluctantly at first, increased our use of these sheets as a teaching tool. However, we design them to facilitate learning processes we value, in which the content and some concepts are contributed by the students, rather than take students down a predetermined path of reasoning to a prespecified knowledge learning outcome. The sheet in Figure 7.1 aims to promote good discussion, first about deciding the most significant features to be noted in spaces provided and, second, about the overall process.

There are other contexts as well as conferences, in which we want the situational understanding of a group's members to be used in discussion to advance each other's sense of how they are getting on. We want them jointly to develop informed *feedback of a formative assessment kind*. Taking care with language, we would not normally use terms like 'formative' or 'assessment' either in worksheets or in our talk with students. This is to avoid the possibility that formal terminology, particularly that associated with making judgements, would create apprehension and inhibit freedom of discussion. However, we want the natural forms of expression that students use spontaneously to be augmented and advanced by including talk which refers to qualities of learning we value. Alongside the encouragement, interest and fresh ideas relating to the content of the inquiry which peers may offer, we want there to be guidance about where desirable qualities are already evident and how they could be strengthened. We want them to adopt our terms, within a common language, to refer to these qualities, and consolidate their understanding of the terms by using them in more and more practical situations.

How well this works obviously depends upon the group's understanding of the criteria, their collective abilities to apply them to each inquiry, and foster development. Alongside the notion of learning partner, we have also introduced the concept of a *critical friend* in this context. When we discuss its meanings, a common difficulty with the word 'critical' is its associations with being destructively negative. Exploring situations in which we need a friend to be honest with us in their feedback, one student said:

> like the friend you'd take with you when you go to buy some knock-out gear to wear on your first date with a guy you really fancy, but you want to know that you'll get an honest answer if you ask them 'Does it make my bum look fat?'.

Students acknowledge that a natural desire to be liked, plus a reticence to offend a peer, can conspire to keep the application of criteria to a fairly low, safe level initially. However, practice accumulates over learning inquiries, of which there may be five across the entire IIL1 module. So, although we normally decline to make *exemplars* or *model answers* available to students, there are many opportunities for considering their progress and comparing it with others' in the light of the criteria. Some virtues of this approach include:

- a person who uses spoken, dramatic, visual and less formal ways of demonstrating their knowing is able to express their whole selves, including their tacit knowing;
- tentative use of academic language can be practised alongside everyday talk, in preparation for the more formal writing expected in the patch;
- using the criteria in low-stakes situations builds up confidence for more crucial ones;
- learning about the criteria is assisted by applying them to a range of different inquiry contexts.

We encourage a person-centred style of feedback, which does not feign objectivity with impersonal language such as *'the argument is weak'* or *'the concepts are not clear'*. Instead, the person giving feedback shows ownership and honesty combined with positive regard: *'I was interested in your thinking about X but I found it a little difficult to follow at this point because I wasn't sure what you meant by Y and how it links with the idea of Z'.*

We are striving to establish self and peer formative feedback as a natural part of the collaborative talk within learning. It is important to be clear that this is fundamentally different from the serial summative assessments which fit a behaviourist pedagogy and its training aims. We are not repeatedly digging up the seedling to inspect its roots and assess its growth. The qualities of learning to be developed, on which feedback is valued, have to be interpreted anew in each context of their use, to specific items of study, so as to be able to strengthen those qualities in the learning process next time. The learner is in the best position to judge how well they are getting on, ultimately by assessing themselves *ipsatively*, that is, in comparison with their own previous achievement of these qualities. In this sense, as Lawrence Stenhouse (1975: 95) put it:

> The worthwhile activity in which tutor and students are engaged has standards and criteria immanent in it and the task of appraisal is that of improving students' capacity to work to such criteria by critical reaction to work done. In this sense assessment is about the teaching of self-assessment.

Between one usage of the 'How are we getting on?' sheet and the next, tutors take frequent opportunities to refer to criteria during talk with individuals or groups about qualities in the work being discussed. We want an ethos in which self-evaluative thinking is a natural part of shaping personal expectations of learning. Similar sheets are used elsewhere in the module, particularly when doing a Course Work Assignment (this is the unsatisfactory name which became associated with a task set about halfway through the module).

Self and peer feedback for formative assessment

The so-called Course Work Assignment (CWA) involves writing a Patchwork Text (PT) using patches accrued and Jotter entries made up to that time. Recognising that no students have had prior experience of the PT format, this assignment is an opportunity to find out about it by direct experience, supplementing what they read in the Module Handbook and advice posted on the Virtual Learning Environment (VLE). It indicates a student's progress in the module thus far and creates a situation in which giving and receiving feedback can be practised. Each student brings to the session two printed copies of the assignment, identified by their university registration number. Feedback sheets (reproduced in Figure 7.2) resemble the appearance of sheets used to assess the final Patchwork Text assignment. Careful discussions at several stages of this process elicit students' immediate reflections (using questions like those shown in italics below) and explain the value of the process.

1   Tutors collect one copy of each Course Work Assignment (CWA), recording receipt against a class list and making up a class set.
2   Tutors swap class sets of CWAs between groups. Simultaneously, each student is completing Sheet One, a self-assessment form, referring to their retained copy of their CWA.

–   *What is it like to try to try to see your work in a dispassionate way?*
–   *Were you generous or harsh in your comments?*
–   *How confident are you about your views?*

3   Each group organises working pairs of students who do not routinely work together. Each pair is given two CWAs from students in another group, ensuring anonymity. They read both assignments separately and, for each one, complete Sheet 2, a peer feedback sheet, with the following guidance.

a   Read the text carefully and have empathic discussion of its content.
b   Make your own informal notes about qualities you have jointly noticed in the assignment.
c   Make more notes about what you think is the student's response to and understanding of, the assessment criteria.
d   Complete all parts of the peer feedback sheet provided, indicating your views about the strengths shown in the assignment regarding the assessment criteria, as well as the areas for development.
e   Check that the wording of your feedback is professionally sensitive, accurate, balanced, supportive, honest and fair.

f   Reflect on your shared experience.

g   Discuss with each other the extent to which you recognise the purposes of this task (see above) being achieved in your own learning.

h   Make entries in your own reflective Jotters about what you have learned.

4   During stage 3a to e, tutors give general advice and one-to-one assistance on the appropriateness of language to express feedback which includes constructive criticism as well as appreciative comment.

   –   *How do I communicate something that I think is a mistake or needs improvement in a courteous, non-threatening way?*

   –   *How do I make the feedback professionally sensitive, accurate, balanced, supportive, honest and fair?*

5   Tutors collect CWAs with attached peer feedback sheets, leaving their group to complete stages 3f and 3g, while the CWAs are returned to the group which produced them.

6   Tutors return CWAs plus peer feedback sheets to their authors, still sitting in twos, for discussion. The feedback comments are compared with those on the self-assessment sheet.

   –   *Is the peer feedback helpful?*

   –   *Does it use appropriate language?*

   –   *How does it make me feel about my work?*

   –   *What ideas have I gained about improvement?*

7   Each student then returns to Sheet 1, the self-assessment sheet, to record (in ink of a different colour) further thoughts, perhaps revisions of previous impressions, culminating in assigning their CWA a mark.

8   Tutors collect the CWAs with associated self and peer sheets attached. This concludes the session.

9   Each CWA is read by a tutor, who attaches Sheet 3, 'Tutor comments on feedback', which contains views of the fairness and accuracy of the self and peer comment, and gives an indicative mark. To aid our action research, we may make a photocopy of the sets of sheets.

10   At the next session, each student receives a complete set of all sheets to read and discuss.

   –   *Why might there be similarities and differences between different sets of comments?*

   –   *How has the exercise helped to improve my understanding of the criteria and the accuracy and fairness of my assessment of my learning?*

1 SELF ASSESSMENT of my Course Work Assignment

Inquiry Into Learning 1	Student	
	Mark	%

Title of Patchwork Text assignment:	**Becoming a reflective learner**

Basic Skills, Outcomes and Marking Criteria

Assessment Criteria	Rating					
The extent to which there is evidence of the following in the Text (all criteria are read together and in relation to each other)	Exc.	Very good	Good	Pass	Marginal fail	Clear fail
Involvement, which is about how well you show initiative, engagement, curiosity, perseverance and interdependence across a range of active involvements in your learning						
Awareness of personal development, which is about how well you make progress with being reflective, empathic, positively motivated, self-aware and autonomous in your learning						
Credible, practical knowing, which is about how well you use evidence, ideas from published work, critical interpretation and creativity across a range of practical improvements in your learning and your ability to learn						

Communication and Referencing

	Good	Need to improve	Comments
Spelling			
Sentence structure			
Punctuation			
Vocabulary			
Text organisation			
Referencing			
Word count	YES / NO	Pagination	YES / NO

Figure 7.2 Feedback sheets

Continued overleaf

Continued

Areas of success	Areas for development

General comments

2 PEER FEEDBACK on a Course Work Assignment

Inquiry Into Learning I	Author	*anonymous*
	Reader	*anonymous*

Title of Patchwork Text assignment:	**Becoming a reflective learner**

Basic Skills, Outcomes and Marking Criteria

Assessment Criteria	Rating					
The extent to which there is evidence of the following in the Text (all criteria are read together and in relation to each other)	Exc.	Very good	Good	Pass	Marginal fail	Clear fail
Involvement, which is about how well you show initiative, engagement, curiosity, perseverance and interdependence across a range of active involvements in your learning						
Awareness of personal development, which is about how well you make progress with being reflective, empathic, positively motivated, self-aware and autonomous in your learning						
Credible, practical knowing, which is about how well you use evidence, ideas from published work, critical interpretation and creativity across a range of practical improvements in your learning and your ability to learn						

Communication and Referencing

	Good	Need to improve	Comments
Spelling			
Sentence structure			
Punctuation			
Vocabulary			
Text organisation			
Referencing			
Word count	YES / NO	Pagination	YES / NO

Areas of success	Areas for development

General comments

Continued overleaf

3 TUTOR comments on Peer Feedback on the Course Work Assignment

| Inquiry Into Learning I | Student | |
| | Reader | |

| Title of Patchwork Text assignment: | **Becoming a reflective learner** |

PART ONE Tutor's comments on the quality and accuracy of feedback
Basic Skills, Outcomes and Marking Criteria

Assessment Criteria	Rating					
The extent to which there is evidence of the following in the Text (all criteria are read together and in relation to each other)	Exc.	Very good	Good	Pass	Marginal fail	Clear fail
Involvement, which is about how well you show initiative, engagement, curiosity, perseverance and interdependence across a range of active involvements in your learning						
Awareness of personal development, which is about how well you make progress with being reflective, empathic, positively motivated, self-aware and autonomous, in your learning						
Credible, practical knowing, which is about how well you use evidence, ideas from published work, critical interpretation and creativity, across a range of practical improvements in your learning and your ability to learn						

Communication and Referencing

	Good	Need to improve	Comments
Spelling			
Sentence structure			
Punctuation			
Vocabulary			
Text organisation			
Referencing			
Word count	YES / NO	Pagination	YES / NO	

Areas of success	Areas for development

General comments

PART TWO Tutor's comments on the assignment

Figure 7.2 Continued

Currently, there seems to be a tolerably good balance between giving enough tutor attention to individual students, to sustain our relationships, fostering mutual trust and understanding and monitoring progress on the one hand, and, on the other, giving control and responsibility to students as individuals and groups for this vital component of learning how to learn. It is a difficult balance to sustain with groups of more than 30 when some students demand more and better feedback directly from the tutor. Their perspective is that only the tutor knows if they are learning properly and should say this clearly; anything else is inadequate teaching.

Conclusion

The Inquiry Into Learning approach, with formative assessment integral to its pedagogy, intends to shape students' expectations towards positive attitudes, including a confident sense of self-efficacy. The importance of self-awareness and collaborative effort to making progress in learning how to learn is conveyed by the care and time given to practising it during sessions. Also, tutors model these attitudes and procedures in various ways. For example, from time to time we end a session with a brief exercise with sticky note papers, inviting students to write feedback such as what they gained from the session, what needs are remaining unmet, etc. Tutors respond immediately orally and, if appropriate, in the subsequent session, with actions. Also, as teacher-researchers, we regard the insight we gain into students' self and peer assessment as of great formative value for reflection and discussion of our planning and pedagogy.

We are aware of several areas for development, such as doing more to train students to give and receive more and better formative feedback with wider use of information technology and increased depth and meaning arising from better use of key concepts in the topics (see Chapter 4). However, we believe that these methods do improve students' learning by helping them to know what we think counts as improvement, to see how their current achievement compares with it and to take action on closing the gap. This is intended to strengthen a student's belief that they can influence their achievement in future, which, among other things, helps to improve the rate of retention.

Questions for reflection on formative assessment to advance *learning how to learn* in other contexts

The following questions provide starting points for thinking, talking and writing about designing a new module or programme or adapting an existing one.

1   Does the programme or module have ways of eliciting students' situational understanding of their learning, including their expectations of tutors and what they perceive tutors' expectations of them to be?
2   Does the programme or module provide, or does it develop through negotiation with students, an explicit set of students' and tutors' expectations of each other's roles? (see Chapter 4 under *Summary of the processes of the module*).
3   Does the programme or module provide contexts in which students already do give and receive constructive feedback on each other's learning?
4   If not, are there other existing situations or tasks which could be adapted or extended to create opportunities for peer feedback?
5   If so, when and how does peer feedback happen?
6   How do students express qualities they think are valuable in their learning and what are those qualities?
7   How do the learning qualities which the students value compare with those espoused by the programme/module?
8   How do these learning qualities relate to the criteria for assessment of the formal assignment (see also Chapter 9)?

Chapter 8

Enriching processes and products of learning with information technology

Patricia Wallis

In previous chapters we have outlined how students undertake a number of learning inquiries. They write a 'patch', which is not formally assessed, about each inquiry after much personal reflection, investigation and collaborative discussion with other students. IIL tutors explicitly value the collaboration component, encouraging an inquiry to use contributions from a range of sources, including that of fellow students. It is particularly during seminar conferences that students have opportunities to share their thoughts and ideas. As technology is becoming a larger part of our and our students' lives, we reflected on whether the use of technology could provide another valuable platform for students to share their learning inquiries.

This chapter outlines how we have endeavoured to incorporate the use of technology into Inquiry Into Learning, in order to provide students with an additional platform on which they can share ideas and experiences.

In the beginning

During their studies of both the IIL1 and IIL2 modules, students' inquiries are shared with other students in their own seminar group. The patches derived from the inquiries then become a valuable resource for their final assessment: their Patchwork Text. We wanted students to share their learning inquiries with other students in other seminar groups so we needed to consider how this could be done. In 2006, the university introduced a Virtual Learning Environment (VLE) as a document repository where tutors could place various module-related documents, electronic copies of book chapters, etc. enabling students 24/7 access. The IIL team investigated the possibility of placing students' own learning inquiries on the VLE, providing them with the opportunity to read each other's inquiries. However, as with all new procedures, there were be some inconveniences that we needed to overcome.

- *Problem 1*: At that time, it was impossible for students to be given permission to post their own material to the VLE.

- *Resolution*: Students would email their learning inquiry to an administrator who would then post the investigation to the appropriate location.
- *Problem 2*: How would students locate learning inquiries?
- *Resolution*: A folder entitled Inquiry Into Learning was created, inside which were three further folders, Seminar Group A, B and C. Students' work would be placed into their own seminar group folder. The documents would be clustered within the folder so that, for example, all the 'motivation' learning inquiries would be together (see Figure 8.1). Students would have 'read only' access rights for all folders.

Students were given clear instructions regarding saving and submitting their learning inquiries.

1   Use Microsoft Word.
2   Name the saved document with your surname and the focus of your learning inquiry (e.g. KELLY : MOTIVATION).
3   Email the document, together with information about your group, to the administrator.

Once placed on the VLE, students had access to read each other's learning inquiries. However, they could not leave comments on each other's work, so seminar group conferences continued to be the only forum for students to share and reflect on their own and each other's experiences.

We were pleased to note from the mid-module feedback that students enjoyed reading each other's work. However, it was not all plain sailing. Although the procedure sounded straightforward, things are never easy when so many inexperienced individuals are involved. There were a number of problems. For

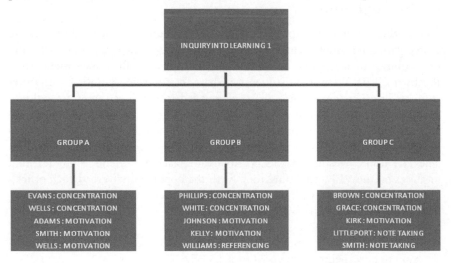

Figure 8.1 Learning inquiry organisation

example, students emailling documents to the administrator often omitted to provide information about either their seminar group or their inquiry focus. This caused difficulties for the administrator, resulting in documents being placed in the wrong folder or simply not posted to the VLE at all. Although students were reminded continually, these problems persisted on and off for most of the academic year.

Blended learning

About this time, 'blended learning' was being discussed more and more within the School of Education. The definition of blended learning is rather vague and, in routine talk, a range of definitions are noticeable, but the general consensus was that it was a mix of methods, some technological, some face to face. But what does 'technological' mean? Is using PowerPoint in a seminar session a form of blended learning? Some tutors said 'Yes' others disagreed. Some blended learning involves students using different media, for example a mix of face-to-face sessions with online technology (Oliver and Trigwell 2005). The School of Education decided that, if we were going to address this shift effectively, we needed a shared definition. Oliver and Trigwell's definition fits well with the School's definition.

> *Blended Learning Guidelines for Nottingham Trent University staff* – There are many definitions of blended learning activities, but in general they blend traditional and technology-based teaching and learning activities and use synchronous and asynchronous interaction with peers and tutors.

IIL tutors were aware of the School of Education's drive to promote the use of blended learning in teaching. With this in mind we contacted the School's newly constructed Teaching and Learning Support Unit (TLSU). This Unit comprised a range of teaching and learning technologists, some of whom also taught part time. They had a wide range of experience of using technology to support and promote teaching and learning. The IIL teaching team worked closely with staff from the TLSU. We outlined our current practice and the aspects that we currently couldn't do, but would like to, such as enabling students to edit their own work and comment on others' work. After much discussion, one of their members suggested the use of a collaborative writing tool, called a 'wiki' (a web-based collaborative workspace). None of the IIL teaching team had even heard of a wiki let alone used one, but the TLSU team were very supportive and encouraging. During 2007–08, IIL adopted a wiki as a way for students to write up their inquiries, reflect and collaborate with peers and, when they felt it appropriate, edit their original work.

One of our TLSU colleagues created what the IIL team felt was a well-designed and user-friendly wiki. It was password protected so only invited participants could access it, and there was a simple 'welcome' page which provided clear information (see Figure 8.2).

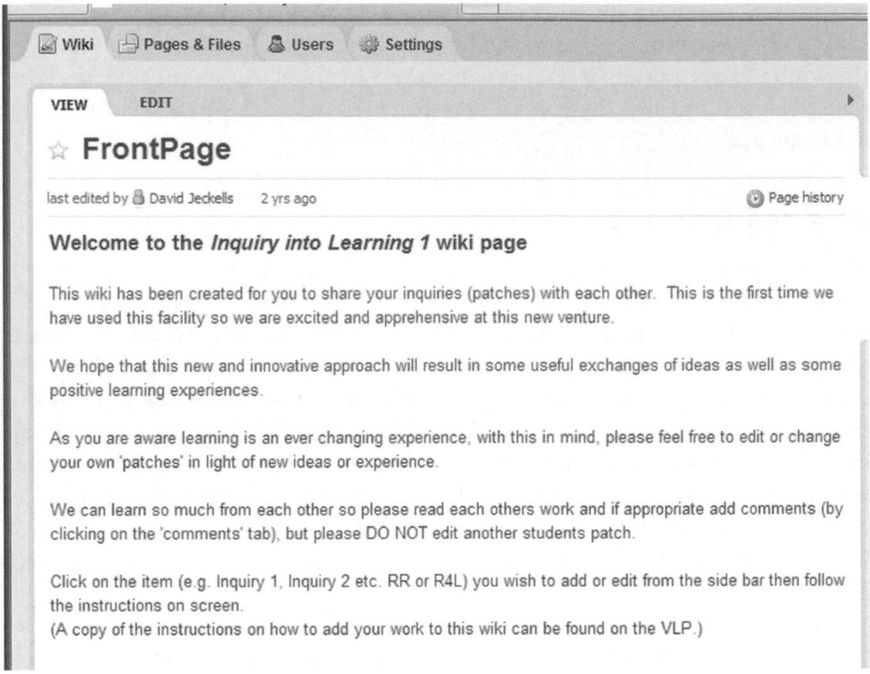

Figure 8.2 IIL1 wiki welcome page

This was followed by clear instructions on how students could post their learning inquiries. A range of predefined and formatted pages allowed students to concentrate on their own writing and reflection, rather than on learning how to use the technology (see Figure 8.3).

During the summer vacation, IIL tutors spent time familiarising themselves with the wiki. At this time we discussed whether we would contribute to the wiki. This posed an interesting moral dilemma between two alternatives, both of which have good and not-so-good characteristics, so it was impossible to choose one alternative which had all the good and none of the not-so-good at the same time. In this case, the good thing about a tutor's written contributions being excluded is that some students aren't prompted to feel that they want to hide from tutors' scrutiny and/or judgement, to which Gatto (2002) refers, but they can 'own' the space. The not-so-good thing is that other students may complain that tutors are not interested enough in their writing to comment on it or join with the exploration of important ideas. On the other hand, the good thing about tutors joining in is that they *can* contribute their own good ideas and/or endorse students' good ideas, but risk inhibiting some students who find this interaction oppressive. We all agreed that we wanted students to view this facility as an area where

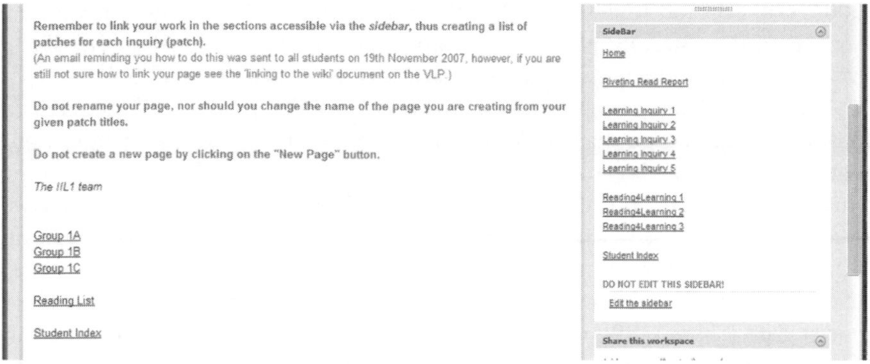

Remember to link your work in the sections accessible via the *sidebar*, thus creating a list of patches for each inquiry (patch).
(An email reminding you how to do this was sent to all students on 19th November 2007, however, if you are still not sure how to link your page see the 'linking to the wiki' document on the VLP.)

Do not rename your page, nor should you change the name of the page you are creating from your given patch titles.

Do not create a new page by clicking on the "New Page" button.

The IIL1 team

Group 1A
Group 1B
Group 1C

Reading List

Student Index

SideBar

Home

Riveting Read Report

Learning Inquiry 1
Learning Inquiry 2
Learning Inquiry 3
Learning Inquiry 4
Learning Inquiry 5

Reading4Learning 1
Reading4Learning 2
Reading4Learning 3

Student Index

DO NOT EDIT THIS SIDEBAR!
Edit the sidebar

Share this workspace

Figure 8.3 Screen shot of document options

they could share their ideas with other students without feeling that tutors were judging their contributions. Our aim was to give students a sense of ownership of this space. We therefore decided that we would not contribute to this public space; however, we would continue to provide verbal encouragement and feedback in seminars or by personal email. In this way, students would be aware that we were interested in their postings and that we were reading them.

Early in the module, there was a session in a computer room to introduce the use of the wiki. A member of the Learning and Teaching Support Team joined the IIL tutor to help students submit their first patches. After an initial introduction and demonstration, the students were guided to decide simple rules and etiquette for using the wiki.

Agreed Rules

1   Only edit or delete your own work
2   Be polite to each other
3   Read other students' posts
4   Provide constructive feedback on each other's work etc.

By the end of this session, all students had learnt how to navigate their way around the wiki and had submitted their first patch, which for IIL1 was their Riveting Read piece (described in Chapter 4). For the majority of students this was the first time that they had used a wiki, so this new environment could have been daunting. Most students' familiarity with online communication had generally been with friends or family. We were asking them to communicate with people they did not know. It is well documented that the lack of non-verbal and visual cues can make this quite a difficult experience for newcomers (Salmon 2006; Garrison and Anderson 2003). Bearing this in mind, writing a book review seemed to be a starting point to develop a sense of online socialisation. There would be no judgements, simply a personal review of their chosen book.

As this academic year progressed, tutors repeatedly encouraged students to post their inquiries on the wiki for other students to read and comment on, but not all did so. During one of our regular meetings we discussed why some students were not contributing to the wiki. We decided to try to improve students' motivation to post their learning inquiries, read and comment on others' work by discussing some of the work posted during seminar sessions. Even the best designed learning experiences will be unsuccessful if students do not engage (Salmon 2006). Some students improved their posting of work but continued to be reluctant to comment on each other's work on the wiki, saying things like *'How can I judge what someone else has said when I'm not sure myself'* and *'I don't have a problem with concentration so I didn't read those'*. This provided an opportunity for tutors to discuss the value of students sharing their ideas, thoughts and personal experience and the usefulness of providing thoughtful encouragement and constructive feedback to others learning inquiries. Peer feedback is discussed further in Chapter 7. An analysis of postings showed that students were more inclined to post comments to learning inquiries posted by members of their own seminar group than postings from students in other groups. As mentioned previously, the lack of visual cues such as body language and verbal notation can noticeably influence online communication. Students who had got to know each other in their own seminar groups had established a social presence within that group. However, they were less familiar with individuals in other seminar groups, so felt that we were asking them to provide feedback to someone they did not know (Salmon 2006; Garrison and Anderson 2003) As discussed in Chapter 7, we endeavoured to support students with this dilemma in seminar sessions.

Overall, the wiki worked well as a collaborative online function, our monitoring of its use showing that most students contributed all their writing to the wiki, and some submitted part of their work. We were pleased that our evaluations indicated that some students found the experience positive, typical comments being: *'I found the wiki extremely helpful and enjoyed reading other's inquiries'* and *'Others' work gave me inspiration when I was lacking it'*. We felt this type of collaborative online forum was something we would wish to develop further.

As part of that year's end-of-module student feedback, we found evidence of more areas for further reflection:

- 40 per cent of students felt that the imposition of deadlines for posting their learning investigations would have increased their motivation to post earlier or even to post at all. Here is another situation in which we experience the dilemma between safeguarding learning autonomy by insisting that students take responsibility for their learning actions, while also wanting to safeguard the learning process by having plenty of writing to be read. What is best? This dilemma is addressed below.

- Most students reported that they enjoyed reading and sharing work with others.
- Some students felt that conferences were the best place to share their work with others: a typical comment being, *'I don't think the wiki is the best way to show your work, it's very impersonal'*. Again, it seems that, for some students, the lack of social presence influences their motivation/ability to engage with this media.
- Our encouragement for students to review their learning inquiry reports was strengthened by the introduction of the wiki because it provided them with the opportunity to edit work after they had posted it. However, analysis of postings at the end of the academic year shows us that less than 17 per cent of students actually did this.
- Some students felt that learning inquiries should be assessed by tutors. The tutors' position is that the learning Inquiry reports (patches) are not assessed; however, they provide the foundation and an essential resource for students' writing of the final Patchwork Text, which *is* assessed. Here is another situation in which we experience the dilemma between safeguarding their internal locus of evaluation by insisting that students take responsibility for their self-assessments, while also wanting to safeguard the learning process by having feedback that improves their learning. This will continue to be an ongoing dilemma for the IIL team.
- Although 66 per cent of students said they never commented on another student's work, 50 per cent of those students who responded said that they welcome comments on their patches, making comments such as: *'I value others' comment on my inquiries; I found it helped to deepen my understanding'* and *'I like to read the comments other students have made about my investigation'*. Tutors noted that students' reluctance to comment on peers' work was also reflected in seminars, where students expressed reservations about what they viewed to be 'judging' or 'assessing' their peers' inquiries (see further discussion about peer feedback in Chapter 7).

In our evaluation of the IIL use of a wiki as a shared online workspace, we reconsidered our decision not to post comments ourselves. On reflection, we wondered if we should have contributed, to model how we wished students to interact with the wiki. This dilemma would be raised again in future team meetings.

Discussion boards

During the subsequent academic year, the university introduced a new VLE, which included discussion boards (see Figure 8.4). The IIL team decided to adopt the 'internally supported' discussion boards as they would give both tutors

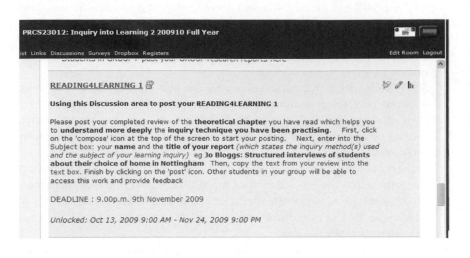

Figure 8.4 Screen shot of discussion board

and students the additional security of technical support. The advantage of using the discussion boards were that the IIL team had more control of what was created, when and how. Discussion boards could be created by any IIL tutor. There were also advantages for the students. The discussion boards were allocated within the Learning Room of the module, giving students easy access to post, read, comment and edit their patches. The summer vacation gave the IIL tutors the opportunity to reflect on previous experience and student feedback. There was more flexibility with the discussion boards, tutors could easily make changes if and when needed, so we decided to start with some quite radical changes.

1   Each discussion board had a deadline date, after which access to the board became 'read only'.
2   We applied some quite sophisticated *release conditions*. For example, the board for Discussion Two would not become available to a student unless they had posted an inquiry and commented on at least two other inquiries on the Discussion One board.
3   Students could see whether a tutor had read a post or not, so tutors would try to open/read as many posts as possible.
4   When it was felt appropriate, tutors posted comments on some inquiries. Sometimes these posts took the form of a simple comment, such as *'Well done for being the first to …'* or *'That sounds interesting, have you thought about …'* or *'You are making some interesting discoveries I wonder if other students …'.*

Some of these radical changes did not fit well with the philosophy of the modules (as discussed in previous chapters) but we felt that we needed to provide well-structured media in which all students would participate. Most students found using these technologies a valuable, enjoyable experience, but for a minority it continued to be a chore. We noticed that these were often the same students who were reluctant to contribute in seminar groups, so it did not seem to be the medium but the activity itself that needed to be addressed. Again, this would continue to be an ongoing dilemma for the IIL team.

When evaluating our use of these facilities we looked at a range of online models but none seemed to fit our rather specific situation. We were using discussion boards, but not in the generally accepted way. Garrison and Anderson (2003) provided us with some interesting points about the influence of social presence and online collaborative activities. Our intention for using the wiki and the discussion board had not been for collaborative discussion in the sense that Garrison and Anderson and Salmon use it, but a number of their points are still appropriate to our experience.

As 'digital immigrants' we found it difficult to find models of blended learning that reflected our practice, that we could use to reflect on, so we looked for other models that we felt would give us a 'best fit'. A popular model at the time was Salmon's (2006) five-stage model for managing e-moderating. We are aware, of course, that Salmon's model is designed for online learning rather than blended learning, but we felt it would still provide us with some useful reflection points.

- *Stage 1: Access and motivation*   Students were provided with easy access and clear instructions on how to post their learning inquiries. Tutors continually encouraged students to post their work, outlining how important their participation would be for developing understand and their final assessment.
- *Stage 2: Online socialisation*   The Riveting Read provided students with an ideal opportunity to post work without fear of being judged. Mutually agreed rules ensured that students respected each other and contributed with supportive and encouraging comments. Initially, there was a reluctance to share work across groups, but with some tutor support and encouragement students did begin to read and comment on postings from other seminar groups. This may have been helped by other modules organising mixed seminar groups for various sessions. In future years we may consider including an 'introduce yourself' section to help with online socialisation.
- *Stage 3: Information exchange*   Our practice does not really address this stage of Salmons' model. The online postings were a mixture of personal learning inquiries and supportive comments. As tutors, we wanted students to see this as *their* learning space so we kept at a distance. We would read their posts but had stated that we would not post our comments as we did not want to perpetuate an idea of tutors giving more valued comment. Whether this is the best thing to do or whether we should take a more active role is a dilemma that we still struggle with. It is not unreasonable to assume

that a space created by tutors, on a university-based platform, means that the students might very well find it difficult to 'take control'. Perhaps we are asking too much of them. Their fear of getting it wrong will, perhaps, always win through. This dilemma will be something that IIL tutors will continue to reflect on. On the one hand, the good thing about tutors keeping a distance is to foster students' sense of ownership of 'their space', but the not-so-good thing is that they may feel we are not interested in or do not care about what they do. On the other hand, if we 'give more', are we reducing their 'ownership'? Salmon talks about the use of a 'lifeguard', a person who could provide email or online help. Could this be a role for a tutor or a proficient student?

- *Stage 4: Knowledge construction*   Salmon sees this stage as 'tutor led'. As our policy was not to contribute to the online discussions, the context in which tutors introduced new theories and/or topics for discussion continued to be the seminar group sessions. They were also where tutors encouraged students to think critically about their own experience in relation to the theory and the practice of their peers, making connections between theories and practice. See Chapter 7 for further discussion. Salmon's link with constructivist approaches to learning can be seen in the final stage of her model.
- *Stage 5: Development*   The IIL modules' alignment to a constructivist approach to learning means that students are encouraged to take responsibility of their own learning and to become independent, reflective learners.

Conclusion

Our reflections on our own practice and from student feedback has raised questions about how we might develop this area for future cohorts. Although pleased with how this technology has given a new dimension to the student learning experience, we are not complacent. The wiki and discussion boards are presented in a purely text form, while we would like students to be able to use different presentation styles (e.g. icons, videos, pictures). This is something we have already done ourselves. Due to a reduction in contact time, we have placed some lectures (the content of which is outlined in Chapter 4) online. This was fairly easy to do by simply adding a commentary to our PowerPoint and converting it to a small video. Each of these lectures gives students some background theory together with independent activities to complete, such as to locate and complete a visual, auditory and kinaesthetic (VAK) learning styles questionnaire. Students are then asked to bring activity results and their notes to the next seminar session.

The ever-changing face of technology means that new opportunities may be just around the corner. For example, should we continue with our 'in house' discussion boards or move to a social network that the students are more familiar with, such as Facebook?

Questions for reflection on information technology support for advancing *learning how to learn* in other contexts

The following questions provide starting points for thinking, talking and writing about designing a new module or programme or adapting an existing one.

1   Does the programme or module currently offer one or more electronic ways in which students can communicate their thinking and learning?

2   Is there sufficient training and coaching to give students a genuinely free choice between different ways of recording their reflections and sharing their writing electronically, to complement more traditional ones?

3   Can electronic methods communicate images and sound as well as writing to assist learning?

4   How is the dilemma about tutor involvement in students' ownership of electronic communications and learning fora resolved?

5   How is the dilemma about deadlines for student contributions resolved?

Part IV

Theoretical and philosophical bases for the Inquiry Into Learning approach

Chapter 9

Patchwork Texts as a curriculum design and assessment method

This chapter is about the design of the IIL curriculum and its distinctive assessment. Some fundamental thinking about what a curriculum is and what the design process can be like opens the chapter. Next, aspects of the story of how the Patchwork Texts approach was developed, to explain and justify its special characteristics, is given. Finally, advice about how to adapt any module and the PT approach to work in a complementary manner is offered. This work has been made possible by the extensive and inspirational contributions to curriculum development by John Elliott and the magnificent leadership of the Patchwork Texts Project by Richard Winter.

Designing a curriculum

As tutors in higher education in the United Kingdom, we have become accustomed to meeting requirements for planning modules and programmes set by institutional, vocational and even statutory authorities. In many situations, we notice the growing influence of technical-rationalistic assumptions about the best way to plan educational endeavour. It has almost become taken for granted that the most important element of a plan is a specific aim, 'broken down' into a set of objectives or outcomes. The ways in which these aims are achieved are always separate, lower down in importance, and may even be merely a perfunctory list of indicative teaching methods, such as lecture, seminar, practical workshop. From our perspective, this separation of aims from the means of achieving them is a fatal flaw. Overcoming another flawed separation, between teaching and assessment, has been addressed in Chapter 7. Although filling in a form with these headings does not necessarily require us to use this kind of planning, it is hardly a stimulus to more integrated or creative approaches. Also, the meaning of curriculum has been degraded from a coherent account of answers to the many various questions about what is to be taught, learned and assessed, and how and why. In worst cases, it is reduced to little more than a statement about content. We begin with a simplified summary of the planning of a module which conforms with technical rationalist assumptions.

'Conventional' curriculum thinking and planning

The aim and objectives are often synonymous with the content which is, in turn, a summary of the knowledge to be taught. Aims and/or outcomes are written in an objectified form, so as to indicate what directly observable evidence can be obtained to prove their attainment by students. The content is presented to students authoritatively as a body of knowledge, maybe hierarchically subdivided and sequenced, with precise meanings, by its custodian, the tutor, against which students' knowledge is in deficit. Content is synonymous with the syllabus: a list of topics, all of which are to be covered. Progression through content is decided by a logical development through simple to complex. Timing is governed by coverage of content, not students' learning. The rationalist epistemological assumptions mean that content knowledge is presented as certain truth, every atom of which has been mastered by the tutor, and should be mastered by the students. There may be a preference for theoretical purity and avoidance of controversy and a tacit assumption that the teaching, when done well, actually *causes* the learning. The assumed learning process of students is passively to receive and replicate the prescribed knowledge in their thinking and knowing so as to be able to reproduce it for assessment. As long as a student is unsure about the accuracy of their reproduction, they remain in doubt about the extent to which it rectifies their knowledge deficit and can only guess at a self-assessment of their learning. This can reinforce feelings of guilt, anxiety and inadequacy, which fuel students' demands for ever greater specificity and clarity in the tutor's *delivery* of the knowledge. This propels intolerance towards doubts, ambiguities, questions or uncertainties in thinking about the knowledge. The learning is like a standardised commodity, produced to match the assessment criteria, made in isolation from other students and in competition with them for grades. Planned learning tasks are tied to specific objectives with no differentiation between students' prior knowledge or development. The most 'objective' way of assessing how well students have achieved the learning objectives or outcomes is by administering tests. Alternatively, some kind of structured essay could be set. A single, idealised version of such an assignment product is presumed to exist, if not on paper, then in the mind and mark scheme of the tutor, to which conformity is prized. The implied way of learning efficiently is by shaping knowledge with rewards and punishments (right and wrong answers) as in behaviourist conditioning. Evaluation of the whole endeavour focuses on inputs and outputs more than any monitoring of events or processes in between. Outcome data are believed to indicate the quality of teaching. Module processes may be assessed for efficiency: to change what is *done to* students, to make it more effective in achieving the fixed, separate outcomes. Ideally, the plan is *person proof*: its success is independent of the people involved.

Students learn from this kind of curriculum that knowledge exists independently of the knower and can be validated authoritatively by the application of rigorous methods appropriate to the subject discipline. They are not deemed to be able to think competently or significantly for themselves about a subject until they have acquired its knowledge in sufficient *quantity* and at sufficiently abstract *levels*. They also learn that theory is pre-eminent over action or practice, that the application of knowledge to practice is a separate, different task, that personal knowledge can be a dangerous source of errors and misconceptions, and that personal evaluations of subject knowledge are inadmissible. Therefore, the values they are encouraged to adopt are *uniformity, structure, certainty, conformity, measurability, standardisation, predictability, authoritarian control, technical efficiency*. The qualities which are notably minimised by, or absent from, this approach are students' prior knowledge, values, interests, questions, experience, interaction, collaboration, feelings such as curiosity, debate of alternatives, areas of doubt or speculation, creative thinking about what might be possible, evaluations and applications of knowledge, links to practice, induction or initiation to an intellectual, academic or professional community.

By specifying standard outcomes in advance, a conventional curriculum plan sets an arbitrary limit on what any students' learning achievement might be, or credit that might be received.

Any particular module or programme can be examined critically to consider how its curriculum has a blend of the characteristics of these two planning approaches. Fundamental differences between them are deliberately contrasted in the following sections to help a planning process to be clearer about what kind of blending is intended.

'Process' curriculum thinking and planning

Unlike the technocratic task of completing a module planning pro forma, which marks the completion of the planning, this approach is an ongoing *process*. It begins with a broad educational purpose or aim, which combines values and ideals with relevant qualities of achievement. This is not like an absolutely clear, fixed, detached target at which to aim. It is more like a vision held by a particular group of tutors, of what good students are like, when they have successfully been inducted and initiated into a certain community of scholars and/or professional practitioners. Tutors consider their vision interactively with how they believe it can be achieved in their current situation. It is as much about the growth and development along the way (of students' learning as well as tutors' teaching) as about the journey's destination. So the educational purpose or aim provides principles which guide the choice and design of learning experiences that are judged to be good, or potentially good, ways to achieve it. Such decisions depend in part on experiential, tacit knowledge, which can be made more explicit through being tested by experience. If the vision is for students to be able to engage wisely with significant questions and problems in a particular field of human endeavour, they need to be inducted into this by doing it at appropriate levels. Tutors refine their understanding of the vision by monitoring and reflecting on how students show the sought-after learning qualities. This part of the curriculum process, monitoring of and collaborative reflective deliberation on the operation of the module or programme, is its action research dimension. Evidence is gathered to consider whether a tutor's actions as a teacher improve any particular set of students' learning in ways that are consistent with the vision. Evidence is also used to reconsider the relevance and desirability of problematic aspects of the vision for *these* students *here* and *now*. Such research not only helps to improve the practice of the tutors involved, but also opens the curriculum to professional scrutiny and facilitates its adaptation by other tutor teams to their different circumstances. It is as if the whole curriculum plan is a complex *human hypothesis* to be tested by the tutors as teacher-researchers. The research offers action hypotheses for others to test in their situations. The completion of a bureaucratic planning pro forma for this kind of curriculum would be like providing a snap-shot derived from a movie.

The educational vision embodies virtues such as *independent thinking* or *creativity*, whose practical manifestations cannot be defined beforehand with specific accuracy, in a behaviourist manner. They are noticeable when they arise, sometimes unpredictably, within students' creative responses to the curriculum. No predefined limit is imposed on what students can achieve. There is no fixed learning path for all students to follow in the sense that different students may progress at their own rates and in diverse directions within the curriculum. Tutors notice student responses as they progress, or as problems in learning arise. It is at this level of pedagogic detail that specific learning objectives and targets are appropriately used. Rather than being tutor-predetermined steps in overcoming a deficit, objectives *emerge* from the monitoring of the learning and teaching process and can be formulated by tutors and/or students appropriately to each situation. Used in this way, an objective or target is not a subdivision of a conventional curriculum's predetermined aim, it is a relevant next step from where a student is now, to move towards the aim. Used in this way, emergent learning objectives are *person centred*, not content centred (see Ovens 2004).

A process curriculum is a way of organising the processes of learning about *something*, so how does it deal with content? The *something* in IIL1 is the practice of learning, about which textbooks and formal teaching (instruction) can be given. We agree with Lawrence Stenhouse's way of thinking about this when he wrote:

> Of course we need instruction. And textbooks too. The key is that the aim of discovery and discussion is to promote understanding of the nature of the concessions to error that are being made in that part of our teaching where we rely on instruction or textbooks. The crucial difference is between an educated and an uneducated use of instruction. The educated use of instruction is sceptical, provisional, speculative in temper. The uneducated use mistakes information for knowledge. Information is not knowledge until the factor of error, limitation or crudity in it is appropriately estimated, and it is assimilated to structures of thinking ... which gives us the meaning of understanding.
>
> (1983: 183)

The content of the curriculum is not treated as a syllabus but as a map of contributory, overlapping skills, attitudes and areas of knowledge relevant to its purpose to guide exploration by tutors and students. There are many ways by which the content can be presented by tutors to enable students to access it purposefully for their learning. Problem-based and inquiry-based methods of organisation, for example, set up practical situations in which students think and act in ways which accord with the educational vision. Learning tasks are set in sufficiently open ways for a range of interpretations, differentiated by student's prior knowledge and current learning development. Instruction is used educatively: with sceptical, provisional and speculative treatment of public knowledge. Assessment of learning is not just a formal, final, summative and judgemental activity, separate from learning, but also an informal, interim, formative part of learning and teaching. Criteria of assessment specify qualities of learning of central importance to the curriculum purpose. Tutors recognise and give explicit attention to them when responding *'critically to students' thinking as it unfolds and manifests itself in often unanticipated ways within their work'* (Elliott 1998: 41). Students could be encouraged to learn what the criteria mean by applying them as personalised objectives to part of their own and each other's learning, extending the influence of the curriculum vision to self and peer assessment of learning. Knowledge is understood as a dynamic interplay of competing theories, practices and value positions, to be explored and linked appropriately to further learning. Tutors present knowledge in the context of its use, as tentative, contested, unstable and open to criticism and revision. Implied assumptions about how students learn are essentially socially constructivist. Underpinning values of the curriculum are plurality, difference, individuality, constructive criticism, productive doubt, sharing control, autonomy, and so on.

A process curriculum plan has, at its heart, tutors' recurring, evidence-based and knowledge-informed deliberation on the interdependent questions:

- What are the good things that we really want our students to achieve?
- Are we doing the best things in our current situation to enable them to achieve it?

This is referred to elsewhere as our action research (see Chapter 11).

The Inquiry Into Learning curriculum

The IIL1 and IIL2 modules described in Part 2 (Chapters 4 and 5 respectively) are planned as process curricula with autonomy as a central value. Each has a vision, translated into learning qualities which provide criteria for assessment of the final assignment and of the learning processes, including their interim products (attention to these, the patches, is given in the next part of this chapter). We want IIL1 students to be aware of themselves *becoming reflective learners*, knowing what that means for them personally, and able to demonstrate qualities of *involvement, awareness of personal development* and *credible, practical knowing.* We want IIL2 students to be aware of themselves *becoming professional inquirers,* knowing what that means for them personally, and able to demonstrate qualities of *inquiry-mindedness, professional engagement* and *credible, practical knowing.* There are no predefined outcomes to which students must conform. The main learning task is to do action research to improve practice as (1) reflective learners and (2) professional inquirers, to develop autonomous capacities to learn similarly in the future when facing difficulties in personal learning or meeting professional problems by inquiring into them. Students develop abilities to select relevant inquiry focuses and ways of finding out and achieving practical improvement. They learn how to exercise a freedom to learn the things that they believe they need. *'They grow into tomorrow, only as they live today'* (this is often quoted as being, but never attributed to a specific publication of, John Dewey).

The careful attention which has been given to curriculum design provided a basis for appreciating the Inquiry Into Learning approach more fully as a process curriculum. The importance of formative assessment and the key role of criteria of assessment has been explained in Chapter 8. Attention now turns to the Patchwork Texts way of organising the course work and assignment, showing its coherence with a process curriculum design.

A Patchwork Texts approach

When he was a Professor of Education at the then Anglia Polytechnic University in Cambridge, Richard Winter was teaching a course on reflective writing for professional practitioners such as social workers, nurses and teachers (Winter *et al.* 1999). Course members were asked to write a series of short pieces with different subjects, purposes and, perhaps, styles, as they progressed through the course, and draw on them at the end, in preparing the assessed assignment. He and his colleagues found that this way of working was helpful in several ways. Most of all, they valued the way in which the final writing conveyed the uncertainty and subjectivity of the personal synthesis derived from the varied perspectives and voices coming together into a unity. They felt it solved problems associated with both of the main alternative methods of assessment: the essay and the portfolio. An essay is likely to be about a relatively narrow part of all the intended learning and lead students' to neglect other parts. Taking time to write it near the end of a module may reduce attendance at later sessions. These are two manifestations of an instrumental and selective attitude to learning which are not addressed by the essay method. Furthermore, essays are associated with the cognitive and logical skills needed to be analytical and evaluative, to the possible neglect of aesthetic qualities and personal involvement such as reflexivity. Portfolio and learning journal types of assignment are not so susceptible to these problems but create others. Since they do not require a student to create an overall synthesis and evaluation of the various entries, which might include too many disparate or trivial items, they are criticised as relatively easy and not an adequate demonstration of academic achievement. The Patchwork Text is a coursework format specifically designed to encourage a critical and personal engagement with the whole of a syllabus, enable students to draw on a wide range of writing skills and build up a complex text through a gradual process of accumulation.

The main ideas

Tutors value students' writing of many kinds, as part of learning, but do we do enough to help them to write? Writing for learning involves thought processes of sorting, ordering, connecting, differentiating, questioning, evaluating and analysing the experiences and ideas which help develop personal meaning. A short piece of writing about a discrete section of learning, before advancing to the next, would help a student to clarify and consolidate thoughts and feelings while they are fresh. However, a student with an instrumental attitude to learning and a dependence on external motivation is unlikely to see it this way. They may not be used to writing for themselves or for learning, but only in high-stakes assessment situations which stimulate anxiety, an inclination to play safe and ultimately even plagiarise.

Conventionally, the only writing by a student read by their tutor is the assessed assignment at or after the end of the module. It can reveal qualities in a student's thinking and learning, good and bad, which hitherto may have remained insufficiently recognised by the student and probably unknown to peers and the tutor. It is not uncommon for a tutor reading assignments to find an outstanding insight, beautifully expressed, or a crude blundering misunderstanding, and wish it had been possible to use them to assist the learning of the group. Conventionally, the only writing by a student which receives formative feedback from their tutor is a failed assignment, when the priority is not so much to learn but to avoid failing again by doing whatever it takes to pass. Except by tutor telling, there may not be encouragement for students to be experimental or exploratory in their writing or to practise drafting and redrafting.

A tutor who is interested in teaching students as much as subjects, may be aware of these self-evident considerations but feel unable to act on them unless they are incorporated into an appropriate strategy such as Patchwork Texts.

Short pieces of writing called 'patches', done regularly throughout a module, could contribute to the final assignment when fitted together into a Patchwork Text. This motivates a reluctant or hesitant student to treat the writing of a patch seriously, since it will contribute to the assessed assignment, while not being as susceptible to a fear of failure as in the final assignment, which can inhibit creativity. It opens possibilities of many kinds; for tutors to require different kinds of writing for each patch, such as story, report, review, commentary etc., to express different aspects of learning, and for students sharing patches in small group discussion. The writing of a retrospective, integrative, reflexive commentary on the whole of the module learning could be the focus of a concluding patch, or a function performed by the 'stitching', the additional text which introduces and links patches, to provide a personal synthesis. The number of patches required and how their word-count length relates to that of the Patchwork Text assignment also need to be decided. If sufficient flexibility in the governance of a programme permits, the full adaptability of a Patchwork Texts approach can be exploited. For example, if a student or group suddenly shows a lot of flair and industry about an aspect of their learning, which the tutor would like to turn to their (and the whole group's) advantage, it could be expanded into an impromptu project which leads to its own patch. Obviously, there would have to be consistency with the module aims and so on, but the attraction would be the ease and simplicity with which students and tutors are set free to transform an unplanned show of enterprise into a benefit to the assessed assignment. The final section in this chapter provides philosophical questions and practical decisions involved in adopting a Patchwork Text approach.

Other parts of this book describe how the Inquiry Into Learning approach uses a Patchwork Text assignment structure for formative and summative assessment. It is liked by many of our students, who recognise it as a significant antidote to their tendency to get into a last-minute panic of assignment writing, which can limit their achievement. But, for a few students, the familiar tendency persists, to appear to give little effort and only superficial thought to patch writing. A very few students evade the patch writing procedure altogether and submit an essay-type assignment about reflective learning (in IIL1) which inevitably lacks the qualities defined by the assessment criteria! An outstanding advantage for tutors is that the Patchwork Text approach expands their access to students' developing thinking and ideas, which enables a tutor's picture of the progress in learning, otherwise based only on listening to their contributions to discussion, to be enriched. A significant difficulty, particularly with large class sizes, is for the tutor to allocate enough time to be able to read enough patches and give enough feedback to meet the student complaint that it is not worth writing anything which is not marked by the tutor.

These Patchwork Text ideas have been adopted and adapted in many different kinds of modules, courses and programmes across a wide range of subjects and academic levels in many colleges and universities.

A Patchwork Texts approach and understanding learning

The PT approach is a fine example of the interconnectedness of everything in an educational endeavour. It works well, not just because it is a clever way of structuring assignment writing, or a powerful stimulus to peer and self assessment, or a way of coaching students' writing for learning, but also because it is in harmony with how students learn *well*.

Insufficient space is available here to do justice to theorists' ideas about learning which provide a resource for developing Patchwork Texts, particularly by IIL. Here are some of the ideas we find relevant and thought-provoking.

Talking about learning as a personal, social and moral practice, as tutors and students discuss learning inquiries together, we are developing communities of practice (Lave and Wenger 1991). We want students to be learning apprentices: learning how to learn through practice and participation in collaborative action inquiry to improve their practice as learners in a social network of inquirers. Our use of *apprenticeship* is similar to Barbara Rogoff's (1991) in that students are using the intellectual tools of inquiry within a socially constructed activity. A difference is that in IIL, the tutor's role as a *senior learner*, is a more distant one, because of the large group size, than in the examples studied by Rogoff. However, tutors do take every opportunity to disclose examples of their own learning which relate to the students' learning inquiries, at the time they arise. We try to be role models for combining evidence of critical moments in significant events in our own experience, with our personal reflections, tacit understanding, helpful concepts from public knowledge and our own evaluative comment. The three interrelated dimensions of a Community of Practice (CoP) described by Etienne Wenger (1998) can be seen in IIL, as follows:

- *Mutual engagement*: students as learning partners are expected to relate to each other collaboratively and help each other's reflections on their learning.
- *Joint enterprise*: shared understandings of each other's learning development are forged through discussion of each other's learning inquiries.
- *Shared repertoire*: communal resources develop in the form of the patches written about each learning inquiry, containing evidence and ideas from reading.

Tutors set tasks for each group, functioning as a CoP, to perform at each stage of doing an inquiry. For example, students help each other to find a focus for the next inquiry or critically examine the latest evidence of improvement in a learning practice. Discussion is influenced by what learning partners know about each other as persons: aspirations, fears, strengths and difficulties etc. Therefore, the CoP does not aim to be like a project team which is task-focused, driven by targets and outcomes, but more like a free association of friends, including *critical friends* (see Chapter 7) with common interests and shared purposes. This has obvious implications for how tutors manage the formation and continuation of learning partnerships and groups. Ground rules are negotiated with students to govern practices such as taking turns to speak and confidential treatment of material in small groups from the whole group as distinct community spaces. A specific procedure such as *Intervision* (see Chapter 6) may be followed. Regular attention is given to how groups see their interaction and its value. At the time of writing, a recent source of food for thought is Marcia Baxter Magolda's (2010) concept of '*developmentally sequenced learning partnerships*'.

Most IIL patches, but not all, are accounts of learning inquiries, for example: '*How dyslexia affects my note taking and concentration*' or '*Becoming a better reader by reading more effectively*'. A patch about an inquiry such as one of these is expected to have some qualities which can be labelled 'scientific' or 'objective' such as evidence-based description, logical thinking, analytical and evaluative reasoning. Other qualities are personal, such as one's values, dispositions, interests, self questioning etc. and yet others could be called 'aesthetic' or 'subjective' such as fit-for-purpose, imagination, integrity, wholeness and creativity. Since students differ in such qualities in their learning, we expect variation in how they blend in any patch and encourage each student to represent their understanding by using their various, differing qualities. We think it is important to ensure that the assessment process recognises this variety in IIL. In another programme, such recognition may not possible within one patch, but would be achievable in the Patchwork Text if briefing for different patches is appropriately set (an extract of the IIL requirement is given below). As a reflective aside: only very bold or foolhardy students dare risk as much imaginative creativity as this in writing a traditional essay. If they interpret it as a demand to master other people's knowledge hastily, they are tempted to pretend to understand fully, hide their own knowledge or doubts as probably naïve and only reproduce conventional evaluative comments or criticisms!

The PT is particularly powerful in encouraging students to integrate diverse elements in their study and grasp its underlying or emergent structure. Using PT in a module for science specialist primary school student teachers, Peter Ovens (2003a) found a step change was achieved in their critical understanding of science. The Patchwork Text assignment written by one of his students, Josephine Quinn (2003), entitled 'Becoming a science specialist teacher' shows how she integrated her reading about the nature of science with examples of science in society and in the media, with a personal interest in science's relationship with religion and her professional interest in how to teach science to young children.

As teachers, we encourage students to revise their existing personal frames of reference in order to accommodate new knowledge, as a genuine process of assimilation. We want their learning to be a process of *constructing meaning* as opposed to merely mastering *information* and to experience the acquisition of knowledge as a personal process of *'self-exploration'* and *'self-questioning'* (Barnett 1997). As tutors of IIL, we experience continuing frustration that this vision is not more fully achieved by more of our students. We have always taught IIL with a Patchwork Texts assignment, so it is impossible to compare it with a different kind of assignment. However, we hold faith with PT partly because of its consistency with our values, and partly thanks to the encouragement we have received from discussion with students, colleagues and our further theoretical reading. For example, there is an interesting distinction between engineering and *bricolage* made by Claude Levi-Strauss (1966). Engineers, he says, produce their structures by operating within a fully pre-planned, closed system of concepts, procedures and components; whereas *bricoleurs* consult what they happen to have in their own shed in order to improvise new structures from materials that were originally part of something else. They *'engage in a sort of dialogue with the various tools and materials they have to hand to widen the possible answers ... to discover what each of them could signify'* (Levi-Strauss 1966: 17–18). If our vision incorporates an image of learning more like *bricolage* than engineering, then we must set assessments which reward students' construction of their own learning through improvisation with the resources they have and can find close to hand. Our task is to overturn their assumption that *learning as engineering* is the name of the game. Assessment must discourage the search for a flatpack solution from the Internet, with the resultant discovery that, as usual, they cannot really understand or follow the technical instructions for assembly! By using the PT format in IIL, we anticipate that a student who initially produces an engineered patch or a flatpack patch will be confronted with patches showing the authenticity of *bricolage*, which will become recognised as *real* learning through discussion with peers and legitimated by our assessment criteria.

We cannot think of a context for learning more relevant to a new student in higher education than that of *trying to learn better* at this new level of challenge. Remembering Lev Vygotsky's (1978) belief that thinking arises from purposeful social interaction, we expect IIL1 students' discussion of each other's learning inquiries to include constructive social feedback which is intrinsic to the Patchwork Text process. Success depends on convincing them that the kind of knowledge we value is *'not authoritative revelation of objective truths, but a developing, always incomplete conversation among those who recognise the limitations of their current understanding'* (Rorty 1979: 171).

Ultimately, we return to the work of Roland Barnett (1997) and our fundamental intellectual values, which include self-understanding and self-evaluation, a form of *critical reflexivity*. This is what the retrospective commentary element of a Patchwork Text requires, either as a final patch or, as in IIL, the stitching which links patches together. It should convey how a student at the end of a particular phase of learning, sees their *knowing* about the module's purpose and their sense of coherence and significance. This is communicated by the stitching, which introduces and explains each patch, and links them to themes, trends, developments or patterns in learning across the module. In IIL, the formal requirements given to students are:

> The Patchwork Text (PT) brings out and explores theme(s) across the separate pieces of your writing. The patches are chosen for their significance to your main learning achievements. For example, any such theme(s) in the PT may be one(s) relating to your personal questions or problems as they have arisen through the processes of writing your Jotter/Journal, and reflection linked to Learning Partners' group discussion. However, you are not expected to arrive at simple, clear answers to these questions but to give an honest exploration of the issues which you may have or may not have resolved, indicating any new questions which may have been raised, and so on. Overall, the PT should convey significant ways in which your learning has achieved the qualities indicated by the criteria of assessment.

A final thought on this is appropriately provided by Richard Winter (2003: 121):

> The argument that the structure of our knowledge is provisional and person-ally constructed, rather than an external, objective reality is a further rationale for what is perhaps the central feature of the Patchwork Text. The Patchwork Text deconstructs the essay's monolithic, finalising unity into a series of *frag-ments*, with a possible overall 'pattern' that is *waiting* to be synthesised by means of a personal journey of exploration. Thus, it embodies a model of learning as an act of *imagination* (Warnock 1976: 28), i.e. as an essentially creative process of seeing links between matters that may seem initially to be separate.

Questions for reflection on adopting a Patchwork Text approach for advancing *learning how to learn* in other contexts

These questions provide starting points for thinking, talking and writing about designing a new curriculum or adapting an existing one, with a process philos-ophy and/or a Patchwork Text approach.

1   What is the module (or programme) *vision* for what it wants students to achieve? More specifically:

  • What is the educational *aim* of the module?
  • Does it include the *induction* and *initiation* intentions of an education rather than a training (see Chapter 2)?
  • Does the vision imply or state *ideals* of higher education such as *autonomy* or *being critical*? What are they?
  • To what extent is the module aim *vocational* or *professional*: implying attitudes and values related to professional action or becoming members of a community of practice?
  • Does the vision imply a *personal development* dimension to students' learning?
  • What is the blend between a 'conventional' curriculum philosophy, which values knowledge acquisition above all else, and a 'process' curric-ulum, in which *what is learned* is not as important as *how it is learned*?

2   Is the module's *subject knowledge* component seen epistemologically as:
  • the acquisition and mastery of informational knowledge or the develop-ment of understanding types of knowledge, or a blend of both?
  • equivalent to the content *syllabus* which students are required to cover or a *conceptual map* to be explored?
  • regarded as a *resource base* for problem solving, or for application to practice?

- partly generated by *student inquiry* and/or *experiential learning*?

3 Taking into account the tutorial team's *vision, aim* and its *view of knowledge*, what are the

- most absolutely essential *qualities* of the *process* of students' learning?
- *aesthetic* and *personal* as well as *rational* dimensions to these qualities?
- *assessment criteria* which express these qualities briefly and accessibly to students?

4 How is the *module content* organised? Is it:

- separated into conceptual *hierarchies*?
- *contextualised* by organisation around practical professional problems, issues of inquiry and/or controversy and/or areas of experience?

5 What are the general assumptions about *how students learn* the content of this module?

- What do they *do*, practically, in the process of learning?
- How are different parts of module content meant to be *integrated* in the students' own thinking and personal understanding, to develop a deep structure?
- How do students manage their reception of others' *meaning* and create their own?
- Is a student's learning mainly or only an *individual* activity or a *social* activity?
- How do they *reflect* personally on their learning and development as learners?
- How do the assessment criteria influence a *student's evaluation* of their learning?

6 What kinds of *writing* will students do?

- Are they left to decide entirely for themselves or guided to *write for learning*?
- Are there written tasks which relate to session activities such as discussion?
- Are students expected to share pieces of writing with each other?

7 If a *Patchwork Texts approach* were to be adopted:

- how many *patches* would be required?
- how would their *word-count length* relate to that of the Patchwork Text assignment?
- would students be expected to read and discuss each other's patches as part of their learning?
- would the discussion include giving and receiving *peer feedback* related to the students' interpretation of the assessment criteria?

- would there be firm deadlines for each patch or a flexible arrangement?
- would a patch be made available only to the student's learning partners or to the entire cohort as well?
- would it be submitted formally or informally?
- would the tutor read patches and give feedback, with reference to the criteria?
- would students be required to keep some kind of Journal or other way of regularly writing personal reflections on their patch writing, and/or their general learning and its progress?
- would the tutor support students' reflective writing by requiring to read it, or by leaving this to student choice?
- how closely would *focuses* of some or all the patches be set by the tutor's brief, to relate to the different parts of module content or to allow student choice?
- would the *presentational style* be set by the tutor's brief or would variation and creativity in forms of self-expression be encouraged?
- what kind of structure would be set for the discussion of shared patches?
- how would the tutor prepare students for discussion and help them to evaluate it and their participation?
- how much control would a student have over the amount and choice of material extracted from each of their own patches and inserted into the Patchwork Text?
- would a student be permitted to refer to and/or quote material from other students' patches and, if so, under what conditions?
- if a retrospective, integrative, reflexive commentary on the whole of the module learning is required, would it be:
  - the focus of a concluding patch, or
  - a function performed by the stitching, and
  - would it be expected to refer, in part, to the student's interpretation of how the assessment criteria relate to their work?

8   What kinds of *formative feedback*, by tutors and/or by peers, is planned, to help self-assessment of learning?

Chapter 10

Action research for personal professional development

An Inquiry Into Learning team meeting is characteristically a blend of many things. As well as responding to changes in room bookings or fixing problems with the preparation of teaching and learning resources, we talk about how things are going, and what we can think and do, to improve. As part of the conversations about 'One student has said to me that ...' and 'What did we agree we were going to do about ...?', we do our action research. A semi-formal structure which runs through our talk is to turn back from time to time to rethink what we initially thought we wanted and how it was supposed to be achievable, amid the ongoing inquiry into what we think *is* actually happening now, from various points of view, and what we are really doing. The activity may appear to an outsider to be more messy and disorganised than we hope our formal presentations of it seem to be. If we appear to be enthusiastic *amateurs*, there is some comfort in an obsolete meaning of the word as 'a lover of something'. If love includes having understanding, close affinity with and high regard for something, then we do love doing action research into IIL. On the other hand, we would not wish to be called *professional* researchers if this means dispassionate seekers after an ultimate truth. We are trying to improve our professional practice. Then again we wouldn't wish someone to call our inquiry 'action research' if all they mean is that we do conventional, objective research that just happens to be centred on *action*, merely finding out what works or what is effective. This is not a meaning of action research that we have regard for. We see ourselves being like Lawrence Stenhouse's 'teacher-researchers', who do not suspend being teachers to take on a separate, researcherly mantle, but integrate an inquiring approach into their teaching, to improve it morally as well as technically and effectively. We also see ourselves being like Donald Schön's 'reflective practitioners', whose artistic as well as scientific ways of knowing are as much in our *doing* as in our *talking* or *writing*: understanding more fully what we think and believe needs to be considered with understanding what we do and vice versa.

We see ourselves at the centre of this research approach and its products, in the sense that they are bound up with each other, since *'the object or product produced is not something "merely" external to and indifferent to the nature of the producer. It is his own activity in an objectified or congealed form'* (Bernstein 1983: 82). *'Our actions are a complex exteriorisation of a vast range of inner choices and decisions'*

(Poole 1972: 53). We cannot divorce our practice from our values. We are aware that who we are and what matters to us are sources of our academic and professional biases, which influence our actions. To enable their part in the research to be assessed, they are declared and explained below. There is no pseudo-objectivised pretence that this research *knows best* for other tutors teaching other modules and programmes. We have not stated things at the beginning of this book which we found more recently, because we want to contextualise them in our learning journey. We try to convey enough about our idiosyncratic inquiry to enable and encourage readers who would like to develop themselves, their teaching and curriculum, for the gain of their students in their own situation. We hope that our hypotheses and quality indicators about *learning how to learn in higher education* provide helpful contributions to others' action research in similar situations with comparable aims. We hope that our subjectivity is demonstrably open and responsive to theoretical, methodological and empirical criticisms. We take full responsibility for the failings and errors that we address. Nevertheless, we believe we have developed ourselves as teachers through our involvement in this action research as an educational development, for as Lawrence Stenhouse put it:

> there can be no educational development without teacher development; and the best means of development is not by clarifying ends but by criticizing practice. There are criteria by which one can criticise and improve the process of education without reference to an ends-means model which sets an arbitrary horizon to one's efforts. The improvement of practice rests on diagnosis, not prognosis. It is not by concentrating on the analysis of health that we cure our ills.
>
> (Stenhouse 1975: 83)

From this perspective, tutors who claim to develop what they teach without developing themselves as teachers or their curriculum, are restricted, like mechanics, to changes of technical operation which are not educational. Reconsideration of aims independently of how to realise them does not improve practice, it just changes words on a page. We do not see our relentless self-criticism to realise our values more fully as in any way a negative venture.

So, this chapter is about what our research is like. The following section gives a distillation of the action research dimension of IIL for tutors. Subsequent sections have been written by each of us separately. We tell about the kinds of subjectivities that have contributed to the research, what are their origins in significant educational experiences and values, explain how they link with IIL and give a summary of our professional development.

Action research into Inquiry Into Learning

Since the beginnings of the teacher-researcher tradition at the University of East Anglia, John Elliott has made numerous, seminal contributions to thinking about action research, leading many influential action research projects and providing the ideas and direction for so many theoretical advances. The criteria for good action research, which he presented in a brief article in 1995, are summarised here as we have understood and applied them.

1 Our research is *insider*, we are part of the inquiry, including reflection on our motives, values and actions, rather than as outsiders, claiming objectivity.

2 We do *educational* research, which is meant to be educative, seeking improved situational understanding, not *research on education*, seeking knowledge about action.

3 Our research is committed to realising pedagogical aims about *learning how to learn* and educational ideals such as *autonomy*, using teaching strategies such as *learning inquiries* as hypothetical probes into ways of actualising our educational values.

4 We focus on changing our practice to make it more consistent with our pedagogical aim.

5 We gather contextual evidence to test the consistency between our practice and our aim, from many sources, particularly our students, to compare our accounts of our own practice with those of observers and students.

6 We try to reflect on our own actions in ways that include others' perspectives, i.e. be reflexive.

7 We identify and analyse inconsistencies, dilemmas, (e.g. between providing structure which helps students to feel safe but does not diminish their autonomy) critical incidents, etc. to problematise the assumptions and beliefs which tacitly underpin our practice.

8 We aim to generate and test new forms of action while simultaneously reconstructing the theories and values that guide our practice, as a form of curriculum development.

9 We use our research to *find* the indicators of educational quality (not apply prespecified ones) which guide context-sensitive forms of practice that achieve our values, such as authentic learning inquiries, open, learning dialogue, empathic reflection, etc.

10 We teach so that it is a form of research and the research is embedded in our teaching: researching and teaching kinds of activity are often interwoven.

(Based on Elliott 1995)

Drawing on Donald Schön's idea of an *'epistemology of practice'*, we do not see knowledge as *molecular*, or as a *product*. Nor do we think of theoretical knowledge as superior to practical knowledge. Instead, we recognise that in our teaching we have *knowing-in-action* or tacit knowing, which we like to notice, reflect on and discuss, to turn it into *reflection on action*. In his talk to the 1987 Annual Meeting of the American Educational Research Association, as public confidence in the professions was declining, Schön identified the important problem in the study of the professions to be what he calls the *'indeterminate zones of practice: the experiences of uncertainty, confusion and messiness, when you don't know what the professional problem is'.* His solution is a *'reflective practicum'* which *'educates for artistry [in] healing the splits between teaching and doing, school and life, research and practice, which have been so insidiously effective at deadening the experience of school at all levels'* (Schön 1987). His voice in the USA nearly 20 years ago is as relevant here, today. In many aspects of professional and educational life, not least research, the reflective experience and moral delibera-tion of individuals is in danger of being steamrollered by managerialist forms of technical rationality.

Our shared collaborative project has been to improve our practice as a team of teachers of students, assessors of learning and developers of the curriculum, of the Inquiry Into Learning modules in this programme. We do this by knowing and understanding better how we and our students live it, and resolving the prac-tical and ethical problems and dilemmas, so as to realise our values more fully. Within this, we have separately explored particular lines of inquiry or tested certain methods or techniques which were personally relevant, and shared our findings.

Frances Wells

My international educational experience, together with having taught at all phases from the early years to higher education, provide a backdrop against which I have sought to develop a rich learning experience to support IIL students in their learning at university and in their future careers with children. Three themes have emerged as fundamental to my reflection on this module: first, exploring educational principles such as the importance of flexible and transferrable skills; second, the importance of developing reflective practice and moving this to more formalised action research and, third, the importance of holistic learning.

I saw the opportunity within this new degree to develop the attitudes and skills that I felt would support effective learning and professionalism in the changing world of multi-professional working with families and children. Of importance was seeing parallels in what I knew about how to learn with my own educational experience and learning observed when working with young children. Valuing a flexible approach to using transferrable skills and knowledge in different contexts has probably arisen from my experience as a pupil in primary schools in England, and then as a student in secondary education in the USA and India and subse-quently through my higher education in England. I feel a confidence from having successfully moved through these phases, recognising their different contribu-tions. For example, the historical knowledge from my secondary education was very American-orientated and therefore largely started in the eighteenth century. Applying to take a History degree in England, I recall my Professor telling me,

> You have better study skills than your fellow students even though you don't know much British history. I'm happy to take a risk that you will be successful on this course. I've seen the schools in Virginia and know what you will have experienced as a way of learning.

This vote of confidence in the nature of my secondary education in the USA gave me great confidence. He didn't know that for me there was only one civil war that was the one dated 1861 in the USA and not 1642 in England! He'd assessed that I had the research skills and aptitude to be successful and I was pleased to prove that his risk was justified. His view was that the degree was about *'learning to be a historian'* and this was rooted in Elton's view of history, *'the purpose and ambition of professional history is to understand a given problem from the inside ... [based on] systematic research'* (Elton 1967: 31). He considered that, despite my lack of content knowledge, I would have the quality in my learning processes to adapt. So, a steep learning curve in historical 'facts' had to occur but I did feel confidence in my developing application of research skills to the analysis of primary and secondary sources.

This sense of exploration and confidence to move my own learning forward has shaped my belief in the importance of positive dispositions towards learning. When working in the early years phase of education I became very drawn to the ideas of Chris Athey (1989) and Cathy Nutbrown (1994) in Sheffield, with a strong constructivist approach that valued the child and presented a view that their learning 'schemas' might not be as they are presented in National Curriculum linear learning models. Valuing the initiative of an individual to 'grow' their own knowledge in their own ways was a challenging view of young children's learning by stressing that learning does not always occur in adult-predicted ways. As a tutor in IIL, I do not expect to have all the answers but would seek to guide students to find ideas and explanations that they can probe for themselves to determine their validity for them personally; I get excited by student inquiries and findings.

Integral to developing both my own teaching and that of the teams of teachers I have led, has been reflection on significant experiences. Developing the inquiry approach in IIL, for myself and for students, has drawn inspiration from applying and interpreting my knowledge of the international early years perspectives which contain a strong action research element. When establishing a new nursery unit, I adapted the American HighScope approach to working with young children. The Plan-Do-Review cycle that is at the centre of the Weikart's Perry school research (www.highscope.org) reflects an action research model; it is a cycle the children have structured into the daily routine of their preschool environment. Each day when the children arrived at our nursery unit they would 'plan' with an adult what they would like to do that day using the resources that were always available for them and this was recorded on paper either as pictures or words. Later in the session, having carried out their 'plan' they would 'review' what they had done, how the resources had worked, how they had worked with others, what had helped them, what had been difficult, what they wanted to do next, etc. We carried out this review during 'snack time' with artifacts of learning being shared with discussion to promote a shared sense of valuing what children had done. Individual children drove the process with staff support. The HighScope approach saw this as central to enabling children to make decisions they take responsibly for; children see themselves as the drivers in their education so that they do not become overly reliant on others and fall into needing the support of prison or social service systems. A series of longitudinal studies by Weikart supported the development of the HeadStart programme in the USA, seeing positive early learning experiences as vital to a child's development. I found a tangible transformation in children from age three, on arrival, to age 5 when they moved into the primary school, regarding attributes such as independence and confidence or *'dispositions'* as Margaret Carr (2001) has written about them. Having helped children as young as four years old to show these characteristics, I recall a moment of intense frustration during my initial experience of IIL1. Some students appeared to be apathetic and negative towards what I thought were the wonderful, open learning opportunities which IIL was offering. My frustration boiled over in a discussion with colleagues, when I said *'My four-year-olds showed more independence than these students!'*.

As a primary teacher I'd always taken the view that my teaching was a *work in progress*. I was continually developing my insights into the whole primary curriculum, and particularly into cross-curricular links such as in environmental studies or links between mathematics and geographical skills. This approach transferred itself to my work in initial teacher education at several institutions – most particularly under the inspired leadership of Len Marsh at Bishop Grosseteste College. Within its strong, active, workshop approach to cross-curricular learning in primary education, students engaged in learning processes of their own and alongside those of the children, using investigative approaches. Len Marsh's (1970) book *Alongside the Child in the Primary School* influenced me as both a novice teacher and then a teacher educator because the children's responses to learning experiences were documented and valued as the stepping stones in moving personal learning forward. The real world of the environment and range of symbolic representations were explored, such as observational drawing, poems, clay or textile work, to focus thinking so that questions could emerge and be examined, often through peer collaboration. This established the importance of 'time' for learning processes to work creatively and has supported me in being patiently 'watchful' of the students' learning in IIL.

This sense of an ongoing learning journey underpinned my approach to initial teacher training students. Alongside Peter Ovens, I developed an action research module for students to inquire into their own teaching. Students would initiate personal action research on questions such as, *'How can I help ... to concentrate better?'* or *'How can I help some groups of children to work better together?'* or *'How can I support learning by improving my working with teaching assistants?'*. These questions often gave rise to insights that were both totally unexpected and complex; students found that the higher attaining groups felt 'left out' because they did not work with a teaching assistant, some children said they had to fidget to think or that if they looked out of the window it helped them to concentrate, others said they hated the carpet area as they did not like sitting cross-legged but teachers thought they enjoyed its informality. By spending time finding out what children's ideas were through focused observations and interviews, the ideas of novice teachers were challenged and set a strong basis for inquiry being part of their approach to research-orientated teaching. This reflective professional practice informed my decision to work on the IIL module for the new BACS degree to help to create the inquiry approach from the outset of the students' degree programme.

Personal reflection based on observation of children's learning has fostered my holistic awareness of how personal and emotional dimensions interacted with the intellectual in an often complex and unpredictable way. I had seen the impact that motivation and confidence could have on children and sought to acknowledge this openly in the IIL modules in allowing for sustaining personal support through developing both autonomy and collaboration based on noting significant events. My growing sense of the dual importance of the personal and the social dimensions of learning was extended during my work in nurseries by the challenging ideas of Malaguzzi and his co-founder Carlina Rinaldi (2006) in the early childhood centres in Reggio Emilia, Italy and by Margaret Carr (2001) in New Zealand. Some ideas from Reggio Emilia are that:

> Learning does not proceed in a linear way, determined and deterministic, by progressive and predictable stages, but rather is constructed through advances, standstills, and 'retreats' that take many directions. The construction of knowledge is a group process. Each individual is nurtured by the hypotheses and theories of others, and by conflicts with others, and advances by co-constructing pieces of knowledge with others through a process of confirmation and disagreement. Above all, the conflicts and disturbance force us to constantly revise our interpretive model and theories on reality ... theory and practice should be in dialogue, two languages expressing our effort to understand the meaning of life. When you think, it's practice; and when you practice, it's theory.
>
> (Rinaldi 2006: 132)

Through the constant approach of observation–interpretation–documentation there is a valuing of subjectivity in ongoing decision making about how to support the learning of individual children. This method of pedagogical documentation is mirrored by Margaret Carr (2001) in the specific approach taken in documenting 'learning stories' to assess learning that is related to the New Zealand 'Te Whariki' early childhood education curriculum with its focus on learning dispositions such as courage and curiosity, trust and playfulness, perseverance, confidence and taking responsibility. The noticing of detail and use of documentation, especially photography and noted interaction, by children, parents and practitioners jointly helps to unravel the learning process and support its development. This strong focus on *joint* interpretation and linking observation and interpretation requires those involved to be sensitive to the importance of detail and open-ended time to allow depth to develop. For instance, doing a presentation about learning styles in IIL has a limited value if the student is not testing out these ideas and reflecting on their appropriateness to them as individuals in different contexts. The information-collection phase was often easy for students but they frequently conveyed a resistance to the self-monitoring of the actual *practice* phase that we as tutors valued so much, with them revisiting ideas and modifying their use for their own purposes so that genuine learning progress might be made. The importance of these *'noticings'* (Mason 2002) for professional development through 'disturbances' that others can provoke has therefore led me to emphasise both the intrapersonal and the interpersonal reflective processes in IIL sessions (as explored in Chapter 6).

Most recently, awareness of the impact of learning styles has provoked me to consider a wider range of strategies for students to use to develop their reflection through their strongest medium rather than a pre-established required approach. Again, the impact of Malaguzzi's ideas is strong, such as his idea of 100 Languages (Edwards *et al.* 1998), which challenges me to value different approaches to learning using a range of symbolic representations. In every setting in Reggio Emilia, Italy there are *pedagogistas* supporting groups of teachers exploring issues of children's learning and *atelieresta* who support the symbolic exploration with purpose-built art studios. This parallels the issue that tutors in IIL have raised, 'How best to document students' reflection?'. Some tutors naturally felt drawn to writing in Jotters but we have widened our response to student initiatives to document verbally, as diagrams or as pictures. Using a series of cartoons about learning, showing learning as a recipe, as ripples in a pond and so on, we ask students to consider other metaphors for learning. They come up with ideas such as a journey, light bulb going on, a hurdle, being taught. Accessing and representing ideas visually was found to provoke discussion with students wrestling with finding effective language to explain their ideas. Other students work most positively with word-processing their Jotters and putting them into a book; the ability to redraft their thoughts rather than writing them down 'correctly' in a handwritten document often feels more reassuring and familiar to them. Other students developed their preference for an oral approach to reflection and 'think aloud' using a Dictaphone to record reflections. As tutors, we respect students' varying strengths but also challenge them to try alternative approaches to provoke *'disturbance'* (Mason 2002) that can support learning.

Further recognition of the holistic nature of learning has come through acknowledging the emotional dimension of learning that has emerged as a strong feature of students' learning during IIL modules. In the Riveting Read, responses are often powerful, with ideas such as *'a family member recommended* A child called "It". *I have never felt an emotion like this from a written text before and I found it quite difficult to read in parts'*. Many students get a similar response to reading about racial issues in the trilogy written by Malorie Blackman that captures their involvement from the first book *Noughts and Crosses* or entering the world of a boy with Asperger's Syndrome in Mark Haddon's *The Curious Incident of the Dog in the Night-time*. We value books which have opened up issues; for example, reading *Dibs, In Search of Self* (Axline 1964) prompted several students to specifically ask to do a work-placement alongside play specialists, having found a strong motivation to explore that specific area of work with children. Underpinning this motivation is the students' recognition that their own sense of well-being will impact on their own learning and that, as professionals, we have a wide sense of having a responsibility for nurturing the well-being of others. As early years practitioners this resonates strongly with the ideas of Fere Laevers (1998) who identifies and assesses the close link between well-being and involvement in learning activities with young children in his research with experiential learning in early years settings in Belgium. In IIL, building a sense of well-being through reflective practice has been fraught when students see reflection from a deficit or judgemental viewpoint rather than as a process of empowerment or emancipation. Their comments convey '*it is a challenge, which can be daunting, especially allowing yourself to think about negative areas, which in most cases I would generally choose not to think about too deeply*'. Building confidence has been a key aspect of our action planning to support students in taking a risk with their metacognition so that they move on from initial inquiries that often met the needs of 'others' to looking more directly at themselves and personal issues with a stronger sense of 'involvement'.

Taking a broad perspective on my personal action research within IIL I can monitor my attempt to try to overcome my frustration with an education system in which children set off as confident, competent learners at the age of 3 but where, by the age of 19, many of these positive dispositions seem to have been squashed in some students. I have listened to what students say during IIL1 sessions about their learning at school. I have reflected on my knowledge of, for instance, the growth of formalisation and segmentation of the Literacy Hour in primary schools and other increases in teacher direction across a system dominated by tests and league tables. I have developed a better picture of the challenge posed to many students by the contrasting experience of IIL. My action research has focused on how to support them with a 'rebirth' which enables them to be 'reacquainted' with rich learning opportunities and to support them in feeling more empowered to guide this process themselves. I see this as crucial to their development in the BA in Childhood Studies as the reflective practitioners which children and families need to work with in a changing world. More generally, however, these dispositions are needed as part of all education. The Qualifications and Curriculum Authority (QCA 2011) states that:

> assessment for personal development and learning is central to citizenship and values education ... It has to do with a vision of what it is to be a citizen, with personally owned values, with hope and aspirations. It has to do with the negotiation of personal biographies with collective stories, with meaning making and personal growth trajectories over time. Essentially it has to do with the development of the dispositions, qualities and capabilities of effective lifelong learners.

There is clearly a reinvigorated focus on the importance of Personal Learning and Thinking Skills with Learning to Learn initiatives as part of the personalised learning agenda.

At the time of writing, school test results are showing a plateau. Some sections of the state secondary system which are experiencing severe pupil disaffection are moving towards an 'expanded view of learning' as developed by Guy Claxton and that I see as similar to that envisioned by IIL. I would like to see greater continuity in approaches to learning and more valuing of learning dispositions from the age of 3 onwards in the education system. It is something that IIL will need to respond to in the future.

A very significant in influence on my own approach to teaching has been Seymour Papert's (1980) *Mindstorms* research about children's use of LOGO on computers in the early days of computer use in schools, which emphasises education in a changing society to support transferrable and holistic learning based on reflection. It showed me as a teacher that:

- I would never know *everything*;
- the world was changing;
- children need to feel empowered to learn in new contexts;
- and that they would challenge themselves if placed in supportive learning contexts where they could take risks, explore and reflect on successes and failures.

I have tried to take this approach into IIL's approach by recognising, as Papert seems to, that:

> all skills will become obsolete except one, the skill of being able to make the right response to situations that are outside the scope of what you are taught in school. We need to produce people who know how to act when they are faced by situations for which they are not specifically prepared.
>
> (Papert cited in Claxton 1998)

The next generation of professionals working with children and families need these skills, these dispositions and this confidence to face new and challenging situations. IIL's personal inquiry approach has been aiming to give the scaffolding for intrapersonal and interpersonal learning (Gardner 1983) to occur, based on consideration of a wide range of evidence that can be observed, gathered and evaluated by professionals at personal, team and institutional levels.

Patricia Wallis

Having entered higher education later in life, I undertook an Open University degree while working as an administrator. My experiences as a mature, part-time student have influenced my approach to learning and teaching while the academic and professional specialisms I have developed have shaped my participation in this project. I agree with Carl Rogers' proposal that:

> The goal of education, if we are to survive, is the facilitation of change and learning. The only person who is educated is the person who has learned how to learn; the person who has learned how to adapt and change; the person who has realized that no knowledge is secure, that only the process of seeking knowledge gives a basis for security. Changingness, a reliance on process rather than on static knowledge is the only thing that makes any sense as a goal for education in the modern world.
>
> (Rogers 1969: 152)

Reflecting on my school years, I didn't particularly like school and I didn't consider myself to be very clever. I did what I needed to get through the yearly exams and I left at the age of 15, with certificates for 50 metres swimming and cycling proficiency and no idea what I wanted to do with the rest of my life. The careers lady secured me a job in an office at a local pharmaceutical company where I worked as on office junior for almost a year. For the next 10 years I drifted from one administrative job to another, never really feeling happy or secure in any of them. Then I saw an advertisement for an administrator in the school of education at the local polytechnic. If I am honest, the main attraction for me was that I would be able to walk to work. I applied and got the job. I worked with lecturers whose responsibility was to secure places for students' teaching practice and also with students in the student resource centre. I had always thought university was for 'clever' people, certainly not for a 'working class' girl like me. My friendship with one particular mature student changed my life: I'll call her Elsie. Having moved from her native Jamaica to England, married and raised four children, she had decided it was time to educate herself. The enjoyment of helping her own children with their homework had inspired her to become a teacher. As she was working towards a BA in Primary Education, she also encouraged me to study. I started evening classes studying English 'O' level. Elsie would meet me each week to talk about my work, always encouraging and enthusiastic. She taught me to enjoy learning. Fuelled by success, I joined another class the following year and the year after that. Learning had become a hobby. Five 'O' levels and an 'A' level later, I enrolled at the Open University. During the six years it took to complete my degree, I became more involved in taught sessions at university. During this period some tutors encouraged me to present some of the content in their sessions and I found that I really enjoyed working with students. I gradually became more involved with the planning and preparation of taught sessions and then became a part-time tutor. Having had no formal teacher training, my style of preparation and teaching mainly reflected my own personal experiences and that of the tutors with whom I had been working. Interestingly, on reflection there were times when I was teaching in a style that, as a student, I personally had found inappropriate (e.g. transmission), but there I was, repeating the behaviour of others even though I knew it wasn't always the right method for all learners. I loved the challenge of creating practical learning activities for students and would do this wherever I could, but I felt I lacked the skills or the pedagogical know-how to develop this method further.

Away from work I was becoming involved in teaching dog agility and animal behaviour, obtaining a Post Graduate Advanced Diploma in Companion Animal Behaviour Counselling at Southampton University. This also taught me so much about myself as a learner, notably how to accommodate full-time working, part-time teaching and competing most weekends at dog shows. I enjoyed all these varied aspects for different reasons so my motivation and enthusiasm never waned.

I often reflected on my practice as a teacher. It seemed to have a more subject- and tutor-led style than that of some colleagues. My sessions would run like clockwork with every activity timed. Sometimes I would have to cut students off in the middle of an activity to keep track with the session plan. Although I wanted to change my practice, I was not confident enough to do so. I decided it was time to learn more about teaching, I began a Post Graduate Certificate in Higher Education (PGCHE) course. I enjoyed learning more ways of preparing and teaching and started to reflect more on my practice, to re-evaluate my methods. At this time, I was invited to join the Inquiry Into Learning modules team with Peter and Frances. It sounded very different to anything that I had taught before and I was very interested. They suggested I join one or two of their sessions before deciding. I loved the way that the sessions seemed to flow seamlessly, the two hours simply flying by. In the reflective journal I was keeping for my PGCHE course I wrote:

> I am somewhat surprised to be involved in the Inquiry Into Learning modules. To be honest I haven't had a lot of time to think about the commit-ment I've taken on. I hope I haven't bitten off more than I can chew. After sitting in on a couple of the taught sessions my first reaction is that the style of teaching is a lot different to the one that I've developed. I'm used to a tutor-led approach where I've known exactly what the students are going to do minute by minute. I've had total control of the pace and content, whereas this approach is more student-led. It feels more relaxed for both the student and the tutor. This surprised me because I would have thought I'd find the lack of control uncomfortable. Perhaps I'm not such a control freak after all! Whilst observing the first session I found myself feeling relaxed and at ease. I talked with the students as they worked through tasks. I found myself sharing experiences with them. It was good to feel as if you were helping them express themselves in such a secure environment.

Working on these modules has completely changed my approach to learning and teaching. Like some of the students in transition from school to higher educa-tion, I found changing my teaching/learning style difficult, but I loved the chal-lenge of developing and experimenting. As Gillie Bolton puts it:

The responsibility of uncertainty is uncomfortable, until the excitement of discovery takes hold.

(2010: 70)

The unpredictability of some of the sessions is itself a challenge. But I feel that I learn so much from providing the students with opportunities to reflect and talk openly about their learning and understanding. After each taught session Peter, Frances and myself would meet up and discuss how the session had gone. I found this really helpful and my contributions were always received with unconditional positive regard.

Although I know that the transition into higher education is a difficult time for some students, I was initially surprised that so many seem to lack a general motivation and enthusiasm to learn. I was even more surprised that many of them seem to lack interest in reading. I noticed that the realisation of how much they are expected to read had come as a shock to some Year 1 students. So I thought the Riveting Read task (see Chapter 4) would be a good way of meeting their needs. However, I had not prepared for students to choose children's books from the Mr Men series, as two students did. When asked about their choice they stated that they didn't like reading and the books are short! Of course, these students might have misunderstood the task and were too embarrassed to admit this in class. Full details of the Riveting Read can be found in Chapter 4. Some students revealed that this was the first time they had read a book from cover to cover. Several said how much they had enjoyed the reading and were glad that they had been asked to do it. The ensuing discussion explored the many reasons why we might read, which in turn led to talk and an activity about writing for different audiences/purposes.

It is clear that technology is impacting more on our everyday lives. Using my personal interest in Information Technology, I have helped to develop aspects of IIL modules and wish to continue to embrace technological changes for students' positive and rewarding learning experiences. For example, I find it interesting that although many Year 1 students appear to be reluctant readers, they often say they can spend three or four hours each evening on a social networking programme such as Facebook or Instant Messenger. Why do they have the motivation and ability to concentrate on this for such a long time but lack these qualities when asked to read a book chapter? There is now a growing number of publishers producing books online (e-books) rather than on paper. I wonder what our students will think about this? When talking to students about reading academic texts on screen, they all tell me they prefer to read academic work on paper. This is something that really interests me and I am currently researching this area for my MA dissertation.

Working with students through these transitional stages of becoming a university student is rewarding for me. I guess I do see myself as their 'Elsie'. I hope they see me as supportive and encouraging and I certainly make every effort never to dismiss or respond negatively to any comment they make. Inevitably, I get frustrated when less motivated students seem to waste their time and, perhaps, their parents' money, or perhaps spoiling the learning experience of others in the seminar group who do want to learn. However, I also think that sometimes we can only be successful learners when we are ready and want to learn. This is how I approach my dog training, I do believe that *they will learn when they are ready*. I find that when they are not focusing, it is better to leave that activity until another time. I do believe that, if I had gone to university straight from school, I too might have wandered and wasted time. I had to wait until I was ready and eager to learn, to develop and challenge myself as an individual.

As someone who enjoys the continuing challenge of unravelling and changing my understanding of what learning is, I have learned not to make rigid assumptions about students' abilities. Also, I have found that I can adapt to change and am not phased by an apparent lack of structure in teaching plans, because I am confident in what I am doing and how I am doing it. This provides me with the same sense of security that previously my session timetable/plan did, enabling me to focus on their processes of learning rather than my teaching of knowledge, reflecting in and on my practice, to develop and improve.

Cyndy Hawkins

When I joined IIL it was like a breath of fresh air to be part of a team with progressive ideas about learning, one that 'breaks the mould'. My experiences of teaching have been varied, beginning with teaching early years and primary school children in the 1970s, when inquiry and collaborative learning were fundamental to all that we did with children, thanks to the influences of Jerome Bruner and Lev Vygotsky (1978). I considered myself very much a facilitator of learning, helping children to learn for themselves. Then, as I moved on to teach young people and adults in the 1980s and 1990s, I found curriculum content had a much more prescribed, product-based character, emphasising outputs rather than processes. This trend continued, with more use of *standards* to define valid learning, gradually changing how we teach, even though it is against our own philosophy. My teaching was unable to be so creative in responding to the students' spontaneous and incidental learning, which so often provide valid insights and new perceptions on a topic. I felt that I was teaching towards assessments rather than providing an open-ended learning environment where there was opportunity for inquiry. I turned into a teacher who transmits knowledge, and tests declarative understanding through prescribed learning outcomes, rather than supporting students to learn how to learn. It was against my values as a teacher to regard students as in a deficit position, waiting to be filled up with knowledge by me, the expert, when in fact I am far more comfortable working with students as co-researchers in understanding learning.

I have struggled to address the sometimes polarised views about the aims of education. Is it mainly about training people to take part in society, concentrating on society's needs and the disciplines of study? Or is education about learning to learn, no matter what is the subject or context? It seems fundamental to me that if we know how to learn, we can tackle almost anything. Therefore it was like making a rediscovery, when I came across the IIL approach, like meeting an old friend! Its philosophy influenced me to re-establish my approach to students and their learning in a new context. I now embark on a journey of learning like a pioneer, discovering a new place as if for the first time, with all of the excitement and trepidation that brings. It enables me to see how students have been adversely affected by imposed, narrow focuses of learning and empowers me to challenge the restrictions. I agree with commentators who have used terms like 'dumbing down' and 'passive learners'. At the heart of the matter, I think that students have been subjected to a dependency model of learning: dependent upon teachers, and upon the resources they are given, with little emphasis on their own responsibility in the process, to develop their control, their autonomy. This is why IIL can give back the power of learning to learners. I think we should help our students to value the uncertainty of life and prepare them for change in thinking, change in knowing, constructing and deconstructing ideas to celebrate and forge new discoveries.

'Cooking up' IIL

When asked what I think is different about the Inquiry Into Learning approach to learning, I think about cooking and compare it to creating an ideal recipe for different tastes. In this analogy, educational practice can seem like a recipe: a tried and tested technique that works to some extent for some people. However, in IIL, the principal ingredients are less traditional and *the* ideal recipe is yet to be devised. In fact, ingredients can be cooked in different ways, because the IIL dish changes to suit each diner, who is not only the cook but also the foremost critic of a meal. The experience of making IIL *dishes* is that some diners relish the taste and ask for more, some eat it because they are hungry and some hate it and want their money back!

Like all analogies, comparing the IIL approach to a cooking process has its attractions to some people in certain situations, bearing in mind its limitations. It acknowledges that students' learning experiences, like their taste for food, have old favourites, and believes that it is good to become independently able to satisfy yourself as a diner. This will necessitate cooks/diners to experiment with recipes and ingredients. The IIL tutor, as the master chef, does not do all the cooking for everyone all the time, but expects students to become apprentices to the dual role of creator and consumer of learning. The expectation of a creative role is a significant change for students who are used to consuming passively only what they have had served to them.

The first couple of weeks of teaching the IIL1 module to a new group are akin to the cooking scenario, introducing students to *different ways of learning*. Some are adventurous and experimental, while others show a palate which appears to have been dulled by bland and mediocre food. Starting IIL may seem like a sudden change to an untried, untested and uncertain diet, which needs a subtle approach to cultivate appreciation of the flavours and textures on offer. A taster is offered, with a little persuasion to *add your own ideas* or *look for some alternatives that suit you*. The aim is to secure sufficient initial involvement and enjoyment to devise your own. And it is fine if doing a safe recipe doesn't go to plan, because this is sometimes where the best learning happens and the tastiest food appears. Help is given to *reflect* on the *relationships* of the ingredients, the appropriateness or skill of the methods and foster *resourcefulness* to have a better go. We want both cognitive and affective domains to be engaged with courage, faith and trust in collaboration. In anticipation of the fear of criticism and perceived failure, we try to create safe, non-judgmental, trial and error approaches, to learn from things that did not work out and cultivate *resilience*. This is one of the four 'Rs' of Guy Claxton's (2002) *Building Learning Power*. The other three are *resourcefulness*, *reflection* and *relationships*. As non-hierarchical qualities, they can be called upon singly or together at any stage in an IIL learning inquiry to empower and sustain it. It is vital that the student feels themselves not at the periphery looking in, but at the centre of the learning process, expanding outwards.

When I teach IIL, I want all knowledge to be valued but also challenged by students, rather than passively accepted. Changing metaphors, I want students to learn that the currency of knowledge is open to change, so that its present state is no indication of where it may extend. Expansive learning (Claxton 2006) creates a *border-less* realm in which knowledge continuously flows between lay and expert opinion. I want them to see themselves as experts of their own learning. Rather than seeing learning like a *ladder* with a beginning and end fixed at particular points, the idea of life-long learning *expects* knowledge and skills to become outdated. Some students seem aghast at this, thinking that once they have *done their time*, there will be an end to learning. Other students need little convincing of the value of new ideas about learning and recognise the implications for transference and progression.

Our emphasis on students' work with learning partners is not meant to discourage independent learning or independent thinking. Collaborative learning relies on creative and innovative individuals to contribute their distinct ideas for collective benefits. We want IIL students to be active members of as a learning community environment, to share, reflect on and evaluate worthwhile things. We are aware that, having the aim to improve practice, action research can be perceived to assume a deficit model: that an externally defined, ideal form of a learner is one to which present practice should be made to conform. This could appear to invalidate appreciation of what is already successful. For such students, instead of emphasising the starting point as a problem, fault or deficit, we take an explicitly appreciative inquiry approach. This is advocated by David Cooperrider and Suresh Srivastva (1987), who start inquiry from the *strengths* of something rather than the *weaknesses*. Instead of students asking why something doesn't work, we encourage them to question how its successful features can be expanded. At the heart of appreciative inquiry is a dialogue of accomplishments. As a narrative-based process, it aligns with principles of IIL for reflection and non-judgmental communication, extending learning away from our expert gaze to where students explore their perceptions in unique ways, tolerating uncertainty through the fluidity of its approach.

Peter Ovens

Having been a teacher, in schools and in higher education (as a teacher educator) all my professional life, my interests, studies, enthusiasm and commitment to developing my teaching have produced the following values and beliefs. From a scientifically biased starting point, I grew to understand teaching in artistic and personal ways as well as rational ones. Moderating my needs for certainty and to have control, I came to see more clearly the moral dilemmas in teaching. Increasing enjoyment has come from inquiring into the uniqueness of each teaching-learning situation to work out afresh how to re-resolve dilemmas. Revisiting theories of person-centredness in education has affirmed some long-held values, deepened my awareness of learning how to learn and suggested positive ways forward in practice.

In my probationary year as a science teacher in an Inner London comprehensive school, I learned two personal principles of teaching. The inspector responsible for awarding my qualified teacher status observed me teach a class of disaffected, 'difficult', multicultural, 'bottom stream' school leavers in London. Their enthusiasm for learning had been spectacularly reignited by practical investigations of their own choice and design. Tense negotiations had established strict rules for their behaviour, in return for being trusted to work with living plants and animals, hitherto reserved for teaching high-ability pupils. I can still recall a burly African boy's dazzling smile as he observed, measured and documented the life cycle of the large flour beetles he was breeding, as part of learning about gathering and presenting evidence. Not only did I pass my test, but I realised the importance of a rich and stimulating learning environment for the inquiry-based teaching I favoured. The second principle emerging from this experience was the power of a teacher's positive regard for learners to stimulate their willingness to be positive towards their learning. In IIL, there is an infinite variety of learning challenges which students say they face, and I enjoy empathising with them, confident in the value of inquiring into them positively.

Moving to higher education, with responsibility for planning and teaching a new module in science education, I drew upon Open University materials to write objectives for a unit on exercise physiology. Eagerly following the 1970s trend, every session was planned with an exhaustive (and exhausting!) list of objectives for students' learning. My science education had encouraged me to value order, logic, clarity and thoroughness. Objectives seem to add rigour to planning set tasks. A warm glow of *control over the learning* came from watching a room full of students pedalling away on the cycle ergometers, carrying out the Harvard step test of fitness, measuring heart rate, blood pressure etc. It seemed that each task inexorably *caused* the achievement of my long list objectives. A third principle of good teaching, a 'scientific' kind of detailed planning, became established in my practice. But I began to notice that valuable parts of sessions, for me and some students, were our informal conversations about their ideas and thinking. As well as dutifully doing tasks and learning set concepts, some looked for connections with, for example, performance in athletics or experience of sport. They enriched my basic approach with their questioning and creativity. Students' independent thinking about applications and evaluations of the taught subject knowledge was outside the objectives in my plan, and at that stage in my development, they were too uncertain and uncontrollable to be a main aim of my teaching.

However, there was a sharply contrasting influence on my development. I was also learning about primary school education, because the college was training teachers for primary as well as secondary schools. I observed the openness and flexibility necessary in a nursery, to teach responsively and opportunistically. Young children can be wonderfully unpredictable and spontaneous! There is something *artistic* about skilful judgements, made in the moment and the situation, which enable a good teacher of young children to exploit learning opportunities in this way, *as well as* meeting preplanned objectives. They arise from unexpected things that the children say and do. As an example, one of my student teachers responded to the following questions that five-year-old children were asking about the garden snails she was helping them to observe: *'How fast can they go?' 'Why don't they have legs?' 'Do they have friends?' 'What do they live on?' 'Why does the shell have patterns?' 'Do they have sex?' 'How do they see?'* (Ovens 2004: 12). Through skilful, responsive and opportunistic dialogue to clarify the children's meaning, they were helped to sort out those questions which could be answered by closer looking, measuring or testing, from others which need to be answered by an expert person or book. Seeing how well five-year-olds can think for themselves when not restricted by teaching which adheres too closely to predictive plans and tight objectives, helped me realise that *teaching cannot cause learning.* On reflection, I was realising the contribution of what could be called scientific and artistic approaches to teaching. Feeling more competent with one, I became aware that its limitations might be ameliorated by the other. Also, my scientific background led me to assume that good teaching follows one clear model or theory. Not having found one, but reading about the *Dilemmas of Schooling* (Berlak and Berlak 1981) I realised there are many *dilemmas* about what counts as good practice. Since I realised that no single theory is sufficient, I eventually concluded that an integration of a range of 'scientific' educational theories and artistic awareness is needed in planning and in practice, to make teaching good. When asked what *the* theory of good teaching is, to apply it to someone's practice, my response has been to support their own improvement of what they most value in their contextualised practice by talking with them about observations of it and theories to discipline thinking about it and the professional dilemmas embedded in it, and then testing gradual, practical improvements in the realisation of their educational values. In IIL, I help students to clarify their expressed needs and aims in their learning and recast them into their action inquiries for improving their practice.

An example of a simple, ordinary *educational dilemma* which could arise in any classroom, not least in IIL, is 'What is the best/right thing do, when students chat when I think that they should be listening, either to me or to each other?'. If humorous, but pointed comments do not work, I might reprimand them. This may stop the talking, but may damage a cordiality which many students appreciate. Later, if I try to elicit students' thinking about key ideas, and there are no responses, I wonder if I have inhibited students' exploratory talk. Alternatively, I might tolerate quiet talking that is not a distraction, since it might be about the ideas to be learned. Later, if I find that some students do not understand, I may attribute this to them not having listened and wish I had been more strict. I used to see these kinds of dilemmas as problems which should have final, universal, rule-like solutions which a good teacher would know and apply in an automated way to all contexts. Now, I reflect more deeply about each dilemma's situation, and teach so as to develop contextualised improvements. I inquire into the situation. Following this example, I might eavesdrop on talk, to find out if it is social chat or helping learning. To assess students' understanding and evaluation of the task, I ask small groups: *'Do they think the task is worth doing?'* and, if so, *'Why? Do they find personal interest and relevance in the topic, the task and the resources?'* and, if so, *'What is interesting and relevant to them?'* and, if not, *'What kinds of things would be better?'* I see their perspectives and explore what they perceive to be mine. *'Do they understand what I am trying to develop? And how? And why?'*. Such inquiry depends on open and honest answers, which are more likely if the students trust a tutor's motivation and feel they are being treated with respect. Equally, it can encourage students to respect a tutor and to feel responsible for sustaining the trust being developed. These are much deeper qualities of the tutor–student relationship than mere cordiality. Through gaining better understanding, I develop improved learning and teaching. Students can be refreshingly natural and helpful in these situations, dispelling cynical and blaming types of views of students that can develop in a tutor's mind if not tested by inquiry. An undue 'distance' in tutor's and students' perceptions of each other can lead to blaming difficulties on each other, rather than sharing responsibility for them. Often, my inquiries revealed that apparent difficulties were due to a minor misunderstanding which was swiftly rectified and, occasionally, helped to unmask and illuminate more fundamental concerns and issues, including ones connected to important moral dilemmas like those listed below. An inquiry reaching this depth it is not only about my practice as a teacher, but also students' learning, my assessment philosophy, my central assumptions and values as an educator. It is about my curriculum planning.

1   Public knowledge versus personal knowledge – do I value the knowledge in, for example, textbooks as accurate, but usually impersonal, or do I value

personal knowledge that learners express, such as in their talk, even if less accurate, but linked to personal values, beliefs and individual significance?

2   Knowledge as content versus knowledge as process – do I value learning of facts and concepts of subject knowledge or the learning of the skills and thinking processes?

3   Extrinsic versus intrinsic motivation – do I value external rewards (and punishments) of the educational (or social) system to stimulate learning; or learners' creative and questioning thirst for knowing?

4   Knowledge as given versus knowledge as problematic – do I value fixed, clear, definite thinking about subject knowledge; or a tentative, sceptical, critical or doubtful way of thinking?

5   Learning is particulate versus learning is holistic – do I value establishing itemised 'basics' first, as firm foundations for big conceptual structures and then applying them to problems and inquiries; or learning through tackling whole problems or inquiries in real situations first, then learn the 'basics' in the context of understanding how they fit into the whole?

For each dilemma, I value both alternatives. The first epitomise conventional approaches, whereas the second alternative represents an antidote to the limitations of the first. But how do I overcome their apparent contradiction in practice? A feature that the second alternatives have in common is that they involve students in thinking critically and creatively for themselves. This is necessary to achieve Ronald Barnett's (1997) aims of higher education. I learned to recognise, reflect on and resolve these kinds of moral dilemmas in each new context, drawing on past experience and discussion of evidence with peers. There are usually features of a new situation to be noticed, which point my practice more towards one alternative in a dilemma as a first step. And then my latest teaching-cum-inquiry has got itself underway. For me, IIL is about students learning by inquiry how to be better learners, while I simultaneously refine my teaching to meet the needs of this group of students here and now by inquiry-cum-teaching.

About ten years ago, I was finding that I could engage students in critical, reflective discussion that included their *personal* knowledge. But when writing their assessed assignments, these achievements did not significantly affect what they saw as the inevitable necessity: to present only *public* knowledge as the admissible kind of content. There was a barrier to including what they thought and valued about their learning which my encouraging comments did not overcome; nor did my attempts to get students to write about their thinking in short pieces of course work linked to the final assignment. Discouraging a *surface approach* to learning had made progress but it had stalled. Nevertheless, deep immersion in my problem (said to be a precondition for recognising a solution) helped. When I heard about Richard Winter's idea of Patchwork Texts, I instantly saw it as a potential breakthrough and joined his project. Tinkering with my teaching practices alone had been insufficient. Curriculum change would be necessary. When I introduced the PT approach to a module for science specialist primary student teachers, almost miraculously, the dilemmas listed above ceased to be confined to planning and teaching, but were shared with students in the collaborative task of bringing all of their learning achievements to contribute to the assessed assignment. I have documented this work (Ovens 2003a and 2003b) and brought its ideas to IIL (see Chapter 9).

My interest in being a science educator was superseded by meeting the challenges of developing IIL, but I see ideas from science, including its history, philosophy and sociology, as relevant to education generally. I believe features of scientific ways of thinking, such as logical reasoning, objectivism and reductionism, are increasingly exerting an inappropriately large control over some human endeavours. Obsessive and dogmatic applications of technical rationalism by managerialist leaders produce decisions at too high a level of generality and at too great a distance from the action. In professional worlds, this can deny human sensitivity, damage professional relationships and overrule local knowledge and awareness of difference. A growing climate of conformity to others' centralised standards arouses my fear that *emergent objectives* and *responsive teaching* are perceived as rudderless relativism and self-indulgent subjectivity in the face of demands for objectively measured outcomes. A scientific background sensitises me to these features of education currently, in the United Kingdom.

Some of the most intriguing parts of my IIL teaching have been when students learn about themselves as learners. For example, in a learning inquiry about improving mental concentration by examining the environment for her learning, an IIL1 student described how she organised her study room one Saturday. Unsure about what would distract her attention, the mobile phone was on the desk but switched off; a curtain was drawn slightly to obstruct her view of students moving around outside, except when she leaned forwards; the computer had Facebook switched on but reduced from the main screen; books, notes, coffee and sweets were to hand. Following her action research plan, she then noted briefly what she was doing, thinking and feeling at regular intervals of about 20 minutes. A pattern which emerged from discussion with learning partners of this fresh experience of her focus was of someone choreographing for herself a dance between isolation and interactivity. Sometimes a potential distraction, such as the arrival of a text message, was ignored in favour of continued attention on study, while at other times it was attended to immediately. By reflection on many instances like these, she increased her awareness of a need to keep in *some* kind of contact with others, particularly after what felt like too long a period of concentration on work (the actual time varied) had elapsed. Conversely, as the time of lost attention accumulated: gazing, chatting or texting, she grew anxious. Instead of seeing this in a familiar frame of a battle between insufficiently determined will power and insidious distraction, her subjective experience was probed more deeply through discussion with learning partners. Words were sought for what would otherwise have remained mainly as intuitive images and sensations. *Losing oneself* in thoughtful study was not always a pleasant experience because it had connotations of being lost, having disappeared and become disconnected.

Tolerable for short times, it had to be balanced by reconnection. Other students did not experience this in exactly the same way but, easily recognising the difficulty, were able to empathise with it. One played with words: 'alone' and 'lonely' to explore feelings and another introduced 'hermit' and 'herd' to sharpen meanings. The inquiring student appeared to be increasing her self-accepting awareness of a tension between feelings of wanting to be part of her social group and a desire to be her individual self: trying to become an academically successful student. I thought about this learning in relation to the development of autonomy as a form of personal power in which a self-directed individual is free, because of an ability to control the extent to which they are influenced by experiences of people and events in their environment. The opposite is a person whose life is driven by external pressures or by internal needs to satisfy perceptions of what *should* or *ought* to be done, notably to please others. It seemed to me that at the centre of this inquiry was growth of this important area of personal autonomy.

Then I read a person-centred account of human nature, and found that '*autonomy*', a tendency to differentiate oneself as a self-governing entity from others, is seen to be connected to a tendency to be in harmony with others in their social group (among other 'superindividual' units) called '*homonomy*'. Together, they produce a sense of oneself as a whole organism (Tudor and Worrall 2006). This questioned my ideal of autonomy in a learner, which, on reflection, included a hidden *individualistic* element: using one's personal power to oppose interference from 'outsiders' or subdue them to make personal gain. But it is more consistent with my wider values and beliefs as an educator, to use a concept of autonomy in *becoming a reflective learner* (in IIL1, and in the context of IIL2, and *becoming a professional inquirer*) which is connected to homonomy. Personal power, from a person-centred perspective, is a force for the freedom of oneself and of others.

> People with power have no need to control, overpower or get their own way at the expense or cost of another. They are more likely to desire cooperation, collaboration and the organismic actualisation of the other. They are open to the experiential process of being with another, listening and understanding without feeling threatened. They are more willing to see what will emerge from any process when no final result is required other than the one which does emerge.
>
> (Embleton Tudor *et al.* 2004: 126)

Turning back to my understanding of this student's learning inquiry led me to reflect on her deeper motivations for balancing, in the way she did, her mental concentration on studies with the continuing relationships of all kinds, with her peers. Maybe she was learning to discriminate between an internal, compulsive need to please others and a judgement about how to express both autonomy and homonomy in this particular situation. My interpretation may not necessarily be accurate to her case, but it has certainly deepened my way of thinking about autonomy as an ideal in IIL, not with individualistic overtones but as the other, inseparable half of homonomy, making two qualities of being human, which are like the opposite sides of the same coin. It prompts me to look at the practice of learners for the Rogerian description of personal power given above (Rogers 1961) as well as a reconsideration of the concept of *mutualism* in the writing, for example, of Peter Kropotkin (1955). Similar conceptions of personal autonomy, emphasising cooperation with others, are appearing in medical and health services literatures, allied to the concept of *mutuality*, as a cooperative quality of professional relationships with knowledge, colleagues, patients and in society.

Afterword

We would like our accounts to be read from a Gadamerian view (see Bernstein 1983), that understanding is always in the process of coming into being. We have reflected on the values and biases derived from our personal dispositions and experiences. We have suggested how these prejudgements have contributed to progress in our practice of IIL. Elsewhere in the book, we show how we use them to reach out to the subjective meaning of others. Also, we have risked, tested and refined these prejudgements through our reflective dialogues with physical evidence of events, with the accounts of co participants and critical challenges of colleagues. Our claims of improved practice and understanding, each helping to explain the other, are relative to the values and beliefs underpinning our purposes in our context. We see the book as offering a *'projective model'* (Elliott 1990) by which our learning may become accessible to others. We hope there is sufficient vicarious experience and reflection of IIL for readers to form their own interpretations, so as to extend their own *'repertoire of cases'* (Schön 1983). Where our work accords broadly with their aims, values and beliefs, it may be suggestive of hypotheses, questions or forms of practice which could have recognisable links to their own context for action, with potential to improve their practice, or at least to test possibilities for improvement. It is the combination of all these things which makes our 'projective model'.

Questions for reflection on action research for professional and curriculum development to advance *learning how to learn* in other contexts

1   Does the programme or module provide good enough contexts in which tutors in the teaching team feel able, and have sufficient time, to share stories and give descriptions of critical incidents from their educational and professional biographical experience and reflection, which they regard as significant and relevant to discussion?

2   Do teaching team members know enough about each other's values, beliefs and biography to understand the prejudgements underlying their contributions to discussion?

3   Is there a sufficiently stable ethos of inquiry within the team to enable existing practice or proposed changes to be risked, tested and refined against fresh experience?

4   Are the personal, professional and academic differences between team members respected for their distinct contributions, while also transcended by a shared, common purpose, maybe held intuitively but deeply.

Chapter 11

Why Inquiry Into Learning?

This venture began ten years ago. We aimed to help students to learn how to learn at university and, above all, practise and develop their autonomy as learners. Where has our journey brought us? How do we reinterpret our purpose and how to achieve it? Reconsidering aims and means together, here are some concluding reflections, with fresh thinking about *why might an Inquiry Into Learning approach be relevant to today's contexts?* Since our understanding is embedded in our practice, these theoretical and philosophical answers are linked with the previous accounts of what we do.

In recent times, we have received encouraging comments from colleagues teaching in other programmes and at other universities. Naturally, we are gratified that their appreciation of the achievements of our best students is like our own. Many of our students, sometimes later rather than sooner, find and use to impressive effect the personal resources to grow considerably as learners, individually and collaboratively. We believe that the IIL approach has certainly not 'got in their way' of learning how to learn and we think it makes a positive difference for many. Reassuringly, colleagues also recognise the kinds of concerns which we associate with students who do less well and who do not like IIL. It is cathartic to share our dismay about the institutional and social factors which we think contribute to the difficulties. Colleagues often say that the IIL approach offers a fresh way of thinking about, and possibly acting in, their own situation, which combats their sense of powerlessness. We are all too aware, as teachers, that experiences of students who seem to reject, willfully misunderstand or just ignore our efforts to help them learn, can lower our morale and make us doubt our aims or competence to achieve them. A natural reaction is to become negative towards such students and blame them for the problem. We have our own self-esteem to nurture as well! The dilemma is between accepting that some 'have a *right* to fail', as it is sometimes put, and continuing to believe in the potential for good in every student. We *do* want more students to be even better learners, not only to improve retention statistics, boost the proportion of good degrees awarded so they get better jobs, enhance the reputation of the programme and the university; but also because we want these young people to gain learning qualities to enrich their lives and work from having been at university. We see ourselves as teachers of people as much as of subjects, because we believe we can *make a difference* to learners.

It may seem perverse to begin this chapter by looking at the problems and difficulties of learning how to learn in higher education. However, 'it is not by concentrating on the analysis of health that we cure our ills' (Stenhouse 1975: 83). Many tutors experience them to some extent and have their own diagnoses.

What is wrong?

As older people, we may be more prone to make critical judgements of younger people, nevertheless we do not look back at our own student days and see ourselves as having been model learners. Anyway, the world changes and, as teachers, we need to be aware of what kind of world is influencing young people's learning today. At the start of their programme, a large majority of our students seem to use processes of thinking which presume the following views of knowledge, how to relate to it and how to act as learners. Maybe it has always been like this to some extent, but we think it is increasingly prevalent and increasingly wrong for today's world and young people's future.

> Correct knowledge must be learned and appropriate behaviour internalised, so as to gain the rewards of assessment, qualification and, ultimately, employment. The system which produced this outcome is more like training than education. It has behaviourist values of predictability, conformity and control. They do not appear to be open to question. They bestow on learners a heavy dependency on authority and a tendency for a deep fear of failure. There is an apparently uncritical acceptance of a system which defines students as its quantified products, to be placed in a competitive market for employment. Such experience in school leads students to expect the same kind of social market ideology shaping higher education. In such a case, a degree programme would have a curriculum aiming for predefined knowledge and prespecified practical skills of instrumental value to the achievement of behaviouristically defined outcomes, which are in turn geared closely to getting work. Tutors would be technical operatives in the transmission, monitoring and testing of objectivised standards. They would be more 'service providers' than professional people. The expected (possibly demanded) 'student experience' would be the effective delivery of commodified achievement rather than being enabled to achieve autonomous powers of personal and professional development.

We may speculate on the historical, social and cultural contexts from which a perspective such as this may arise. For example, is there currently an undue influence of a business culture on the knowledge which is counted as useful and ways in which it is communicated and used? Does it, as John Gatto claims it does in the United States, induct children into economic values to be avid consumers and compliant employees? Attention turns in the next section in this chapter to the more important question for a designer of undergraduate programmes: 'What is good?. But for now, the question is: 'What is wrong?'.

It is to Gatto's analysis that we now turn. He was a New York City state school teacher for more than 30 years. His book entitled *Dumbing Us Down: The Hidden Curriculum of Compulsory Schooling* claims that compulsory schooling has nothing to do with education as it teaches young people to become a docile, malleable workforce to meet the growing, changing demands of corporate capitalism. His own educational vision is that people who live in a rapidly changing society need to be able to function comfortably with knowledge that increases at a dizzying rate and, to achieve this, a content-based curriculum is entirely inappropriate. Believing in self-motivation and self-assessment in learning, it is wrong that schools focus on external motivating factors, such as rewards and punishments for meeting goals set by others. Since he values communication of experiences, to collaborate, and to exchange information, *conversation* should be a central part of a sound education. He believes that people have an immense capacity for concentration and hard work when they are passionate about what they are doing and that schools must become far more tolerant of individual variation and far more reliant on self-initiated activities.

> Over the past 30 years, I've used my classes as a laboratory where I could . . . study what releases and what inhibits human power. During that time, I've come to believe that genius is an exceedingly common human quality, probably natural to most of us. I didn't want to accept that idea, far from it: my own training . . . taught me that intelligence and talent distribute themselves economically over a bell curve . . . The trouble was that the unlikeliest kids kept demonstrating to me at random moments so many of the hallmarks of human excellence: insight, wisdom, justice, resourcefulness, courage, originality, that I became confused. They didn't do this often enough to make my teaching easy, but they did it often enough that I began to wonder, reluctantly, whether it was possible that being in school itself was what was dumbing them down. Was it possible I had been hired not to enlarge children's power, but to diminish it? That seemed crazy, but slowly I began to realise that the [school] bells and the confinement, the crazy sequences, the age segregation, the lack of privacy, the constant surveillance, and all the rest of the national curriculum of schooling were designed exactly as if someone had set out to prevent children from learning how to think and act, to coax them into addictions and dependent behaviour.
>
> (Gatto 2002: xxxv)

Drawing on his extensive experience, and his desire to question and test assumptions, John Gatto identifies seven ways in which he believes learning is prevented in his school system.

1   *Confusion*: a curriculum dividing knowledge into many little parcels taught in unrelated ways.
2   *Test scores*: to label children and become self-fulfilling prophecies.
3   *Indifference*: I teach children not to care too much about anything … when the bell rings I insist they drop whatever it is we have been doing and proceed quickly to the next subject. They must turn on and off like a light switch … Bells inoculate each undertaking with indifference. (p. 6)
4   *Emotional dependency*: by stars and ticks, smiles and frowns, prizes and disgraces, I teach kids to surrender their will to the predestined chain of command. Rights may be granted or withheld by any authority without appeal. (p. 6)
5   *Intellectual dependency*: good students wait for a teacher to tell them what to do. This is the most important lesson of all: we must wait for other people, better trained than ourselves, to make the meanings of our lives. Successful children do the thinking I assign to them with a minimum of resistance and a decent show of enthusiasm. Curiosity has no important place, only conformity. Bad kids fight this, even though they lack the concepts to know what they are fighting, struggling to make decisions for themselves about what they will learn and when they will learn it. Good people wait for an expert to tell them what to do. It is hardly an exaggeration to say that our entire economy depends upon this lesson being learned. (p. 8)
6   *Provisional self-esteem*: our world wouldn't survive a flood of confident people very long, so I teach the kids self-respect should depend on expert opinion. My kids are constantly evaluated and judged. Self-evaluation, the staple of every major philosophical system that ever appeared on the planet, is never considered a factor … People need to be told what they are worth. (p. 10)
7   You can't hide. I teach students that they are always watched, that each is under constant surveillance by me and my colleagues. There are no private spaces for children; there is no private time. Disloyalty to the idea of schooling is a devil always ready *to find work for idle hands*.

(Gatto 2002: 2–10)

Through talking to our own students, we can judge if and, if so, how this analysis relates to them.

A school run on these lines deserves to be called *psychopathic* in Gatto's estimation and what he calls the *pathological* effects of such schools is to tend to make children:

- *indifferent to the adult world*: nobody wants children to grow up these days, least of all the children themselves, and who can blame them?
- *have almost no curiosity*: what little they do have is transitory. They cannot concentrate for very long, even on things they choose to do
- *have a poor sense of the future*: of how tomorrow is inextricably linked to today
- *ahistorical*: they have no sense of how the past has predestined their own present, limited their choices, shaped their values and lives
- *cruel to each other*: they lack compassion for misfortune, they laugh at weakness, they have contempt for people whose need for help shows too plainly
- *uneasy with intimacy or candour*: they cannot do with genuine intimacy because of a lifelong habit of preserving a secret inner self inside a larger outer personality made of artificial bits-and-pieces of behaviour borrowed from television or acquired to manipulate teachers. Because they are not who they represent themselves to be, the disguise wears thin in the presence of intimacy; so intimate relationships have to be avoided
- *materialistic*: following the lead of school teachers who materialistically grade everything and television mentors who offer everything in the world for sale
- *dependent, passive, and timid in the presence of new challenges*: this timidity is frequently masked by surface bravado or by anger or aggressiveness, but underneath is a vacuum without fortitude.

(Gatto 2002: 27–28)

He uses harsh language and we need not treat this list as a prediction about students we meet, much less as a guide for what to expect in any individual. But, like other distillations of a lot into a little, we can keep it in mind as a possible resource for the interpretation of actual situations in which we find ourselves, to sensitise our noticing and questioning. If we encounter these characteristics, we are better able to imagine what kind of school experiences could have played a part in their formation.

Before leaving this diagnosis of what can be wrong, we can consider John Gatto's advice:

In theoretical, metaphorical terms, the idea I began to explore was this one: that teaching is nothing like the art of painting, where, by the addition of material to the surface, an image is synthetically produced, but more like the art of sculpture, where, by the subtraction of material, an image already locked in the stone is enabled to emerge. It is a crucial distinction.

When I was trying to decide what to say to you that might make my experience as a schoolteacher useful, it occurred to me that ... what I do that is right is simple to understand: I get out of kids' way, I give them space and time and respect.

(Gatto 2002: xxxviii)

This analysis is not about transferring blame for our students' difficulties from them to their teachers while they were at school. We often find school teachers in Britain are just as critical of these difficulties and disappointments as John Gatto in the USA. Teaching which draws out the good which is believed to be there also depends on not creating or perpetuating the kinds of obstacles listed above.

What is good?

Any approach to *learning how to learn* is based upon views of what learning is and what counts as knowledge, which are in turn based on some kind of ultimate sense of human nature. It is to Carl Rogers that we turn for inspiration about this because he applied his person-centred approach to understanding human nature not only to the development of a distinctive kind of psychotherapy but also to understanding learning and teaching. If John Gatto's perspective can help us to understand students' prior experiences as possible factors in their present expectations about learning, Carl Rogers' ideas can help us to work constructively on the potential for good.

In *Freedom to Learn* (1994) Rogers emphasises similar qualities of relationship to those advocated by Gatto. A climate of trust nourishes curiosity, stimulates participation in decision making, helps students to value themselves, and builds their confidence and self-esteem. His image of learning involves the whole person, not just *from the neck up* (p. 35) having qualities of a self-initiated, *reaching out from within*, towards what is personally significant and pervasive to the self, engaging in personal meaning-making, with an internal sense of what is valuable. *Whole person learning* combines logical, factual and linear qualities of the traditional, orderly, cognitive, left brain, masculine image of learning, with the person's own purpose, imagination and intuition. Building personal *freedom to learn* uses problems that are perceived by learners as real, stimulating their intrinsic motivation. This is planned not with objectives but specifications of conditions for learning: qualities of relationships, collaborative inquiry, richness of resources, significance of projects, peer teaching and self-assessment. The design of IIL matches these principles.

Dominant theories of learning lack explicit assumptions about being human. But in Carl Rogers' psychology, a person is in a process of *becoming*, through interaction with the world as they see it. The motivational drive for behaviour is the *tendency to actualise*: the quality of a person as an organism which promotes activity not only for survival, but also for learning and development. Internal conditions for its (unconscious) operation in a person are fostered by external conditions of relationship with significant other persons, such as for a student, their peers and tutors. Conditions include genuineness, openness, caring, acceptance, respect and prizing of each other, using ways of expressing one's own ideas and feelings which do not impose themselves on the other person, and trying to understand how the other person feels about and understands their world. Rogers claims that shared experience enables persons in such a relationship to: explore more deeply, discover previously hidden characteristics, increase acceptance rather than denial of difficulties, value oneself and other persons more, increase self-awareness, immediacy of experiencing, enable more genuineness towards other persons, express oneself with more openness, be less reliant on absolutist views and more willing to think tentatively, and move towards confident reliance on an internal locus of evaluation. The tendency to actualise is not conceived as inherently good in a moral sense, but it can be seen to be good for *learning how to learn* as a springboard for how to address what is wrong.

A person-centred approach assumes a student is to be trusted to take and be responsible for, self initiated action, intelligent choice and self-direction, to be a critical learner, acquire knowledge relevant to solving problems, adapt flexibly and intelligently to new problems, cooperate and work not for the approval of others but for their own socialised purposes. Having asserted the potential for good learning inherent in a person, Rogers claims that '*We cannot teach another person directly; we can only facilitate his learning*' (Rogers 1951). As Gatto says, we get out of such a student's way and enable them to learn for themselves. A misinterpretation of Rogers and Gatto would be that teachers are not needed because everything comes from the learner. With simple learning, of course another person is needed (for example, to *tell* a child what is the conventional spelling of a word which is consistently misspelt). But learning complex things is a process to which only the learner can ultimately bring key contributions to success, notably motivation and awareness, which occur in *enabling* environments and relationships.

But what is Rogers' view of a student who does not seem to show such a positive approach to learning? And what can any teacher do in such a situation?

Rogers' theory addresses effects on a learner of consistently having the positive regard of a significant other person withheld unless their requirements are met. The learner's positive self-concept and self-regard depend on fulfilling the conditions set by the other person, which can become an internalised *condition of worth*. A sense of self-worthlessness can be routinely provoked by situations in which there is fear of failing to meet this or another person's conditions of this kind. For example, a teacher's repeated, hasty and insensitive treatment of spelling errors by a learner who may be oversensitive to this aspect of their writing, may create the expectation that they are unworthy of esteem by the teacher, or anyone, regardless of effort, for their spelling. This can develop into a self-fulfilling prophecy that '*I am no good at spelling*'. Lacking confidence to improve, the learner feels doomed to make more errors, and does so. If their tendency to actualise enables an awareness and acceptance of a difficulty, a learner creates ways to overcome it. Otherwise, defensiveness maintains a self-concept as a *'rotten speller'* which resists rational, external attempts to overcome it. Negative conditions of worth which have become established in a person's self-concept as a learner may present obstacles to the functioning of the tendency to actualise and distort learning.

Why is a person-centred approach helpful?

This way of understanding difficulties with learning reveals hidden, emotional, relational and personal factors to complement the explicit, cognitive, logical ones. A teacher attends to the learner as a whole person, assessing how they perceive the personal, purposeful, relational and emotional contexts of learning. Addressing a learning difficulty about which the learner has a negative condition of worth, requires the teacher to avoid making a rational challenge to the learner's self-concept. Telling them they are wrong to believe they can't do it does not work. It will not be heard as it is meant because the learner will deny and/or distort the message. Even the teacher's wish to do helpful things like re-presenting what is to be learned using a fresh approach, with different language, new resources or a more interesting task, etc. must wait. The learner needs to be listened to empathically, in a trusting, relaxed, non-threatening relationship, so as to empower the *tendency to actualise* to recognise and accept the difficulty. Their negative self-concept may then soften and become more open to possibilities of change.

Quotations of an early piece of Rogers' writing about learning are presented in Box 11.1. They are set alongside paraphrased examples of our own students' perspectives on an aspect of their learning in the Inquiry Into Learning 1 module. They are closely based on spoken and written evidence we have gathered in our research. These are, in turn, set alongside a way of understanding the student's perspective using Rogers' theory.

Box 11.1 Comparative examples of aspects of students' learning

Carl Rogers' theory (with explanatory comments on concepts in brackets)	Examples of different IIL students' perspectives on an aspect of their learning based on evidence	A tentative interpretation
'A person learns significantly only those things which he perceives as being involved in the maintenance of, or enhancement of, the *structure of self*.' (This is the person's set of beliefs and values regarding who they are and what they are like: the self-concept.)	Somehow I just knew that the reflective journal would be the key to becoming a better learner, even if it did seem unusual and was something I'd never done before.	Here, a student intuitively senses that a new task will be helpful because it is compatible with her image of herself as someone who is not threatened by writing reflectively about her learning. Even though she hasn't done it before in such a situation, she is able to assimilate the experience into her *self* and enhance its structure. She feels positively about having a go.
'Experience which, if assimilated, would involve a change in the organisation of self tends to be resisted through *denial* or *distortion of symbolisation*.' (*Denial* is not perceiving properly something that has been experienced and *distortion of symbolisation* is changing its meaning to reduce its perceived threat to the self-concept.)	When they told us about the reflective journal we have to keep I was very confused because they didn't tell us how to do it or when to do it. I walked away from the lecture feeling very confused and lost.	This student sees herself as able to respond dutifully to close direction. She did not seem to hear the direction which was offered. She feels unable to adapt to an unfamiliar challenge or risk making a response that might/ might not be acceptable. To protect her image of herself in an unsafe situation, she may either *deny* to her conscious awareness the direction which was given by the tutor or she may *distort* it as *incomprehensibly vague*.
'The structure and organisation of self appears to become more rigid under threat.'	The idea of becoming an independent thinker was very daunting for me and seemed like a concept that was way out of my reach and so this heightened my worry about this module.	This seems like a consolidation of the perceived unsafe-ness of the IIL situation, that it expects her to achieve something that she believes to be personally unattainable, prompting feelings of helplessness.

Continued overleaf

Box 11.1 **Continued**

Carl Rogers' theory (with explanatory comments on concepts in brackets)	Examples of different IIL students' perspectives on an aspect of their learning based on evidence	A tentative interpretation
'Experience which is perceived as inconsistent with the self can only be assimilated if the current organisation of self is relaxed and expanded to include it.'	Over the past couple of weeks I have noticed a change in my efficiency and enthusiasm as a learner. Who would have thought that eating properly before sessions and getting a good night's sleep would have had such an impact?	A student's initial scepticism that changes in personal habits could improve critical qualities in her ability to learn led to surprise and pleasure. An initial self-image that she would not be able so easily to improve her practice was held in a relaxed way, in what she perceived as a non-threatening situation.
'The educational situation which most effectively promotes significant learning is one in which 1 threat to the self of the learner is reduced to a minimum, and 2 *differentiated perception of the field of experience* is facilitated.' (This is a change in how a person perceives an experience which is enabled by using their own or another person's ideas which assist in noticing new or finer differences in experience.) (Quoted text is from Rogers 1951: 123)	I felt that the most satisfying aspect of the discussion with other students was my realisation that others often share the same concerns as me. We can empathise with each other, share good ideas and support each other through the difficult times. As I began to write my reflective journal I realised that it was the little things I found about myself, that made a big difference once I took action. For example, by sitting at the front in lectures I focused more and it felt more like a seminar, making the new experience of lectures less scary. I shared this idea with one of my learning partners and she has since taken the same action. Seven months later I am still using this practice and it seems to work every single time.	A significant part of this student's learning is achieved by empathising with other students' concerns as learners. Her self-concept, as a person who is susceptible to difficulties in her learning which arise from her unique inadequacies, has been reorganised, allowing that, in this situation at least, other learners have similar difficulties which make it a less blameworthy event. She has also noticed that empathic talk was a helpful factor in the learning process by which a perceived threat was reduced to a minimum. Her previous experience of attending lectures might not have allowed her to consider that the choice of where to sit might be a factor in enhancing learning which was worth attending to, but it is now clearly differentiated as a significant one, also reducing perceived threat.

This analysis is offered as an example of how Rogers' ideas help us: first, to understand students' perspectives; second, to avoid a blaming attitude towards the negative impressions they may create and; third, to sustain our intention to offer in our relationships with students an *authentic and empathic valuing* of them as learners. It affirms our belief that *most students are doing their best for most of the time*. It can help a hard-pressed tutor who wants to retain this article of faith, to consider examples of students' difficulties in this way. We have found that problematic incidents often fit this kind of explanation. These speculative explanations are not trying to name a difficulty and make it into some kind of medical problem which will require a set treatment to be administered by an expert. This is not about trying to medicalise learning, but precisely the opposite. In Rogers' theory, the *tendency to actualise* is the internal resource for development, as part of being human, which functions better when there are particular external enabling conditions. We do not need to know with certainty what are the precise causes of a difficulty, before practising and fostering the enabling conditions which Rogers advises. He said that his theory is not meant to be explanatory, telling us what is really happening, but *descriptive*, helping us to notice more perceptively. It is not necessary for the tutor to be the only or even the main person with whom the most productive relationships are made, to enable a student to flourish.

To summarise, as IIL tutors:

1 in our relationships with students, we practise:

- a non-judgmental accepting and respectful regard for each person as a learner, valuing their expressions and contributions as well meant
- an empathic attitude towards their perceptions of their experiences as learners and what they believe they can do about difficulties
- genuineness and openness of our own presence in the situation, making comments about the situation which are clear and honest while also intended not to impose ourselves on the other person

2 we also explicitly intend our practice to be a model for students' relationships with each other
3 following Carl Rogers, we adopt practices of student-centred teaching, including:

- the creation of an acceptant, non-threatening climate
- the development and refinement of individual and group learning purposes

- a dynamic role as leaders of learning: giving control over their learning to students and, from time to time, temporarily taking it back, to renegotiate tasks and give feedback
- cultivating the freedom to learn what, when and how is appropriate to each student

4   within this overall frame, we look for students' individual needs to unlearn a negative condition of worth in themselves as learners, as they emerge in their learning inquiries.

We believe that these are good ways to help students to learn how to learn and are pleased when they say and write things like:

> Looking back, I felt so self-conscious that I did not want to draw any attention to myself when it came to asking questions. I did not want to seem unintelligent. At the time, I believed that I was the only person in the room to have issues raised by the concept of 'thinking about my own learning'. Before I'd started university I never really thought about how I learn best, or what my strengths and weaknesses were when it came to learning. I guess I took my learning for granted.

When a student says that they don't understand this approach and feel unable to respond as expected, we find ourselves in the situation described by Donald Schön:

> I can tell you that there is something you need to know, and with my help you may be able to learn it. But I cannot tell you what it is in a way you can now understand. I can only arrange for you to have the right sorts of experiences for yourself. You must be willing, therefore, to have these experiences. Then you will be able to make an informed choice about whether you wish to continue. If you are unwilling to step into this new experience without knowing ahead of time what it will be like, I cannot help you. You must trust me.
>
> (Schön 1987: 93)

In emphasising *'the right sorts of experiences'*, Schön denies that the learner is not understanding merely because the teacher is lacking skill in *'telling'* the learner what they need to know. To be the *'right sort'*, the *'experiences'* must be perceived by the learner in the right way. If they are unwilling to trust the teacher, to *'step into this new experience'*, then progress is blocked. This sounds like whole-person learning in which the learner is offered control over purposes and methods, in a non-threatening situation.

In his consideration of how to educate professional people in reflective practice, Schön prefers what he called *'coaching'* to conventional teaching (by which he probably means mainly telling). The coach of a complex practice listens, reflects, engages in dialogue with the learner about their initial attempt and guides the next try, aware that there are many possible ways of making progress. In so doing, the coach exposes their own thinking, making reasoning explicit in order to clarify it as much for the coach's benefit as for the learner. The coach's legitimacy does not depend on scholarly attainments or proficiency as a lecturer but on *'the artistry of the coaching practice'*. Therefore a fellow student who knows something relevant or has helpful insights based on similar experiences can also be a good coach. A potential advantage of peer coaching, in Rogerian terms, would be a *'minimum of threat to the self of the learner'* combined with *'differentiated perception of the field'* provided by a peer, co-learner who can point out unnoticed helpful features of an experience arising from their own, parallel learning using their own language.

These ideas from John Gatto, Carl Rogers and Donald Schön, point to a way of learning how to learn which compares well with IIL students' discussion of each other's learning inquiries to improve their practice as learners. Gatto characterises some common learning difficulties associated with features of a school system. Rogers suggests that, if the difficulties have become part of the learner's self structure, they will be more susceptible to change in non threatening situations within helping relationships. Schön suggests that a climate of minimal threat is aided by collaborative learning with helpful peers who show artistry of coaching practice. The structure of IIL intends to create many situations in which this can happen. The best example is probably in the seminars at which a student is discussing with a small group of critical friends or learning partners the interim progress of their current learning inquiry. Acting on the tutor's trust to select a meaningful inquiry focus, a learner is engaged in a reflective examination of their evidence of what they do, in comparison with what they want to be improved, what peers say about their evidence, interpretations and descriptions of what they do, plus appropriate ideas from reading. Discussion in a climate of minimal threat may enable the difficulty to be detached from the learner's self structure so that a less defensive reaction is provoked, which reduces disempowerment of the student's inner *tendency to actualise*, to liberate creativity and energy towards overcoming the difficulty.

Key concepts in the pivotal role of students' discussion of learning inquiries are now examined more closely.

Knowledge, thinking and knowing

The most troubling questions and intractable difficulties which have recurred throughout our reflections on IIL experience and within collegiate discussions about our practice, are to do with *'How do we think about knowledge?'* and *'How do we want our students to think about knowledge?'*. Having relegated *knowing* from a position of central and overriding importance to one aspect among others of being a learner, in our perspective, it nevertheless remains as the most problematic aspect in the students' perspective. What we all think knowledge is like and how we think about experiences and ideas are crucially important.

Rationalism

Western traditions of thinking, not least in academia, have been heavily influenced by rationalism, but are becoming increasingly open to alternatives of various kinds. We are tutors in a higher education system which is deeply imbued with rationalist assumptions. Even though they are not formally justified, we have to conform to them and try to do so creatively. For example, since the 1960s in the United Kingdom, a teacher is likely to believe, as a self-evident truth (implicitly using a rationalist view like Paul Hirst's (1965) *'forms of knowledge'*) that knowledge really is, by its very nature, divided into categories called 'subjects'. Having become a kind of orthodoxy, it was astonishing to find in 1983 that Hirst himself rejected his own rationalist perspective for a utilitarian one. In his *Education, Knowledge and Practices*, he argues that we do not need to believe that a theoretical idea is something that actually exists, but just use it when it is helpful. For example, I do not have to plan my person-centred teaching by thinking about a Rogerian idea such as *a condition of worth* as if it were a real, distinct *thing* that my student actually has. It matters less whether it exists in the world than whether it helps to make learning and teaching better. Hirst says:

> we must never confuse such analytically discrete elements for distinct existences. We shall never make sense of ourselves if we cannot overcome those dualisms that separate the activities and achievements of reason from those of other mental capacities, or those of mind from those of body.
>
> (Hirst 1983: 190)

So, knowledge is not truly in academic subjects, it *begins* in practice, related to satisfying wants, and is in the form of practical principles – mainly tacit 'know-how' of skill and judgement. Replacing a rationalist by a utilitarian approach, Hirst now says that practice comes first, not propositional reasoning of a theoretical kind.

> Reason can put into propositional form only what is necessarily a limited element in any situation, trading in any given instance in categories that necessarily strip practical realities of all their other aspects, excluding unique particularities, and ignore all tacit considerations. What is more there are no good grounds for believing that any array of such general principles, however extensive, could even in principle capture the full character of practical situations.
>
> (Hirst 1983: 191)

IIL students' learning inquiries are about the *full character of practical situations*. They can be illuminated by, but never reduced to, any array of general principles. We want them to use propositional knowledge from theoreticians not as a starting point but as a resource to enrich what we (and Hirst) value more, which is a student's thinking about the practical realities, including unique particularities and tacit considerations. He goes on to argue:

> not merely for the priority of practical knowledge in education, but rather for the priority of personal development by initiation into a complex of specific, substantive social practices with all the knowledge, attitudes, feelings, virtues, skills, dispositions and relationships that that involves.
>
> (Hirst 1983: 197)

Following Hirst's utilitarian philosophy, planning begins with initiating students into relevant social practices, which in IIL include noticing what we do when we learn, talking about why we do it, thinking about how we would like it to improve and trying out ways of learning better (however the learner perceives 'better').

Thinking

According to Paul Hirst, the existence of a word does not inevitably imply the existence of what it refers to. There is no independent evidence that words used to describe thinking such as 'deciding', 'imagining', 'remembering' really exist as actual mental functions, activities, processes or structures. In his book *To Think: In Language, Learning and Education*, Frank Smith urges caution: *'All these proliferating "thinking" terms are only words ... Their relevance is semantic, not psychological'* (Smith 1992: 8) and other ideas, such as *levels of thinking* are: *'fictitious and prejudicial concepts, favoured by people with vested interests in finding ways of categorising individuals – usually school children – in discriminatory ways'* (1992: 26). We may mistakenly assume that thinking is a specialised activity, which happens when not doing other things or appearing to do nothing, whereas Smith believes that commonplace thinking is a smooth, effortless, continuous process with complexity and skill, which permeates all we do. Saying he follows the philosopher Karl Popper, he declines to *define* thinking in absolute, general terms, but prefers to *describe* how he uses the word on particular occasions. This is a good teaching and learning practice during discussion: when a significant word is used, to ask the speaker for a description of its meaning for that person in that situation.

Smith claims another mistaken assumption is that thinking is primarily an intellectual ability or is skill based. He asserts, in a person-centred way, that thinking always involves feeling, and is determined more by emotional and personality considerations than intellectual ability. This suggests that teachers should not neglect these aspects in a rush to focus on knowledge. It also suggests other reasons than a lack of intellectual ability for a student not appearing to think well enough. Indeed, he claims that classroom situations, like bureaucratic ones, have a rare power to immobilise a person's thinking, if they are contrived situations for which learners have little purpose, interest or control. This is a good reason for a student's learning inquiry *not* to be a contrived one, to please the tutor or a peer, but to be about what they genuinely what to learn. During a learning inquiry, a student's thinking is helped most by finding an appropriate way to think, by understanding the problem more deeply, by knowing more about it. Smith's advice is to gain more knowledge about we are trying to think about. It is a common difficulty with students who dislike IIL to have little knowledge of the kind that would help them think better. They see knowledge as inert – for remembering, not for thinking.

Knowing

In his article 'The role of theory in a pedagogical model for lecturers in higher education', Stephan Rowland (1999) presents a learning process for a different kind of course from IIL, but one with a similar approach. He advocates that learners engage in a form of *critical interdisciplinarity*, which Roland Barnett (1997: 165) has argued should be part of all students' experience of higher education. This is developed when course members discuss their diverse personal theories and value positions that they bring, to develop each other's understanding and practice. This happens when IIL students discuss their learning inquiries. Three kinds of knowledge are brought into dynamic relationship: knowledge which is public, knowledge which is personal and knowledge which derives from the present experience of communicating together. Each has a critical influence on the others and, together, they constitute the curriculum of the module. Having distinguished public and personal knowledge with IIL students, we find that Rowland's third kind of knowledge deserves closer examination.

> The third source of knowledge ... derives from the shared context ... the process of the group's work, ... the process of interaction itself. ... In one respect, this context is even more public for the participants than the public context, since they each have an equal access to it. Any sharing or disputing of knowledge from this context can always be related back to the shared experience. It is the only context which has a shared reference. In another respect, however, it is even more personal than the personal context, for the way in which any individual responds to the process, interprets it, and feels about it, may often be intensely personal and revealing of their feelings and identity. Perhaps the most important criteria for engaging with this context is openness.
>
> (Rowland 1999: 311)

Rowland's view is that learners' engagement with each other's learning through interactive processes within a shared context is so important as to name it as one of the three sources of knowing on which to plan a course. In IIL, we call it 'discussional knowing'. Students bring their personal knowledge of their practice as learners, plus relevant items of public knowledge or theory, into a shared context for critical debate, at a level appropriate to first-year undergraduates. This activity is at the centre of a student's action research into their practice as a learner, to improve it. In the best examples, students, in their initial experience of group discussion of each other's learning inquiries, find their ideas taking on *'a sharper and more immediate reality'* (Rowland 1999: 312). In this way, *'the process of the course becomes a subject of its reflection and is thus transformed into the course content'* (Rowland 1999: 313).

For example, an IIL1 student describes a practical attempt to improve how they organise and manage study time, gather evidence of practice and find ideas from reading about factors which affect practice and offer explanations of difficulties. These elements are all brought to a social context in which several students listen empathically and question or challenge or endorse the evidence of practice or the ideas from reading which have been brought to the group, using their own personal and public knowledge of this aspect of the practice of learning. They share a common aim of improvement, which takes a unique form anew in each person's learning inquiry. Each group member interprets the learning inquiries discussed, developing their own practical understanding of these particular situations by learning to interpret them better, as a resource for improved practice in future situations. Students who expect to engage in talk of this kind, as a way of learning, adapt to IIL more easily than those who expect that IIL is either about finding a theory to implement, or getting a practical quick fix which can be dressed up with quotes afterwards. Even the best idea from theory or the hottest tip from a learning skills resource, still need to be *interpreted* personally and appropriate ways of incorporating them into that person's practice need to be worked out. As well as reflecting on and discussing what could be called these 'externally oriented' ways of improving learning, there are 'internally oriented' ways, such as addressing recurrent fears, noticing habitual use of stereotypical excuses, recollections of past humiliation, denial of praise, routine affirmation of a negative self-image of oneself as a learner, and so on. Given the enabling conditions explored above under the heading 'What is good?', notably openness, these kinds of limitations on learning can be discussed in the context of experiencing them in particular learning situations.

We have held underlying assumptions about what this kind of knowing is like, which students generate during discussion about learning inquiries. We have come to understand it better, as Stephen Rowland describes, using hermeneutics, the study of the art of interpretation, which is summarised by John Elliott in the following way:

> From the hermeneutic perspective one does not derive practice from theory as rationalism suggests. Nor does one reduce theory to practice as behaviourism suggests. The basic principle which underpins the hermeneutic

perspective is that of *situational understanding*. This principle implies that practice is grounded in interpretations of particular situations as a whole and cannot be improved without improving these interpretations. Moreover such interpretations are not 'objective' in the rationalist sense of detached from the biases and prejudices of everyday practical cultures. ... The herme-neutic understanding of situations is improved not by detachment from one's biases but by being open to aspects of the situation which may render them problematic in some respects as a basis for interpretation. In order to arrive at an understanding in these circumstances one has to accommodate the discrepant data by modifying ones' initial biases. Situational under-standing is improved not by eliminating bias but by modifying it.

(Elliott 1993: 18, emphasis as the original)

A student's situational understanding of the aspect of learning practice which they are trying to improve needs to be advanced in an accepting context which enables openness. A student's peers, and sometimes also the tutor, who know the student's habitual ways of interpreting events and ideas, are in a privileged posi-tion to assist with problematising the interpretations and exploring the prejudices and biases which impinge on finding a way forwards.

We also value a hermeneutic description of the relationship between theory and practice.

The hermeneutical perspective implies the dependence of behaviour on situ-ational understanding. Intelligent responses in a practical situation often cannot be specified in advance of it. Such situations are very complex and unpredictable in the way they develop. Judgments about what to do and how to respond in them have to be made *in situ*. Hence the practical signifi-cance of the situational understanding. Good practice is not a matter of reproducing pre-programmed responses but responding intelligently and wisely to a situation as it unfolds on the basis of discernment, discrimination and insight. Moreover, the relationship between understanding and action is an interactive one. One does not first understand and then act. Understanding is developed through actions in the situation, and those actions are them-selves improved as understanding develops.

(Elliott 1993: 18 emphasis as the original)

Tutors try to model this *way of being* in their relationships with students. The openness built in to IIL session planning and our pedagogy intends to create opportunities for students' responses, and initiatives. We react to the unexpected by explicitly making on-the-spot checks of our own and the students' situational understanding and we think aloud about how to proceed, in negotiation with the students. Some students show they value this by giving appreciative cooperation and interest, while a few see it as evidence of our incompetence as planners and teachers, getting impatient with what they perceive to be a waste of time in endless talk, saying *'I just don't get it!'*. Since we are not putting theory into practice, it seems contradictory to give these students a theoretical justification for our approach, but we sometimes do. We also say we are inducting them into a practical approach which underpins their life-long learning as persons, their current practice as learners and their future practice as professional people.

Reasoning and knowing for Inquiry Into Learning

This chapter has tapped the most powerful intellectual resources which are relevant to our reflections on ten years of accumulated experiential knowing about and practising IIL. We are doing what we ask IIL students to do: problematise practice, reflect on evidence of it and discipline our thinking with better knowing. In one sense, we have come back to where we started, seeing it as if for the first time. This is meant to refer to the fertile soil of early years education in which strong roots of IIL grew, to which we return now, with a description of a 'teachable moments' pedagogy as a summary of something at the heart of IIL.

> For us, teachable-moment-oriented curriculum practice combines teachers' emerging purposeful actions with those of the learners in their charge. Teachable moments arise when teachers observe, recognize and interpret the spontaneously occurring interests of diverse learners. As curricular opportunities, these spontaneous moments represent a confluence of students' unique cultural identities, developmental growth and change patterns, together with their particular needs, interests and curiosities. Teachers' careful observation, recognition and interpretation of these opportunities (from the students' perspective) help to form an emerging purposeful instructional action (curriculum practice) that is equal to or relevant as a 'learnable moment'. Once this kind of emerging and purposeful instructional action becomes an inherent and pervasive daily practice within teachers' continuous consciousness of what they are doing, teachable-moment-oriented curriculum practice has taken root.
>
> (Hyun and Marshall 2003: 113)

This chapter has presented a scholarly study of significant features of the IIL approach, to develop our intuitions and partial awarenesses, to make them clearer, more coherent and open to further development. It provides: a more explicit rational basis for our practice and ideas; a better differentiation of the IIL approach; affirmation for some central values and beliefs; encouragement to sustain some aspects of present practice; stimuli for deeper probes into existing lines of inquiry; growth points for new inquiry and development; and a better substantiated platform from which to critique current educational policy and argue for radical change.

Conclusion

Conclusion

Chapter 12

Beginning anew

When concluding their Patchwork Text assignments, students quite often write a comment like: *'I don't know why all schools and colleges don't teach you to reflect since it's so important for developing you as a learner'*. We know how large has been the change which enabled certain students to reach this view.

Issue 1

We have inquired into ways of helping students learn how to learn, by developing their personal reflection in the initial phase of an undergraduate degree. The first emergent issue of importance to the continued development of IIL is appreciating the enormous challenge posed by a reflective process approach to learning. Some students find it difficult to develop an appreciation of the relevance of IIL to their learning, either on the degree programme or their future professional roles. At times it was not just an *expanded* view of learning that we seemed to be asking them to embrace but more of a *paradigm shift* in their expectations of learning. Most students' experiences of learning at school seem to have been so completely knowledge-driven and teacher-controlled that passive learning is almost inescapable. The *unlearning* of dysfunctional ways to learn is an even more challenging part of IIL as a precursor to the *relearning* of autonomous ways. We are more alert to the destabilisation for some of our students which *unlearning* provokes: strong affective responses, possibly as an unconscious self-protection that can appear to be defensiveness. We will redouble our efforts to justify to IIL students the value of reflective adaptability and independence to learning and practice in professional work. We will continue to point out the parallels between their development and enabling young children to develop autonomy and well-being as learners, involving similar dispositions and skills. Obviously, young learners are unlikely to need to unlearn an approach to engage in reflective, process-orientated learning since that is the natural way human beings learn as babies and toddlers.

Issue 2

The second, closely related issue is that many students find it very hard to reintegrate knowing with thinking in their learning. It is as if a specialised ability to acquire and reproduce inert knowledge as a commodity to be served up for assessment purposes, can function completely independently within a person from the rest of themselves: their creative, questioning, analytical, empathic and evaluative thinking and feeling.

> We produce through education a majority who are ruled by knowledge, not served by it – an intellectual, moral and spiritual proletariat characterised by instrumental competencies rather than autonomous power.
>
> (Stenhouse 1978: 11)

Unlike John Holt's children who *'pleased themselves'* with a love of learning (Chapter 3) too many students today deeply dislike learning, as if alienated from it, with a fragile self-esteem and disempowering dependence as learners. However, compared with transmission teaching, IIL's pedagogy enables us to know more accurately what students' learning is like and understand its frustrations and disappointments.

These issues seem to be intensifying, year by year. If our suspicions are correct, they are a grim harvest of 20 years of school education having been in the vice-like, technical rationalist grip of National Curriculum, Standard Attainment Tests, OfSTED, league tables and performance management. As its influence spreads through our society, affecting higher education in the form of managerialist quality assurance, competency based objectification of student assessment, and so on, it makes the climate for innovative teaching and expansive learning increasingly hostile. We would like to see this influence replaced by acknowledgement that:

> The more complex a professional activity becomes, the more policy interventions have to take into account the views of the practitioners and leave space for local adaptations. This assumption is based on the understanding that in complex modern societies many local practical problems cannot be solved for the institutions by central regulations. Instead, the problem solving capacity of these institutions and of the persons working in them has to be improved ... Innovations in complex situations cannot be cloned ... The principle implies that any substantial innovation must be 'acquired' by teachers in a very personal sense. This means that they must be able to transform it.
>
> (OECD 1996: 11)

We reaffirm our commitment to students developing this expanding view of learning and knowing, because we believe it is necessary to becoming an educated, professional person in a rapidly changing world.

We continue to inquire into practice related to our vision, through the development of:

a   our own empathic understanding of the effects on students' expectations for learning of having grown up in such a technical rationalist dominated education system

b   deeper appreciation of manifestations of students' *autonomy* (expression of personal difference, free from inner and outer compulsions) bound to *homonomy* (expression of sense of belonging) to sustain their own and others' *mutual development* in a *Community of Practice*

c   improved students' valuing of and expertise in *discussional knowing*, at the heart of learning through doing learning inquiry

d   develop a collection of *educative case studies* of students' learning inquiries which show unusual, challenging or profound learning achievements, as a cumulative learning resource

e   improve ways of extending students' world view beyond a restricted modernism to include *hermeneutic or postmodern* beliefs about interpretation, knowledge and action.

Current developments

Regarding point e above, we are using a response sheet to inquire into, and simultaneously develop, students' awareness of their beliefs about what tutors want them to think about their learning.

Four statements of belief are presented in Box 12.1. Students are asked to allocate a rating to each one, of how well it matches what they believe: Poor, Not so good, OK, Good, Very Good.

Box 12.1 The four student beliefs about what a tutor wants students to think

1   Public knowledge is fixed, certain and true. A good tutor is an absolute authority who knows everything that's right and wrong and tells students about the knowledge clearly.

   'So my tutor wants me to learn and remember it and reproduce it exactly and correctly.'

2   Some public knowledge is uncertain and authorities do not know everything. A good tutor helps students to understand how some knowledge changes and what is more valid or less valid knowledge.

'So my tutor wants me to learn what authorities say and are finding out, as knowledge develops and is evaluated.'

3   Authorities often do not have all the right answers and best decisions. A good tutor helps students to discuss and decide what to think and do with public knowledge.

'So my tutor wants me to know about the different ideas that different books, tutors and students think about which help us to develop our own knowledge.'

4   Knowledge is relative to the context. A good tutor helps students to learn that the best knowledge is what fits the situation, to meet the purpose, and how to work out what that is, in any particular context.

'So my tutor wants me to value what I and others know and think, be willing to reconsider ideas and rethink what to do in each situation.'

The sheet concludes with a Question about whether students think their belief has changed and, if so, why.

So far, we found about one-third of the current first term Year One students are not sure what the four statements mean. They usually ignore the Question, or say their beliefs have not changed. Most students do show *some* understanding. About one-third seem to understand well enough to rate statements 3 and 4 as closer matches to what they believe tutors want them to think. Also, they are quite likely to say their beliefs had changed. They quite often recognise a change of expectation in the direction that IIL aims for, giving reasons typified by: 'I believed my teacher wanted to give me facts I had to learn, now I know my tutor wants me to learn independently and apply my knowledge to practice'. One response contains an ethical slant: 'I used to believe that tutors didn't really care for the development of a student and their knowledge and uncertainties, but tutors do care and do believe in students and their development – I have witnessed it myself'. Another shows apprehension triggered by the change: *I used to believe they'd teach me to help me pass my course, but now I feel a little less supported, they'd prefer me to do most of my learning by myself, I believe this is to develop my independence? I don't like the responsibility!!'*.

We intend to feed these findings back to the students for exploratory discussion, to increase their awareness of different responses, to think about the statements again and reconsider the value of the distinctions and meaning. We may find it worthwhile to repeat the exercise near the end of the IIL1 module, and with IIL2 students to make further comparisons.

As mentioned in Chapter 10, the purpose of all evidence gathering for action research is not to seek objective knowledge dissociated from practice. This response sheet is not primarily a 'research tool' and the data are not for 'outsiders'. We want to find ever-better ways of probing into what is really going on, to improve what we do. So, the data are fed back into the teaching–learning process to enrich it. In time, the sheet may become as much a stimulus for student learning as for our research. Hopefully, it will help to realise more fully our vision for students to learn in a way which uses knowledge as follows:

> The most important characteristic of the knowledge mode is that one can think with it. This is in the nature of knowledge – as distinct from informa-tion – that it is a structure to sustain creative thought and provide frame-works for judgement.
>
> (Stenhouse 1975: 82)

Our recommendations for *learning how to learn in higher education*

Sometimes, the 'findings' of action research, summarised as lists of recommenda-tions, risk sounding like glib statements of the obvious. They are understood more fully when read with an awareness of the practices, experiences, deliberations and personal values through which they have emerged. We commend these principles to guide endeavours to help students learn how to learn in higher education.

For students

- Be *open* to learning, seeing it partly as an area of knowing and a set of skills, but mainly as a *personal practice*, which you can improve (see Chapter 2).
- Be alert and sensitive to your *feelings, moods and emotions* related to your *whole person* learning as they are at least as important as the ideas, reasoning and thinking aspects (see Chapter 11).
- Look closer at your experiences of learning, to find out if they are as they seem, to become more interested in, and to *know yourself* better as a learner.
- *Be yourself* as a learner: don't feel you have to pretend to do or be anything to please or impress anyone else; be true to yourself and your authentic experi-ence (see Chapter 2).
- Notice how others learn; talk with them about learning and read about learning.
- Seek particular students with whom mutually enabling, trustful and caring relationships are sustained as *learning partners*: to share interests in learning and to help each other try improvements (see Chapter 4).
- Nurture your own and each other's *positive esteem* as learners, to be more confident and open (see Chapter 11).
- Notice too narrow or defensive a preoccupation with *pleasing oneself*, or too strong a desire for the feeling of belonging to, and acceptance by, your group of peers and needing to *please others* (see Chapter 11).

- Nurture your own and each other's *honesty* and *courage* to ask difficult questions, to make hard decisions/tough choices, and be prepared to disagree, when you are inclined to agree just to be nice (see Chapter 7).
- Maintain a *reflective conversation with yourself* about your experiences and developments as a learner by keeping a written Jotter, a blog or making regular voice recordings (see Chapter 3 and 4).
- Raise *questions* about improving your learning, and seek answers to them by noticing significant events in your practice and asking expert sources for better knowing (see Chapter 4).
- Face learning *difficulties* in a relaxed way, describing them to learning partners, asking questions and searching for significant, relevant public knowledge that helps (see Chapter 4).
- Be *sceptical* of 'quick fix' but trivial solutions to difficulties and smart but superficial answers to questions (see Chapter 4).
- Practice high-quality talk which prizes *discussional knowing* that brings together each other's personal knowing with significant public knowing relevant to the immediate learning experience (see Chapter 11).
- Practice *diversity* in learning, particularly reading and talking, accepting and prizing *difference* in each other's personal experience, and using it to *develop intrapersonal and interpersonal modes of learning*, notably using *Intervision* (see Chapter 6).
- Develop your abilities to notice and coach each other's reflections about learning in many varied situations, help each other to *see yourselves as others see you* (see Chapter 6).
- Don't mistake *acquiring information* for *authentic thinking, knowing and understanding* (see Chapter 4).
- Cultivate looking hard for public *knowledge and understanding* that really makes a difference to what you are trying to think about and achieve, and ignore the rest (for now at least!) – its not what the knowledge means to someone else that makes the difference but what *you* do with it for your own purposes (see Chapter 11).
- To nurture your *confidence* and belief in yourself as a learner, notice the learning that is most satisfying to you, feeling good about having done it your way – and well (see Chapter 3).
- Combine all the above into one collaborative activity: do a *learning inquiry*, to improve the aspect of your learning practice that is currently most important to you (see Chapter 4).
- *You*, and to some extent your learning partners, are in the best place at any given moment, to take into account all the relevant factors that help you to decide *what* to improve next in your learning, *how* to try, and what would count as *progress* (see Chapter 4).
- Recognise and cherish all signs of better learning practice, to *prize* your own and each other's progress (see Chapter 3).

- As you always knew, deep down, it is *ultimately down to you*. What *really* matters in your learning are qualities that no one can give you. No one will tell you exactly what to do or how to do it. But you do already have within you what really matters, the qualities listed above. They just need noticing, nurturing, coaching, with peers and tutors you trust to help you.

For tutors

- Develop *collegiality* in the teaching team, which acknowledges each tutor's values and beliefs as their contribution to developing a shared vision and common purpose for the module/programme (see Chapter 10).
- Thinking and talking about the most profoundly important *educational aims* of a programme or module, such as student autonomy and learning how to learn, tutors should think of them as qualities of being human which cannot be taught directly, but require enabling conditions for them to develop (see Chapters 2 and 9).
- Deconstruct policy and planning documents for *behaviouristic* assumptions and *instrumental* reasoning which separates means from ends (see Chapters 2 and 7).
- *Comply creatively* with other technical rationalist/social market driven procedures while blending educative with training dimensions of the module/ programme (see Chapter 11).
- Aims need to be distilled into statements of the fundamental qualities of learning, processes and products, which students should develop, which are expressed as *criteria* to be used in formative feedback (see Chapter 7) as well as summatively, for assessing the assignment.
- *Authentically prize* students' personal interest, and motivation for learning, during activities which show tolerance to uncertainty and ambiguity.
- Notice students' *learning processes* and consider how well the module/ programme provides appropriate support for their promotion (see Chapters 2 and 6).
- *Assess general progress* in a student group's learning with evidence of qualities of learning processes (see Chapter 7) as well as how much content has been covered or whether externally set targets are being hit.
- *Give students a voice* as progressively active participants in learning and inquiry (see Chapter 6) encouraging them to give and receive feedback on each other's ideas and progress, in a variety of ways including electronic ones (see Chapter 8).
- Interpret students' behaviour as manifestations of by their expectations (see Chapter 7) and *situational understanding* (see Chapter 11) of their learning in this module/programme, and provide ways to harmonise their expectations with the module/programme aims (see Chapter 7).
- *Listen* to accounts of their attempts to improve their learning, accept their

perceptions of difficulty and find *non-threatening* ways to challenge them to gain better knowledge of the difficulties (see Chapter 6).

- Encourage students to write to learn and consider incorporating it into a Patchwork Text approach to the curriculum and assessment (see Chapter 9).
- Be committed to *changing* one's own teaching practice through action inquiry (see Chapter 10) treating the curriculum of the module/programme as a human hypothesis to be tested (see Chapter 9).
- Meet regularly to discuss evidence of critical incidents, current concerns and progress, reconsider aims and ways of achieving them and plan collaborative improvements (see Chapter 10).
- Give careful attention to the *integration* of teaching and learning informed by the ideas, values and practices in this book (such as a teachable moment curriculum – see the end of Chapter 11) with those in use across the degree programme, to develop a *coherent* approach.

We offer these recommendations to future educational policy:

- Recognise the damaging excesses of a target culture in which the hidden curriculum of compulsory schooling, and increasingly in higher education too, is personal compliance, control and a dehumanising kind of standardisation.
- Restore trust in professional and academic collegiality to make innovations, adaptations to different situations and local problem solving, particularly through inexpensive collaborative action research for personal, professional and curriculum development.
- Rebalance the blending of artistic and personal dimensions with technical and rationalistic ones, to moderate the excesses of the latter, in managing, assessing and evaluating tutors, systems and students.
- Rebalance the relative contributions of discussion, intuition, personal authenticity, democracy and subjective diversity in contrast to documentation, impersonal formality, distant hierarchy and objectivity in educational, working relationships.
- Transfer substantial resources from central controlling forces and structures, as the guardians of quality in teaching and learning, to local and regional, human-scale initiatives, which generate multiple kinds of improvement in diverse centres of excellence.

Bibliography

Askell-Williams, H., Lawson, M. and Murray-Harvey, R. (2007) 'What happens in my university classes that helps me to learn? Teacher Education Students' Instructional Metacognitive Knowledge', *International Journal for the Scholarship of Teaching and Learning*, Vol. 1, Issue 1, January, pp. 1–2.

Athey, C. (1989) *Vertical Schemas* pre-publication draft.

Axline, V. (1964) *Dibs: In Search of Self.* London: Penguin.

Bandura, A. (1977) *Social Learning Theory.* New York: General Learning Press.

Barnett, R. (1997) *Higher Education: A Critical Business.* Bristol: Open University Press.

Baxter Magolda, M. (1992) *Knowing and Reasoning in College: Gender-Related Patterns in Students' Intellectual Development.* San Francisco, CA: Jossey-Bass.

Baxter Magolda, M. (2010) 'A tandem journey through the labyrinth', *Journal of Learning Development in Higher Education*, Issue 2. http://www.aldinhe.ac.uk/ojs/index.php?journal=jldhe&page=article&op=view&path%5B%5D=61&path%5B%5D=37 (accessed 24.2.11).

BERA (2004) Revised Ethical Guidelines for Educational Research.

Berlak, A. and Berlak, H. (1981) *Dilemmas of Schooling.* London: Methuen.

Bernstein, R. (1983) *Beyond Objectivism and Relativism.* Oxford: Basil Blackwell.

Black, P., McCormick, R., James, M. and Pedder, D. (2006) 'Learning how to learn and assessment for learning', *Research Papers in Education*, Vol. 21, Issue 2, June, pp. 119–132.

Blackman, M. (2001) *Noughts and Crosses.* London: Corgi.

Bloxham, S. and Boyd, P. (2007) *Developing Assessment in Higher Education: A Practical Guide.* Milton Keynes: Open University Press.

Bolton, G. (2010) *Reflective Practice: Writing and Professional Development*, 3rd edn. London: Sage.

CARN (Collaborative Action Research Network) (2007) Conference notes, Nottingham University, November.

Carr, M. (2001) *Assessment in Early Childhood Setting.* London: Sage.

Claxton, G. (1998) *Hare Brain, Tortoise Mind: Why Intelligence Increases When You Think Less.* New York: Fourth Estate.

Claxton, G. (2002) *Building Learning Power: Helping Young People Become Better Learners.* TLO: Bristol.

Claxton, G. (2006) 'Expanding the capacity to learn: a new end for education', Opening Keynote address, British Educational Research Association Annual Conference, 6 September.

Claxton, G. and Carr, M. 'A framework for teaching learning: the dynamics of disposition', *Early Years*, Vol. 24, No. 1, pp. 87–97.

Claxton, G., Edwards, L. and Scale-Constantinou, L. (2006) 'Cultivating creative mentalities: a framework for education', *Thinking Skills and Creativity*, Vol. 1, pp. 57–61.

Cooperrider, D. L. and Srivastva, S. (1987) 'Appreciative inquiry in organizational life', *Research in Organizational Change and Development*, Vol. 1, pp. 129–169.

Council of European Judges. www.coe.int (accessed 9.3.11).

Dearden, R. (1975) 'Autonomy as an educational ideal'. In S. C. Brown (ed.) *Philosophers Discuss Education*. London: Macmillan.

Department for Education and Skills (2003) *Every Child Matters.*

Dewey, J. ([1916] 2010) *Democracy and Education: An Introduction to the Philosophy of Education*. New York: Dover edition.

Donelan, H., Kear, K. and Ramage, M. (2010) *Online Communication and Collaboration: A Reader*. London: Routledge.

Dweck, C. (2000) *Self-Theories: The Role in Motivation, Personality and Development*. London: Psychology Press.

Edwards, C., Gandini, L. and Forman, G. (1998) *The Hundred Languages of Children: The Reggio Emilia Approach*. New York: Ablex.

Elliott, J. (1975) *Developing Hypotheses About Classrooms From Teachers' Practical Constructs*. Cambridge Institute of Education, Ford Teaching Project.

Elliott, J. (1990) 'Validating case studies', *Westminster Studies in Education*, Vol. 13, pp. 47–60.

Elliott, J. (1991) *Action Research for Educational Change*. Milton Keynes: Open University Press.

Elliott, J. (1993) 'Professional education and the idea of a practical educational science'. In J. Elliott (ed.) *Reconstructing Teacher Education*. London: Falmer Press.

Elliott, J. (1995) 'What is good Action Research? Some criteria', *Action Researcher*, Vol. 1, 10–11.

Elliott, J. (1998) *The Curriculum Experiment: Meeting the Challenges of Social Change*. Milton Keynes: Open University Press.

Elton, G. R. (1967) *The Practice of History*. London: Fontana.

Embleton Tudor, L., Keemar, K., Tudor, K., Valentine, J. and Worrall, M. (2004) *The Person Centred Approach: A Contemporary Introduction*. Basingstoke, Hampshire: Palgrave.

Faculty of Arts, University of Groningen, Netherlands. www.imaginal.nl (accessed 24.2.11).

Foster, E. (2008) Verbal report on 'Welcome Week at NTU' to Nottingham Trent University School of Education staff meeting.

Friere, P. (1996) *Pedagogy of the Oppressed*. Harmondsworth: Penguin.

Gardner, H. (1983) *Frames of Mind: The Theory of Multiple Intelligences*. New York: Basic Books.

Garrison, D. R. and Anderson, T. (2003) *E-Learning in the 21st Century*. Abingdon: RoutledgeFalmer.

Gatto, J. T. (2002) *Dumbing Us Down: The Hidden Curriculum of Compulsory Schooling*. Gabriola Island, BC: New Society Publishers.

Haddon, M. (2003) *The Curious Incident of the Dog in the Night-time*. London: Random House.

Hendricksen, J. (2002) *Intervision: kollegiale beratung in sozialer arbeit und schule 2*. Weinheim, Germany: Beltz Verlag.

HighScope. www.highscope.org (accessed 24.2.11).

Hirst, P. (1965) 'Liberal education and the nature of knowledge'. In Archambault, R. (ed.) *Philosophical Analysis and Education*, pp. 113–138. London: Routledge and Kegan Paul.

Hirst, P. (1983) 'Education, knowledge and practices'. In R. Barrow and P. White (eds) *Beyond Liberal Education: Essays in Honour of Paul H. Hirst.* London: Routledge.

Holt, J. (1991) *How Children Learn.* London: Penguin Education.

Hyun, E. and Marshall, J. D. (2003) 'Teachable-moment-oriented curriculum practice in early childhood education', *Journal of Curriculum Studies*, Vol. 35, No. 1, pp. 111–127.

Jasper, M. (2003) *Beginning Reflective Practice.* Cheltenham: Nelson Thornes.

Kropotkin, P. (2009) *Mutual Aid: A Factor of Evolution.* New York: Dover.

Laevers, F. (1998) In http://www.european-agency.org/agency-projects/assessment-resource-guide/documents/2008/11/Laevers.pdf (accessed 24.2.11).

Lave, J. and Wenger, E. (1991) *Situated Learning: Legitimate Peripheral Participation.* Cambridge: Cambridge University Press.

Levi-Strauss, C. (1966) *The Savage Mind.* Chicago: The University of Chicago Press.

Marsh, L. (1970) *Alongside the Child in the Primary School.* London: A. & C. Black.

Mason, J. (2002) *Researching Your Own Practice: The Discipline of Noticing.* London: Routledge Falmer.

Meijer, Dr. P. C. www.onderzoekinformatie.nl (accessed 24.2.11).

Milgram, S. (1974) *Obedience to Authority.* London: Tavistock.

Morley, C. (2007) 'Engaging practitioners with critical reflection: issues and dilemmas', *Reflective Practice*, Vol. 8, No. 2, February, pp. 61–74.

Northedge, A. (2005) *The Good Study Guide.* Milton Keynes: Open University Press.

Nutbrown, C. (1994) *Threads of Thinking: Young Children Learning and the Role of Early Education.* London: Paul Chapman.

Nyerere, J. (1973) *Freedom and Development.* Dar es Salaam: Oxford University Press.

O'Connor, A. and Diggins, C. (2002) *On Reflection: Reflective Practice for Early Childhood Educators.* New Zealand: Open Minds.

OECD (1996) 'An overview of the Organisation for Economic Cooperation and Development work on teachers, their pay and conditions, teaching quality and the continuing professional development of teachers'. A paper to the 45th International Conference on Education, UNESCO, Geneva, 30 September to 5 October.

Oliver, M. and Trigwell, K. (2005) 'Can "blended learning" be redeemed?', *E-Learning*, Vol. 2, No. 1, pp. 17–26.

Open University. www.open.ac.uk/skillsforstudy/being-reflective.php (accessed 24.2.11).

Ovens, P. (2000) 'Becoming scientific and becoming professional: towards moderating rationalism in the initial teacher education curriculum', *The Curriculum Journal*, Vol. 11, No. 2, pp. 177–197.

Ovens, P. (2003a) 'Using the patchwork text to develop a critical understanding of science'. In *The Patchwork Text: A Radical Re-Assessment of Coursework Assignments: A Special Issue of Innovations in Education and Teaching International*, Vol. 40, No. 2, pp. 133–143.

Ovens, P. (2003b) 'A patchwork text approach to assessment in teacher education', *Teaching in Higher Education*, Vol. 8, No. 4, pp. 545–562.

Ovens, P. (2004) 'Suggestions for a SANE way to encourage creativity in science learning and teaching', *Primary Science Review*, Issue 81, Association for Science Education.

Papert, S. (1980) *Mindstorms: Children, Computers and Powerful Ideas*. New York: Basic Books.

Petzer, D. (1995) *A Child Called 'It'*. London: Orion.

Please, S. (2002) *The Making of a Meritocrat: Good Luck Versus Personal Effort*. Windsor: Short Run Book Company.

Poole, R. (1972) *Towards Deep Subjectivity*. London: Harper & Row.

Qualification and Curriculum Authority (2011) BeCal Learning Centre for Education and Values. www.becal.net/lc/assessment/assessment.html (accessed 9.3.11).

Quinn, J. (2003) 'Becoming a science specialist teacher', *Innovations in Education and Teaching International*, Vol. 40, No. 2, pp. 144–151.

Rinaldi, C. (2006) *In dialogue with Reggio Emilia: Contextualising, Interpreting and Evaluating Early Childhood Education*. Abingdon: RoutledgeFalmer.

Rogers, C. R. (1951) *Client-Centred Therapy*. London: Constable.

Rogers, C. R. (1961) *On Becoming a Person*. London: Constable.

Rogers, C. R. ([1969] 1994) *Freedom to Learn*. Columbus, OH: Charles Merrill.

Rogoff, B. (1991) *Apprenticeship in Thinking: Cognitive Development in a Social Context*. Oxford: Oxford University Press.

Rorty, R. (1979) *Philosophy and the Mirror of Nature*. Princeton, NJ: Princeton University Press.

Rowland, S. (1999) 'The role of theory in a pedagogical model for lecturers in higher education', *Studies in Higher Education*, Vol. 24, No. 3, pp. 303–314.

Salmon, G. (2006) *E-moderating: The Key to Teaching and Learning Online*. London: RoutledgeFalmer.

Schön, D. (1983) *The Reflective Practitioner: How Professionals Think in Action*. London: Temple Smith.

Schön, D. (1987) *Educating the Reflective Practitioner*. San Francisco: Jossey-Bass.

Smith, F. (1992) *To Think: In Language, Learning and Education*. London: Routledge.

Social Care Association. www.socialcareassociation.co.uk (accessed 24.2.11).

Stenhouse, L. (1975) *An Introduction to Curriculum Research and Development*. London: Heinemann.

Stenhouse, L. (1978) 'Towards a Vernacular Humanism' (unpublished paper).

Stenhouse, L. (1983) *Authority, Education and Emancipation*. London: Heinemann.

Teacher Education Department, Masaryk, University, Czech Republic. www.muni.cz/research/publications/230086 (accessed 9.3.11).

The International Association of Facilitators. www.iaf-methods.org (accessed 24.2.11).

The Nodes Committee of the Global Diversity Information Facility. www.gbif.org (accessed 24.2.11).

Torrance, H. and Pryor, J. (1998) *Investigating Formative Assessment*. Milton Keynes: Open University Press.

Tudor, K. and Worrall, M. (2006) *Person-Centred Therapy: A Clinical Philosophy*. London: Routledge.

University of Ottawa, Canada. www.saea.uottowa.ca (accessed 24.2.11).

University of Surrey Centre of Excellence in Learning and Teaching (2007) Learning in a Complex Society Conference, June.

Vygotsky, L. S. (1978) *Mind in Society: The Development of Higher Psychological Processes*. Cambridge, MA: Harvard University Press.

Warnock, M. (1976) *Imagination*. London: Faber & Faber.

Wenger, E. (1998) *Communities of Practice: Learning, Meaning and Identity*. Cambridge: Cambridge University Press.

Winter, R. (2003) 'Contextualising the patchwork text: addressing problems of coursework assessment in higher education', *Innovations in Education and Teaching International*, Vol. 40, No. 2, pp. 112–122.

Winter, R., Buck, A. and Sobiechowska, P. (1999) *Professional Experience and the Investigative Imagination*. London: Routledge.

Index